POSTCARD HISTORY SERIES

Postcards from the State of Jefferson

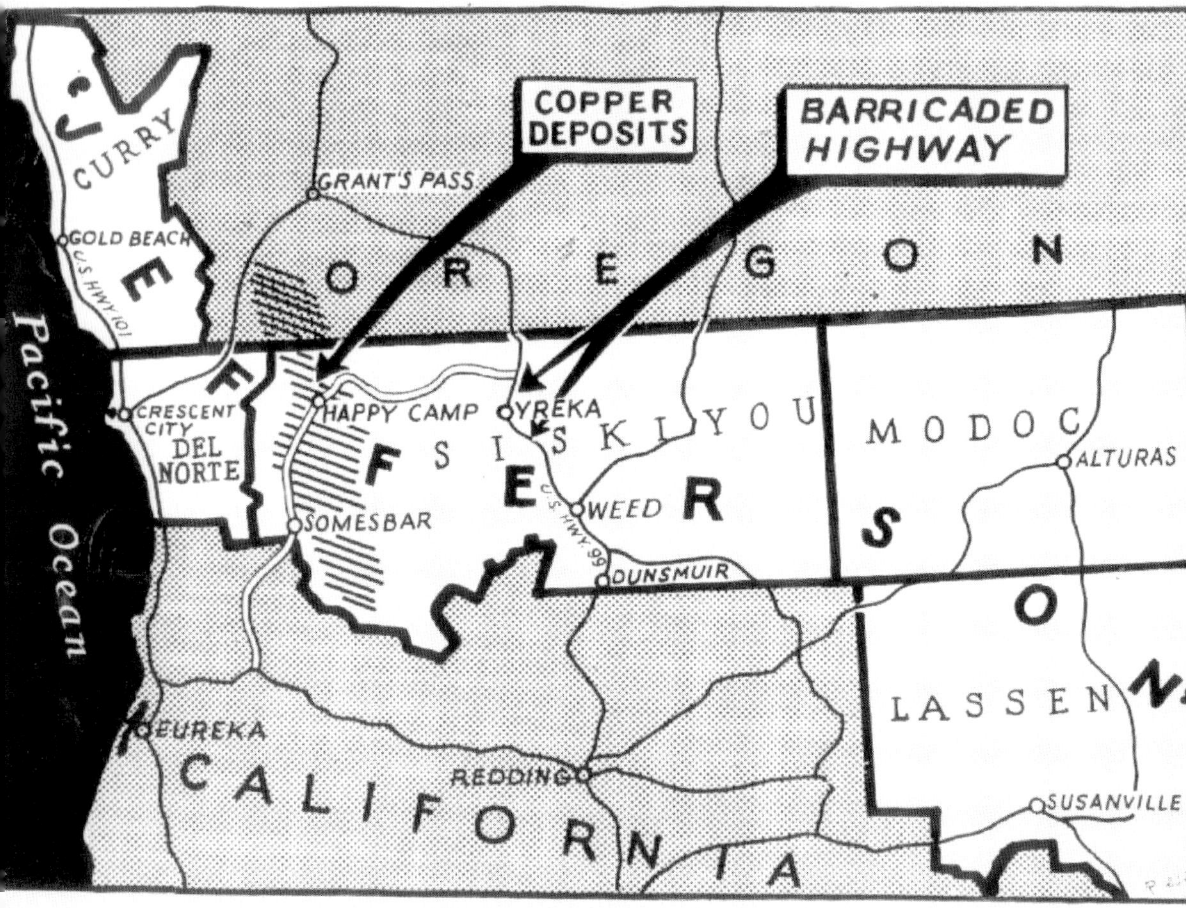

This December 1941 map shows those first counties in southern Oregon and northern California calling for the creation of the State of Jefferson only days before Pearl Harbor was attacked and the movement was derailed. Since then, more and more counties on either side of the border have declared themselves part of the "mythical" State of Jefferson. (Courtesy of the authors.)

On the Front Cover: Driving freight was dangerous work but critically important to miners and settlers in the north. The August 10, 1861, *Sacramento Union* reported: "From Shasta to Yreka, a distance of 115 miles, with the exception of about twenty miles through Scott Valley, the road . . . has been made by artificial means, crossing Trinity and Scott Mountains, each at an elevation of nearly three thousand feet above the valleys." Some of these roads were treacherous. (Courtesy of the authors.)

On the Back Cover: Mount Shasta can be seen from points near and far. It rises 14,179 feet and its snow-covered ridges often collide with the clouds that encircle it. Legends about the majestic peak are part of Shasta tribal history. (Courtesy of the authors.)

POSTCARD HISTORY SERIES

Postcards from the State of Jefferson

Gail L. Fiorini-Jenner and Bernita L. Tickner

ARCADIA
PUBLISHING

ISBN 978-0-7385-9666-2

Published by Arcadia Publishing
Charleston, South Carolina

Printed in the United States of America

Library of Congress Control Number: 2012948661

For all general information contact Arcadia Publishing at:
Telephone 843-853-2070
Fax 843-853-0044
E-mail sales@arcadiapublishing.com
For customer service and orders:
Toll-Free 1-888-313-2665

Visit us on the Internet at www.arcadiapublishing.com

To our beloved children and grandchildren, and all those who come after—
may a glimpse into the past reveal something of the future.

Tempus fugit.

Bernita L. Tickner
1928–2013
Historian, Storyteller, Friend

Contents

Acknowledgments

It is impossible to thank all those who have supported us over the years as we gather old photographs and postcards, interview neighbors and acquaintances, and seek out those less-told stories that are being lost or discarded far too quickly. We want to especially thank those who have provided photographs for us to use in this volume, particularly Hazel Davis Gendron; Sandra Elam; the Fort Jones Museum and Cecelia Reuter and Debbie McCully, its curators; the Betty Jane Young family, in particular Dona Young Farnam; and our own families for our historical collections. Unless otherwise noted, the photos included here come from our personal collections.

We also want to thank Tasha Staton, who tirelessly supported us during the gathering and research process. We hope this inspires her to always continue learning and searching.

In addition, we want to thank our editor at Arcadia, Jared Nelson, who invited us to again participate in putting together a third volume on the State of Jefferson. It's a subject we find both fascinating and challenging. Jared provided continual assistance and encouragement and corrected our errors and omissions. Finally, but not lastly, we want to thank our husbands and families. They have endured late nights and late suppers; they have helped to keep us organized and cleaned up while we worked to meet our deadlines, and most of all, they have supported us and believed in us without reservation.

Though we have tried to cover as much of this varied and diverse region as possible, we recognize that there are many locations and/or incidents and individuals we have not been able to include. This, being the third volume about the State of Jefferson, has photo postcards that differ significantly. We hope it will thus add to the understanding and appreciation we feel for the history—perhaps still untold—that waits to be included in the pieces of recorded history. Story is, after all, something that all people have in common.

As this volume goes to print, it is with heavy heart that I say goodbye to my writing partner and friend, Bernita Tickner. Her passing is a loss impossible to measure.

INTRODUCTION

The great Gold Rush of 1849 opened the doors to the State of Jefferson. Harry L. Wells, in his *History of Siskiyou County, California*, credits the first mining in this region to Lindsay Applegate, who traveled south from Jacksonville, Oregon, in 1849 to mine along Beaver Creek and the Klamath and Scott Rivers. In June 1850, prospectors from Trinity River crossed the Salmon-Trinity Alps and found enough gold to whet their appetites.

With the unique characteristics of the geography and climate, this region lent itself to the rugged nature of the people drawn here. From the Cascade Range to the Siskiyou Mountains, from the top of Mount Shasta to the top of Mount McLoughlin or Mount Lassen, the people here have lived in close proximity to the rivers and forests and peaks and valleys.

Within a year of the first gold strike, these northern mines were drawing prospectors from every part of the world. Without roads, however, travel was by foot or mule train and later by wagon, boat, or train. Populations and towns grew and then diminished, and only the hardiest stayed. With conflicts raging between the numerous tribes who called this region home and the hordes of miners and settlers moving in, life was not easy, and tragedy reared its ugly head time and again. But time brought the certainty of change.

As early as 1852, the settlers and miners who settled the borderlands from southern Oregon to northern California called for the creation of a new state. The movement gained momentum into the 20th century, when residents felt "betrayed" and overlooked by both state governments. In 1935, John Childs, a Crescent City judge, declared himself the new governor of a new state, citing neglect and oversight by Sacramento. After this, Mayor Gilbert E. Gable of Port Orford, Curry County, Oregon, joined in the protest, this time rallying support against Salem and the politicians of Oregon.

Finally, in November 1941, on Old Highway 99 outside Yreka, California, protestors staged a "revolt" by stopping traffic and handing out proclamations. Those present declared that the State of Jefferson would "secede every Thursday" until it finally became recognized as the 49th state. Gable appointed himself an interim governor and announced his proposed platform: no sales taxes, income taxes, or liquor taxes. Income would come from the region's natural resources, including mining, timber, ranching, fishing, and more. Anything extra would come from red-light districts.

John Childs joined the movement. Yreka, in its enthusiasm, was selected as the proposed state capital. A state seal was designed: a mining pan with two *X*s, representing the double-cross by both Oregon and California.

On December 4, 1941, an election was held and John Childs won the governorship. There was a parade and rally, speeches, and even a dancing bear. Newsreel companies filmed the event, and Stanton Delaplane, of the *San Francisco Chronicle*, wrote such impassioned articles on the new state and its cries of abuse and neglect that he went on to win a Pulitzer Prize for his writings. Residents decried bad roads as "impassable, hardly jack-assable!"

The great clamor for statehood was cut short, however, when Pearl Harbor was bombed on December 7, 1941. With the nation drawn into war, the battle for statehood slipped into the past. Residents mustered together and jumped into the fray. Locals considered themselves patriots first, rebels second.

But the dream of a State of Jefferson has never really died.

Residents tote banners and flags and wear hats with the Jefferson state logo; bumper stickers declare boldly, "Resident of the State of Jefferson." Businesses are labeled Jefferson this or Jefferson that, including the local public radio station, Jefferson Public Radio, which is located on the Southern Oregon University campus in Ashland, Oregon. There are road signs, publications, and musical groups that include "Jefferson." There is even an official State of Jefferson flower—"anything but a pansy"—and a Jefferson state beer. Articles have appeared in magazines, and television shows have highlighted the frequent cry for statehood.

Residents today who continue to support the idea of a separate state point out that the over-reaching arm of state government has once more compromised their independence. What this points out, of course, is that the dream lives on, and the notion that this region is somehow different—unique, set apart—is part of the identity that citizens of the "mythical and magical" State of Jefferson have painted for themselves.

Perhaps this identity is best characterized by the following anonymous poem, written and published in August 1884 by the *Coquille City Herald*:

The Song of the Workers

I sing the song of the workers, the men of
the brawny arm:
Who giveth us daily bread, and keep us from
hunger's harm;
Who labor afar in the forest, who leaven the
fields with toil,
Who take no heed of the sunshine, and
mind not sweat or broil.

I sing the song of the workers, who harvest
the golden grain,
And bind it, and thrash it and sift it, nor
care for the sting and stain;
Who load it in creaking wagons, and stoutly
their oxen drive,
And bid them good-bye as they go, like the
bees flying home to the hive.

I sing the song of the workers, the men who
struggle and strain,
Who give us their muscle and nerve, as they
guard the loaded train:
Who give us their sinew and brain, as they
watch the poisoned steam,
And run the risk of their lives, as they pass
the perilous stream.

One

Spring

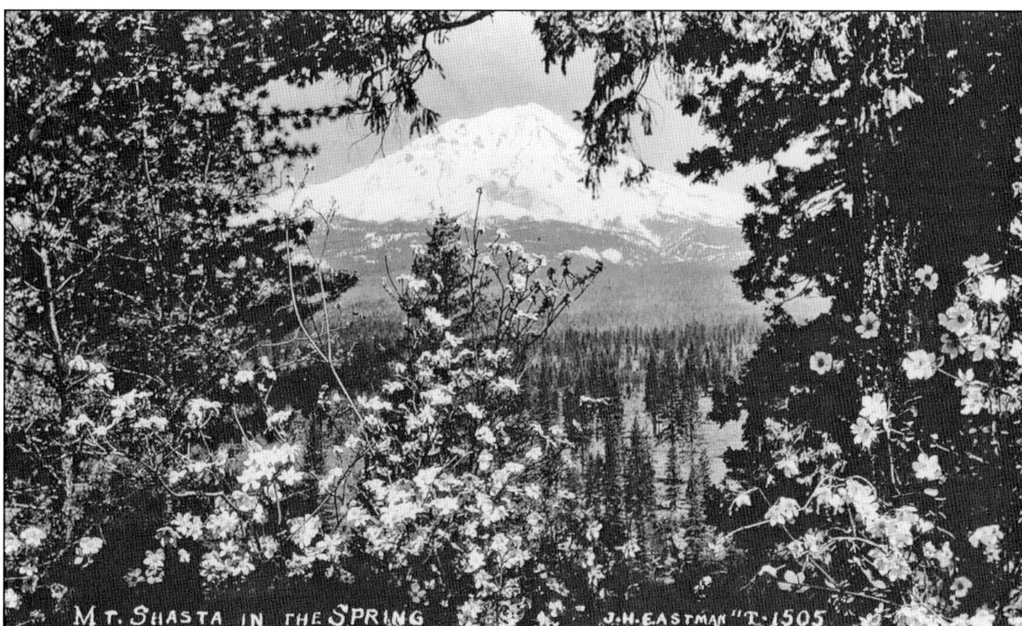

Spring rides no horses down the hill, but comes on foot, a goose-girl still.
—Edna St. Vincent Millay

Mount Shasta, now reported to be 14,179 feet high, reigns over the landscape. Visible from 150 miles away, it is the second highest peak in the Cascade Range and the fifth highest peak in California. Poet Joaquin Miller wrote, "Lonely as God, and white as a winter moon, Mount Shasta starts up sudden and solitary from the heart of the great black forests of Northern California."

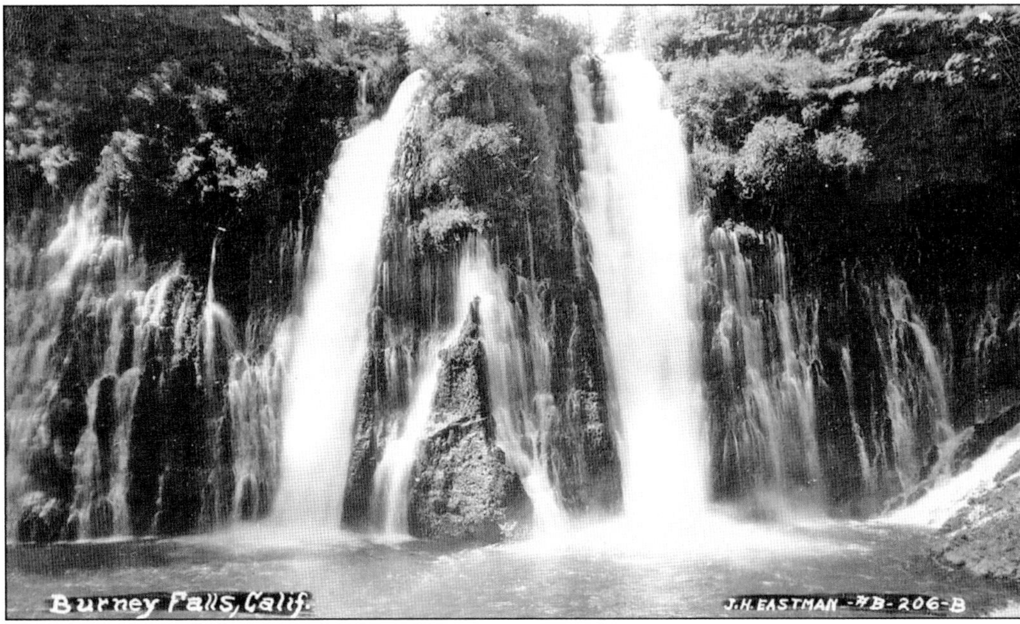

Located along Highway 89 in Shasta County, Burney Falls is part of McArthur–Burney Falls Memorial State Park. A spectacular waterfall, it flows year-round from three underground springs located a half-mile above the falls. The height of the falls is officially 129 feet, and there's easy access down to them. Visitors often follow the easy 2.4-mile loop, which crosses the Pacific Crest Trail.

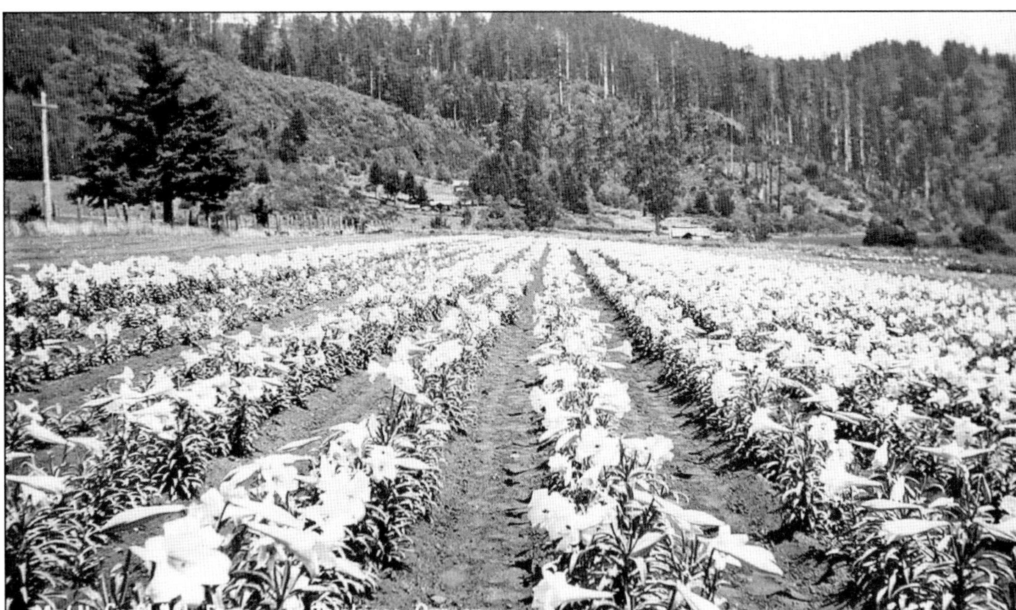

Brookings, Oregon, is the southernmost town on the Oregon coast. Although it was originally a redwood logging company town, the town fell on hard times after timber operations were terminated in 1925. In the 1930s, the production of Easter lilies began to boost its economy. The bulbs grew easily in the fertile coastal soil. Into the 1990s, the lily farmers of Brookings produced more than 90 percent of the world's Easter lily crop.

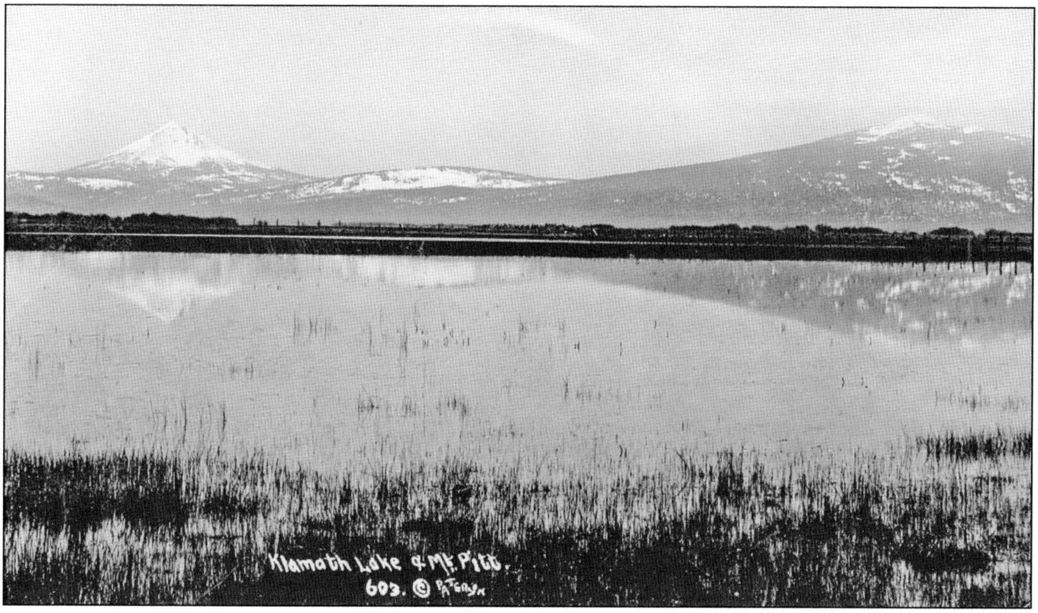

Upper Klamath Lake is a shallow freshwater lake approximately 20 miles long and eight miles wide. It is the largest such body of water in Oregon. The lake is fed by several streams, and drains into the Link River. To protect local and migrating wildlife, the Upper Klamath National Wildlife Refuge has been created along its northern shore. In the background stands "Mount Pit," officially known as Mount McLoughlin.

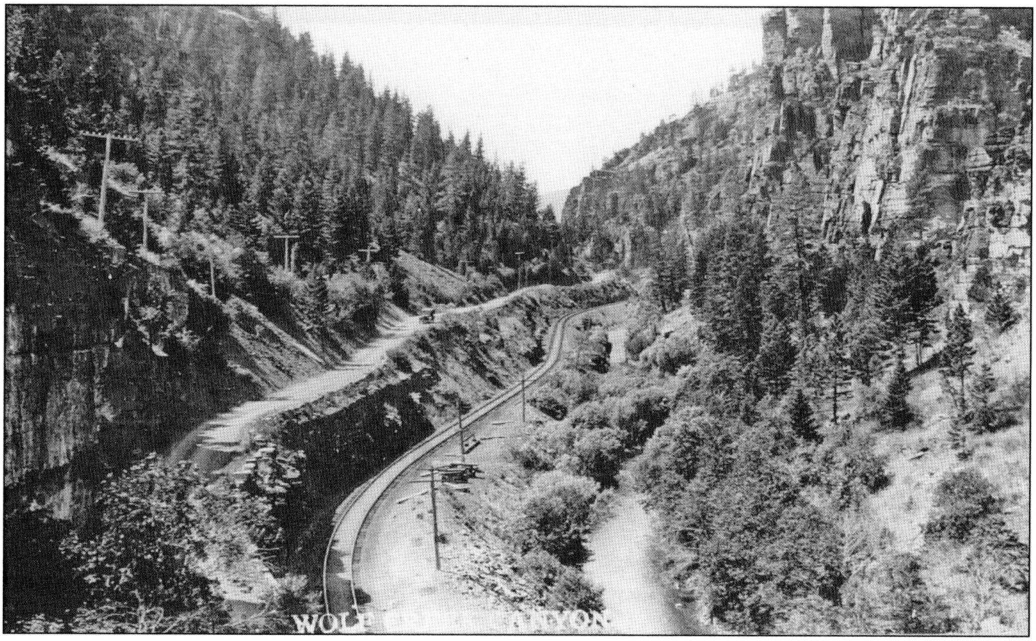

Interstate 5 parallels much of Wolf Creek Canyon. Sandstone cliffs tower 400 feet above the river. Today, kayakers run the rapids in winter, while rock climbers rappel over the cliffs year-round. Although a number of creeks in Oregon were originally called Wolf Creek, the official community of Wolf Creek was established in 1883 as a lumber and supply center for the nearby Wolf Creek and Coyote Creek mines.

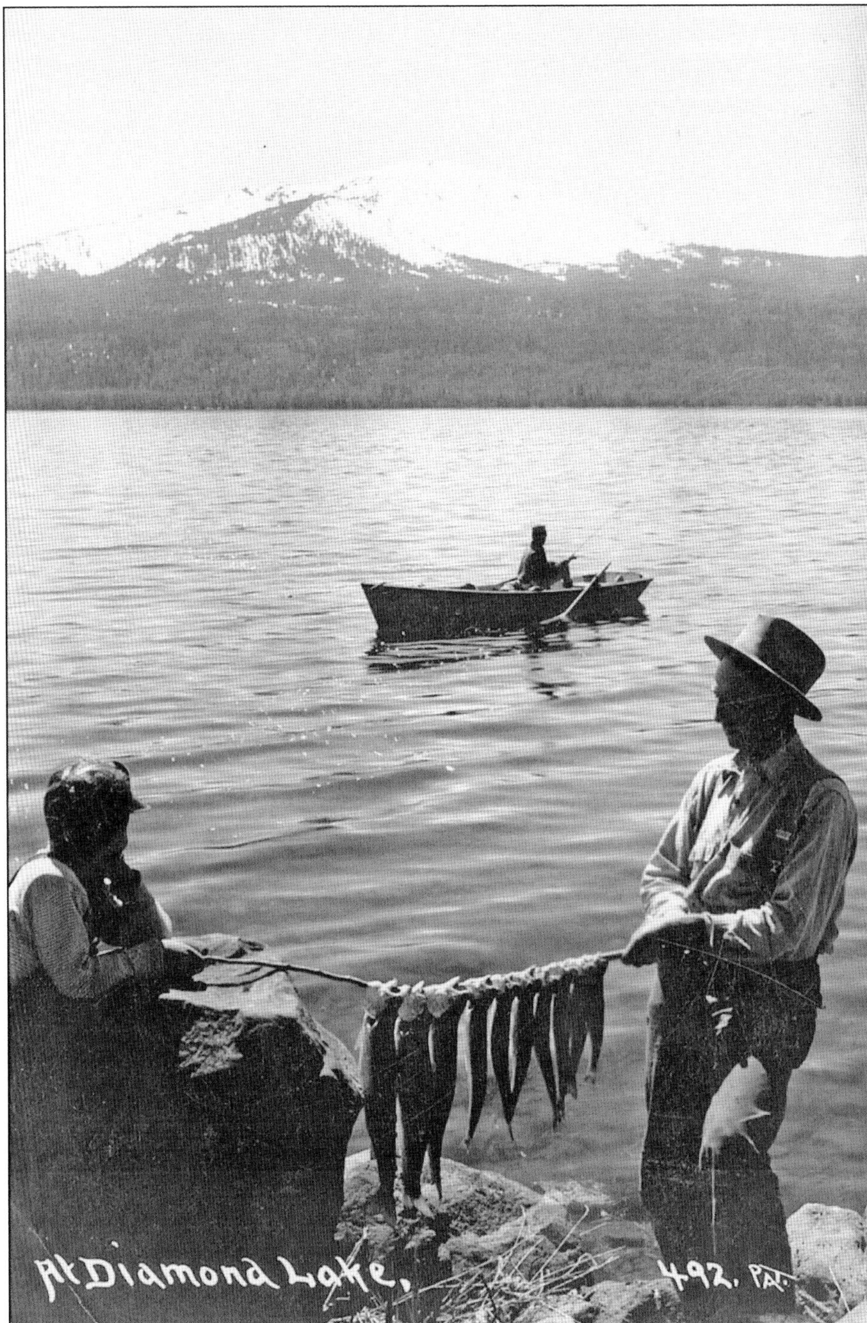

Diamond Lake has been called the gateway to the eastern entrance to Douglas County, Oregon. It is a natural body of water within the Umpqua National Forest and is situated between Mount Bailey to the west and Mount Thielsen, the highest point in Douglas County, to the east. It lies north of Crater Lake National Park and flows into the North Umpqua River on its way to the Pacific Ocean. The lake was named for John Diamond, who discovered it in 1852 while working on opening a road between the Middle Fork of the Willamette River and Idaho. Water from Mount Thielsen is the starting point for the North Umpqua River.

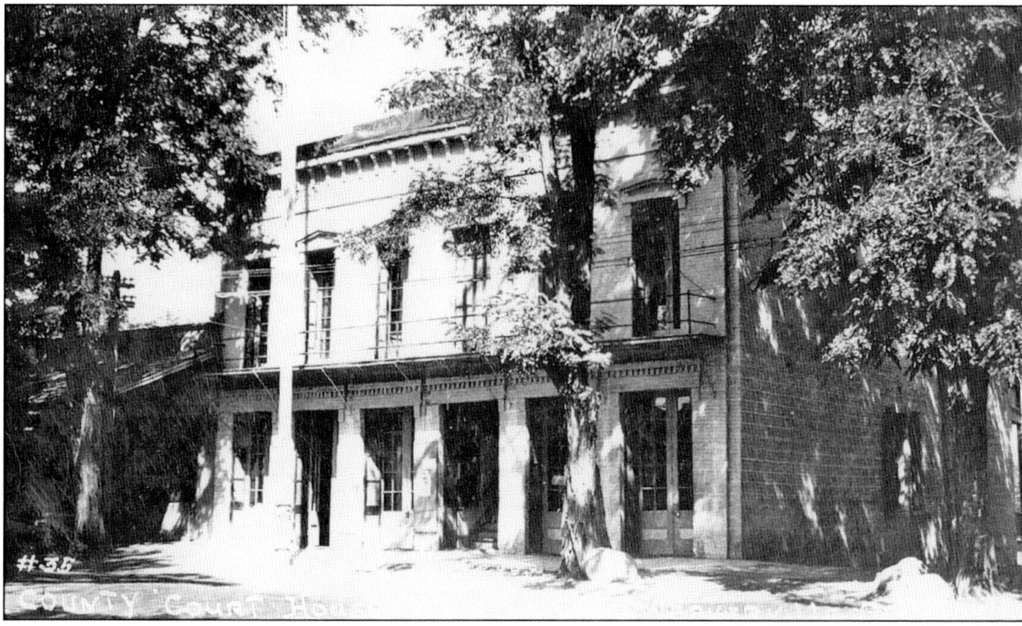

Weaverville, California, sits nestled below the Trinity Alps. The historic community was settled during the Gold Rush of 1849–1850. Fire destroyed many of the wooden structures, so by 1854, eight "fireproof" brick buildings were erected. The Hocker Building, constructed by Henry Hocker in 1854–1855, became Weaverville's courthouse, the second oldest in California. Originally it was a store and hotel. Across the street stands the restored 1901 bandstand.

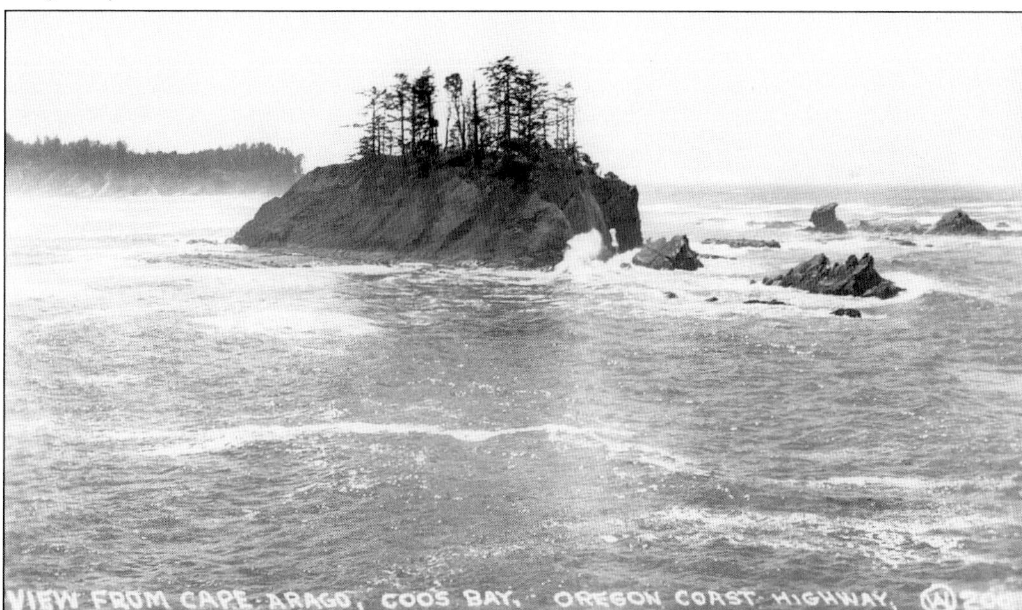

Coos Bay, Oregon, is a coastal town in the southwestern portion of the state. Along with North Bend and Charleston, the area is known as Oregon's Bay Area. Coos Bay is the largest natural harbor between Seattle and San Francisco, and until recently, it was also the largest timber port in the world. There are three state parks located here and a rugged but beautiful coastline that attracts visitors.

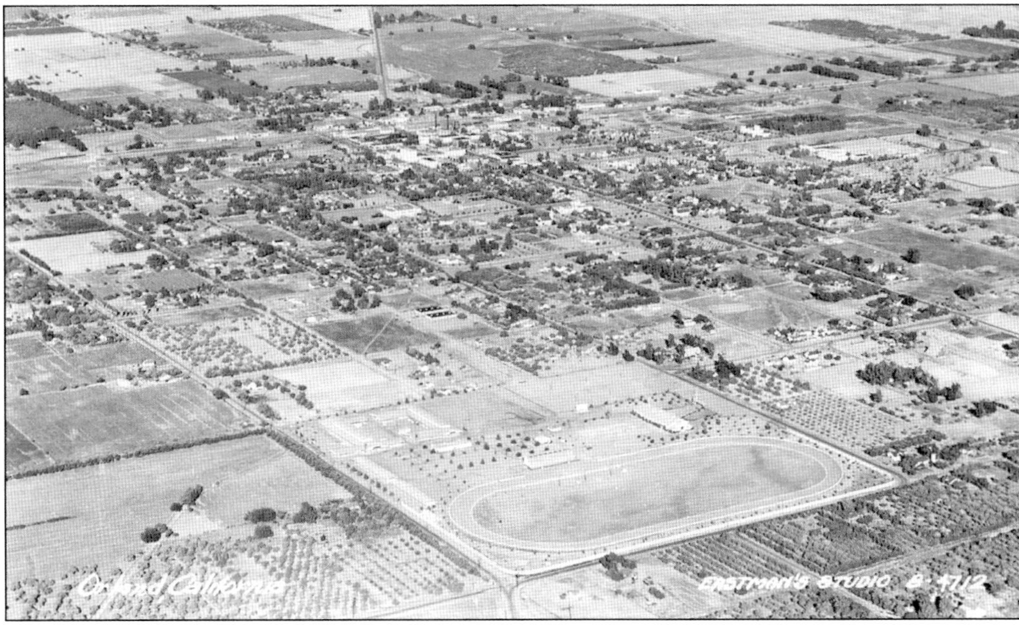

Orland, California, is located along Interstate 5 in Glenn County. Its earliest recorded history was built around cattle ranching, which was established by Granville Swift in the 1840s. Grain production led the Central Pacific Railroad to lay track between Colusa and Red Bluff. By 1880, Orland's population was 292. By the 1920s, the population had increased to 1,600. Still an agricultural area today, the city's population numbers 7,500.

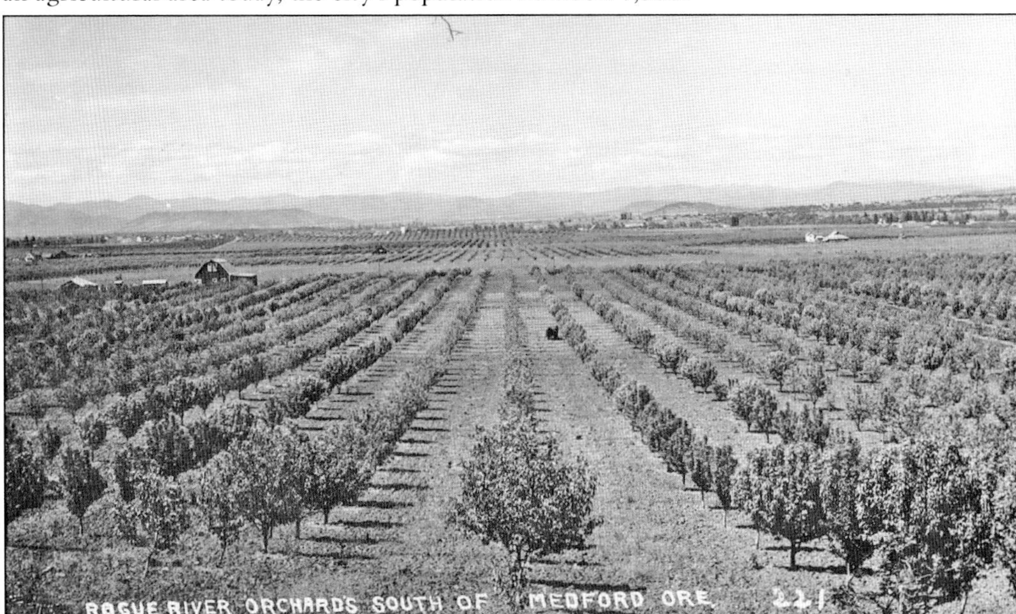

The first fruit trees in Rogue Valley were grown from seeds brought across the plains to Ashland, Oregon. J.H. Steward and J.D. Whitman planted the first commercial apple orchard in 1885. By 1930, however, 94 percent of the apple trees had been replaced by pear trees. Unfortunately, today, Rogue Valley's orchard ground has been reduced by urban sprawl, but higher-density orchards continue to produce quality fruit.

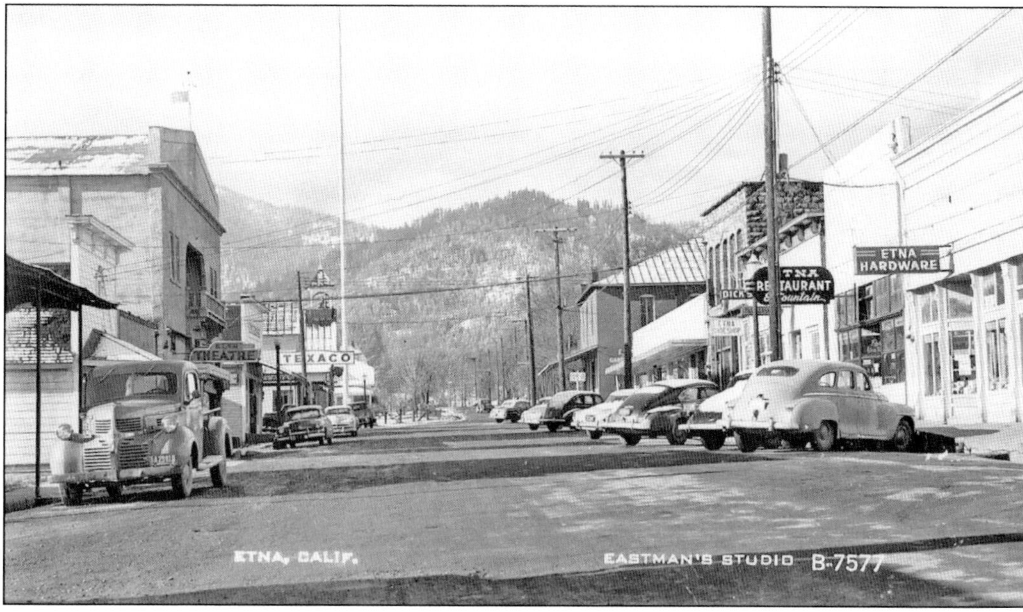

Spring in Etna, California, is characterized by cool weather. Etna grew in response to the need to supply miners; for a time, two communities, Aetna Mills and Rough and Ready, competed for business. When a flood destroyed much of Aetna Mills, the remaining businesses, including the post office and the town's name, moved a mile down the road to Rough and Ready. Etna was incorporated in 1878.

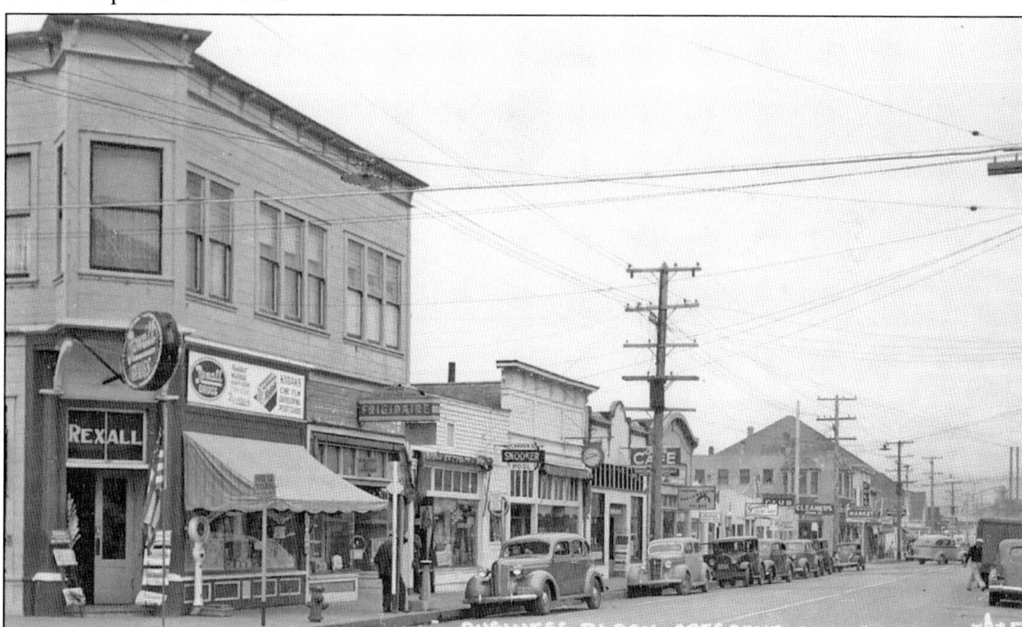

Crescent City, California, is the county seat and the only incorporated city in Del Norte County. Located 20 miles south of the Oregon border, it was named for its crescent-shaped stretch of beach. Commercial and recreational fishing is Crescent City's most important industry, with salmon, tuna, and cod the most popular catch. Because of its geography, Crescent City has been susceptible to tsunamis. The last one occurred after Japan's 2011 earthquake.

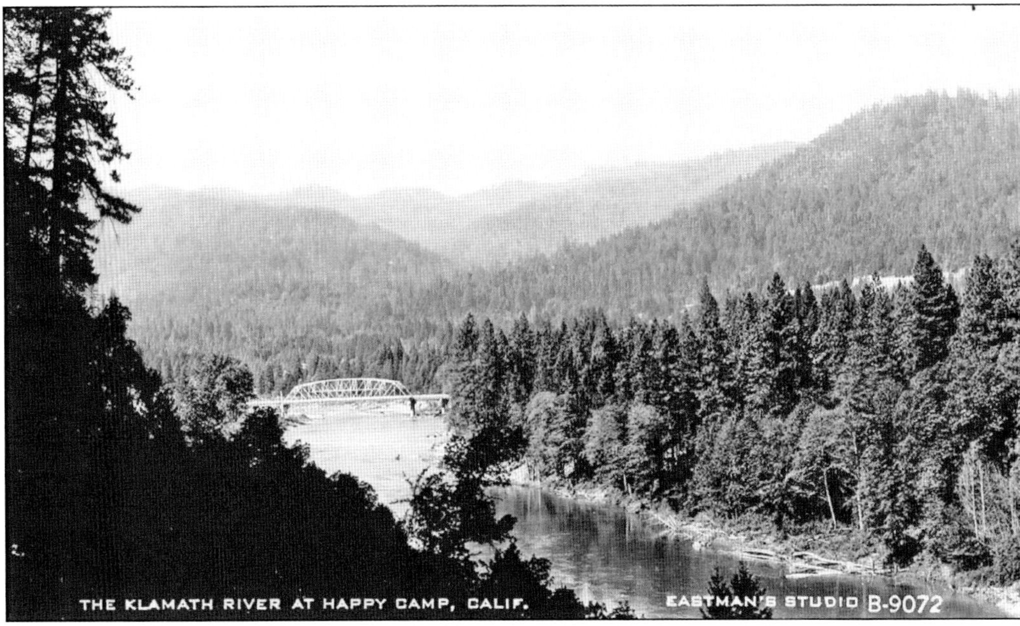

Happy Camp, California, is situated along the Klamath River and is almost completely enveloped by mountains. A number of creeks flow into the river, including Elk Creek, Clear Creek, and Indian Creek. The Karuk, who have lived here for generations, originally called the area *Athithufvuunupma*. The town is located 70 miles west of Interstate 5 on Highway 96, also called the State of Jefferson Scenic Byway.

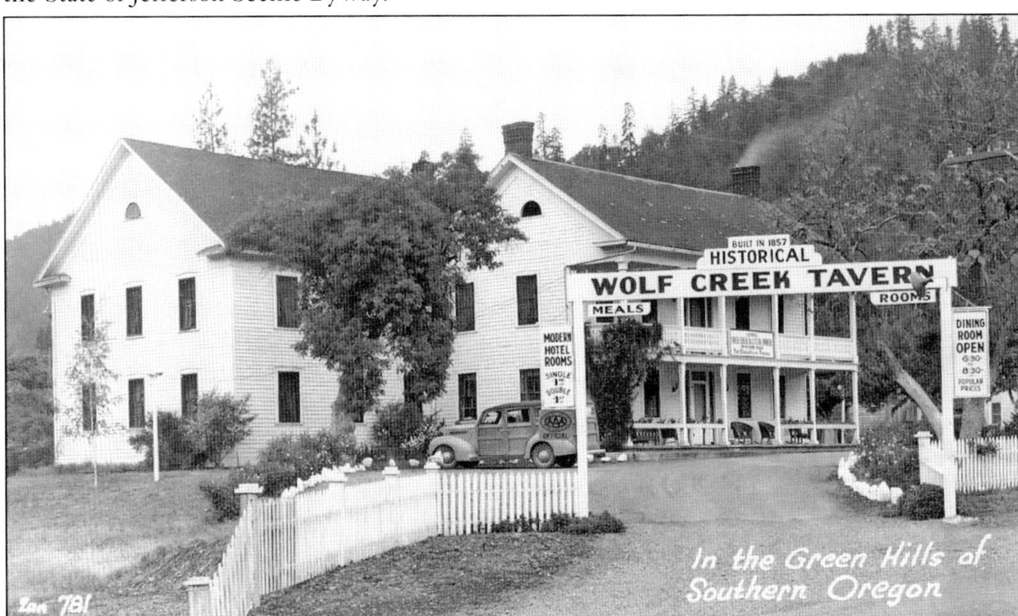

Wolf Creek Tavern, 20 miles north of Grants Pass, Oregon, was a popular stop along the old stage road. An earlier roadhouse, the Six Bit House, was built around 1853, while Wolf Creek was built in 1883. It later became famous for its visitors, including Clark Gable and novelist Jack London. Listed in the National Register of Historic Places, Wolf Creek Tavern is one of the oldest continuously used inns in Oregon.

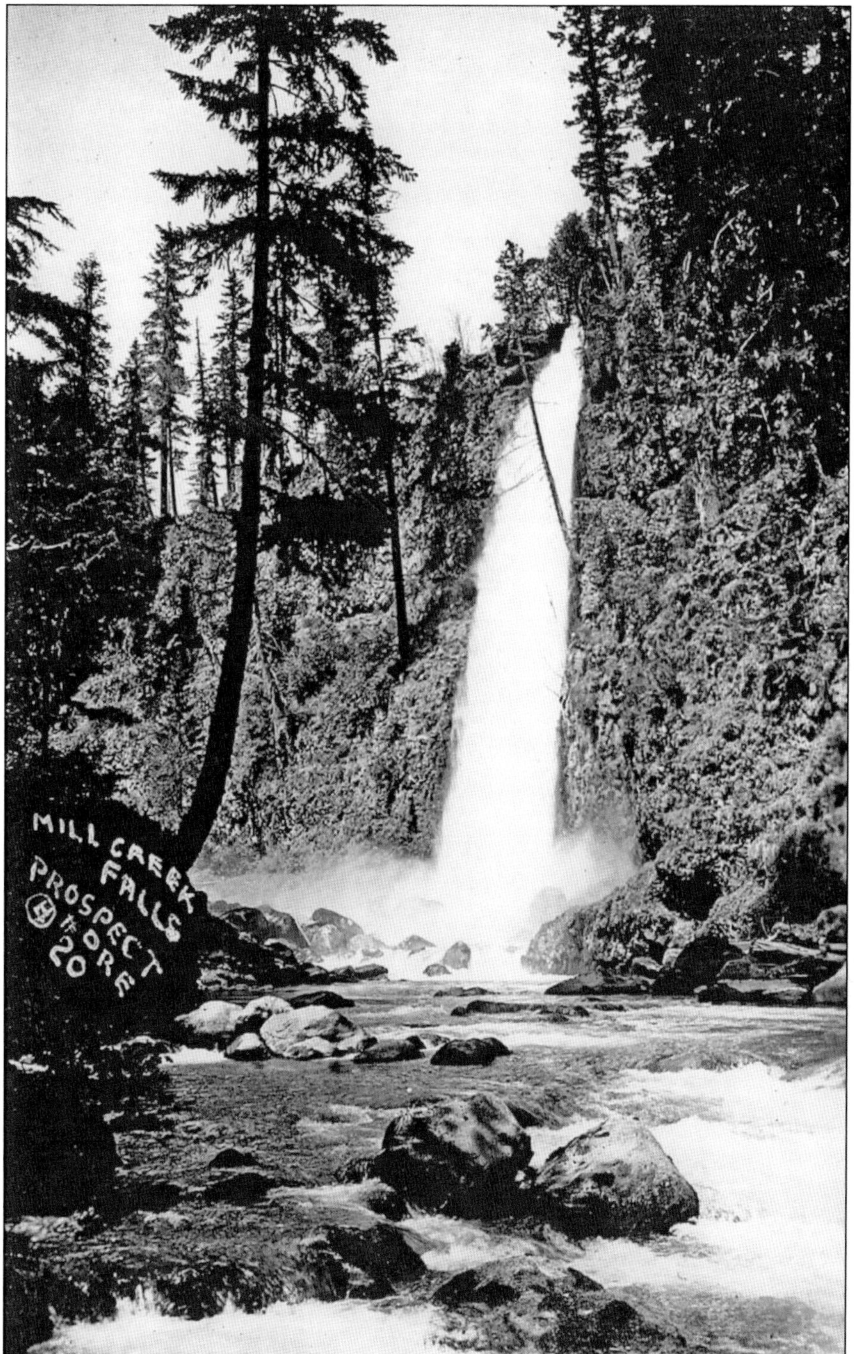

Mill Creek Falls is a 175-foot-high waterfall located along Oregon Route 62 outside the town of Prospect and on the way to Crater Lake. The amount of water does not fluctuate dramatically during the year but cascades into the Rogue River Gorge below throughout the seasons. It is not known who first noted the falls, but the town of Prospect was settled in 1882. The trek to the falls is less than a half-mile long, and the parking area is only a half-mile from the turnoff. A few hundred yards from Mill Creek Falls is Barr Creek Falls, one of Oregon's tallest waterfalls.

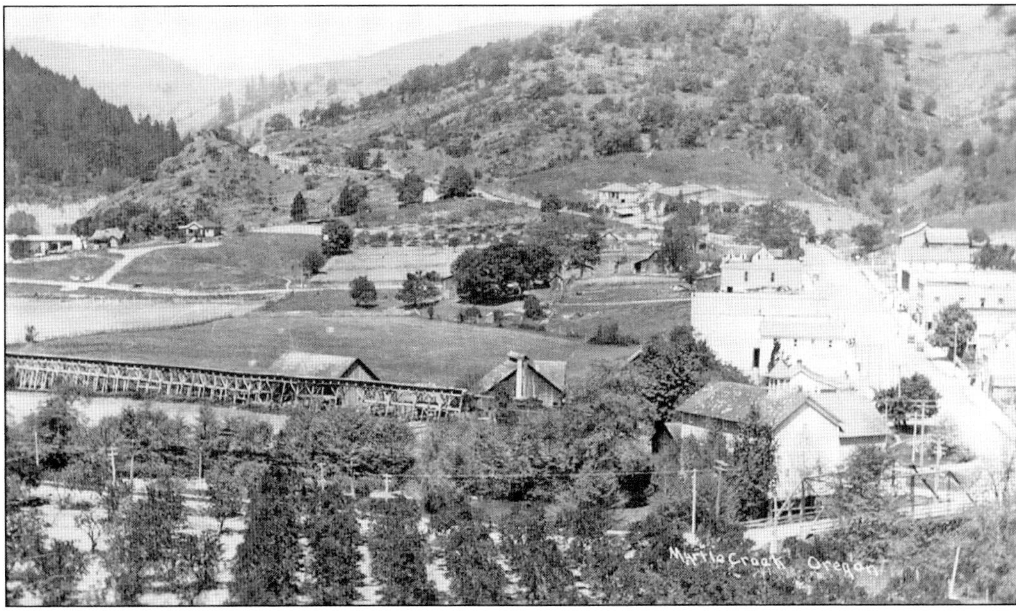

Myrtle Creek, Oregon, was named for the groves of myrtle that grew in the region. With the Gold Rush, miners flocked here. In North Myrtle Creek, two hydraulic "giants" or water "guns" worked around the clock during the summer months. By 1891, more than 200 Chinese laborers were hired to construct a ditch to carry more water to the mines. The China Ditch is still the largest 19th-century man-made landmark in Douglas County.

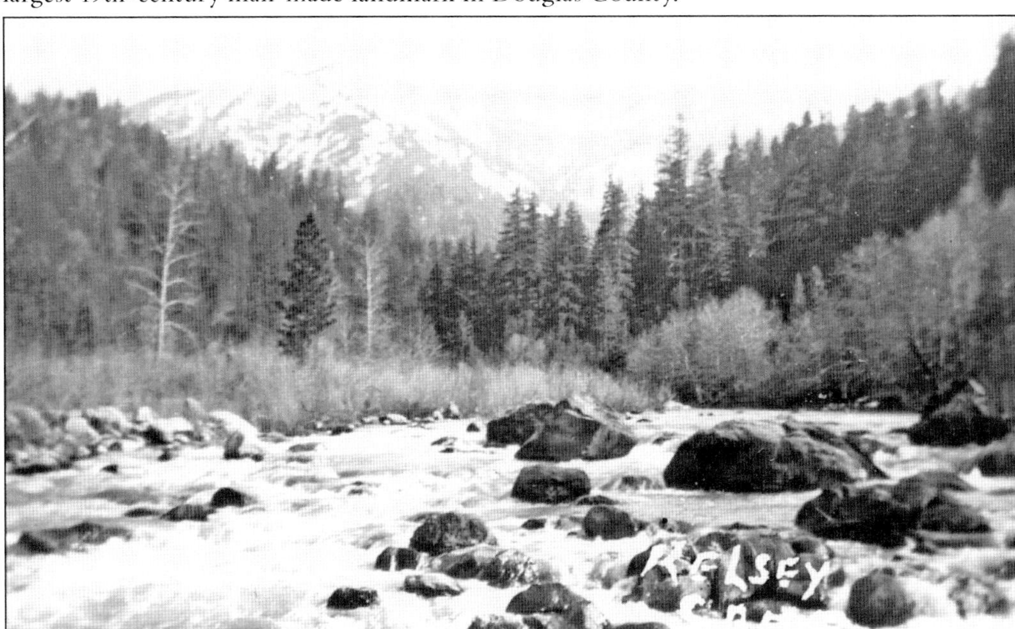

Kelsey Creek is located in the Marble Mountain Wilderness in Siskiyou County, California. The Kelsey Creek Trail was an 1850s trail that led from Crescent City over to Fort Jones and Scott Valley. Pack trains, sometimes numbering 60 mules or more, would lumber up and over the mountains packed either with supplies for the miners and soldiers stationed at Fort Jones or with gold and commodities for the ships at Crescent City.

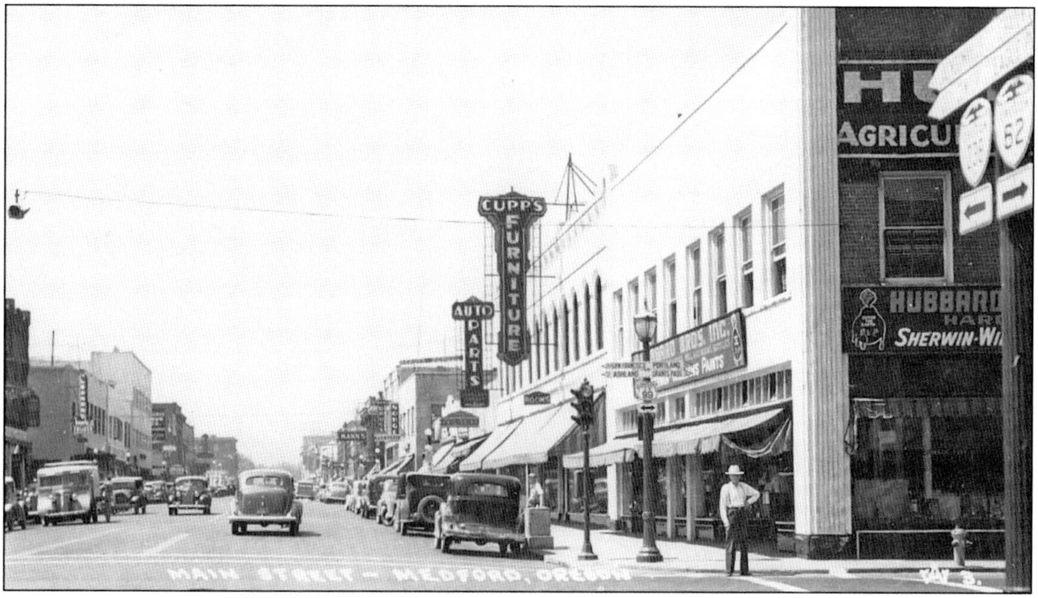

Medford, Oregon's history is linked to the establishment of the Oregon & California Railroad. In 1883, four men deeded portions of land to the railroad for a depot and town. By 1884, Front Street boasted several businesses, as did Seventh Street down to Main Street. As with the railroad, the surrounding orchards boomed, and fruit became the valley's major commodity. Today, Medford is the medical and commercial hub for southern Oregon and northern California.

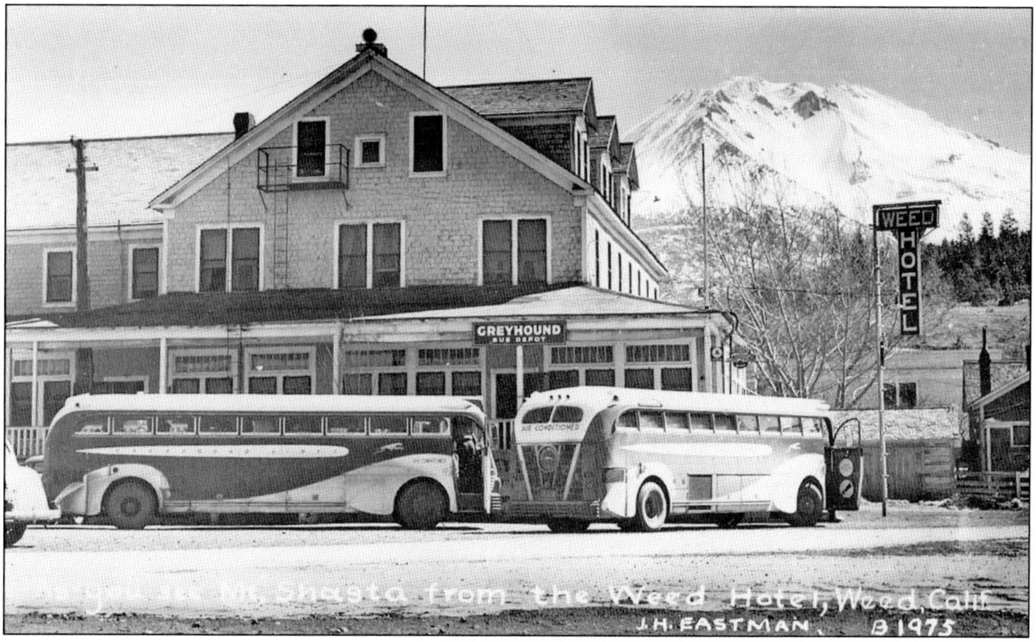

Weed, California, got its name from Abner Weed, pioneer and founder of the town's original lumber mill. Today, even more than in the past, the community relies on tourism. Weed lies 10 miles from Mount Shasta and the Pacific Crest Trail and is located at the junction of Interstate 5 and Highway 97. College of the Siskiyous was built here in 1957 and is the only community college in the state north of Redding, California.

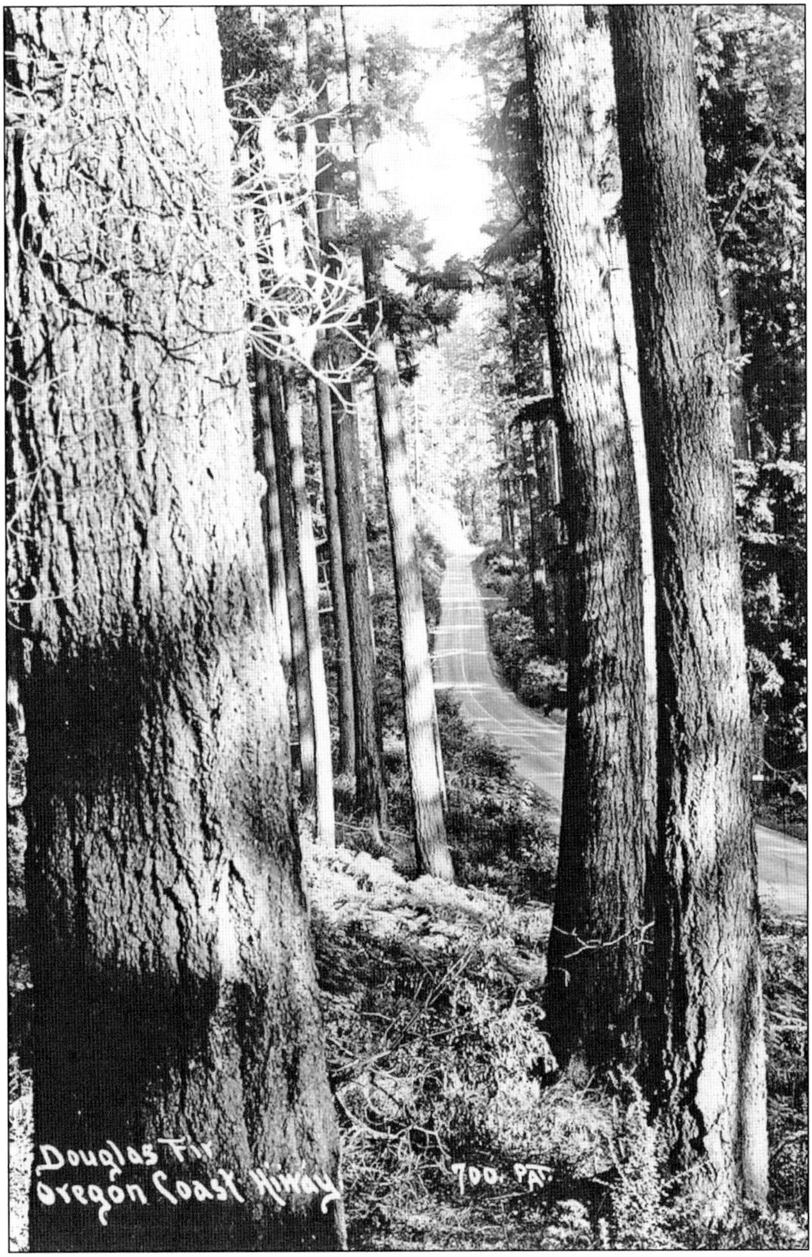

Douglas-firs grow in all states from the Rocky Mountains to the Pacific Ocean. Medium to large evergreen trees, Douglas-firs, also known as Oregon pines, are found at elevations 1,500 feet and higher. The largest trees, 200 feet tall, grow along the coast near Vancouver, British Columbia; they are second only to the coastal redwoods. The leaves are flat and needle-like, much like other firs; however, the Douglas-fir is not a true fir, hence the hyphen in the name. It is a prolific seed producer, however, and used for more lumber products than any other tree on the continent because of its characteristic strength, durability, and availability. It was named for David Douglas, the Scottish botanist who introduced its cultivability in 1827. He also introduced other native North American conifers to Europe. Douglas-fir is used for timber in Europe, New Zealand, and parts of South America. It is Oregon's state tree.

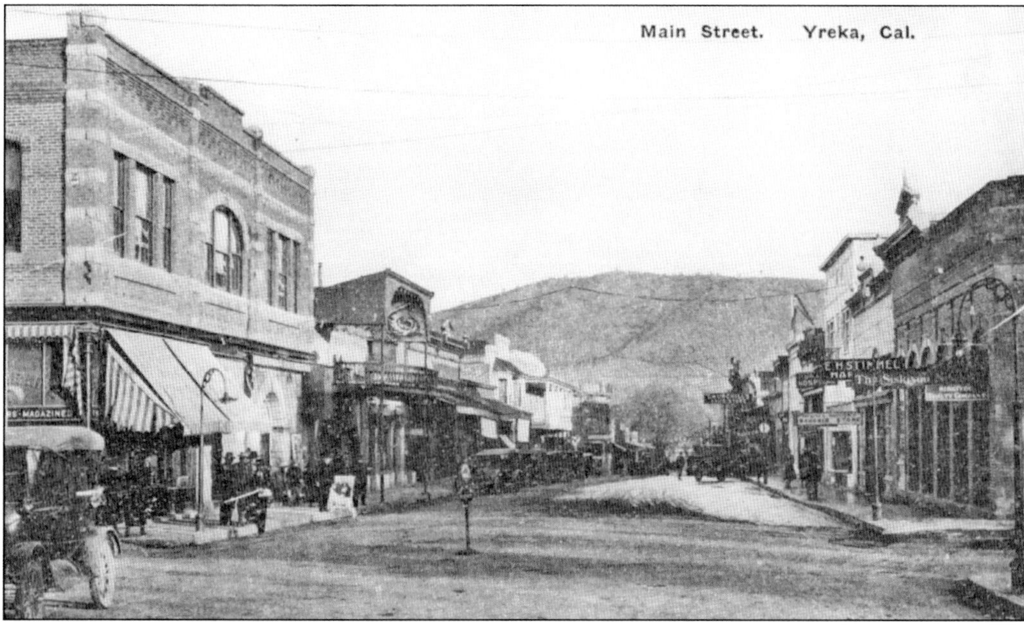

Yreka, California, is the county seat of Siskiyou County and sits 16 miles from the Oregon border. Miner Street in Yreka is listed in the National Register of Historic Places. In 1851, Abraham Thompson and company discovered gold while traveling south, and his discovery launched a rush into northern California. By 1851, two thousand miners had established a tent city.

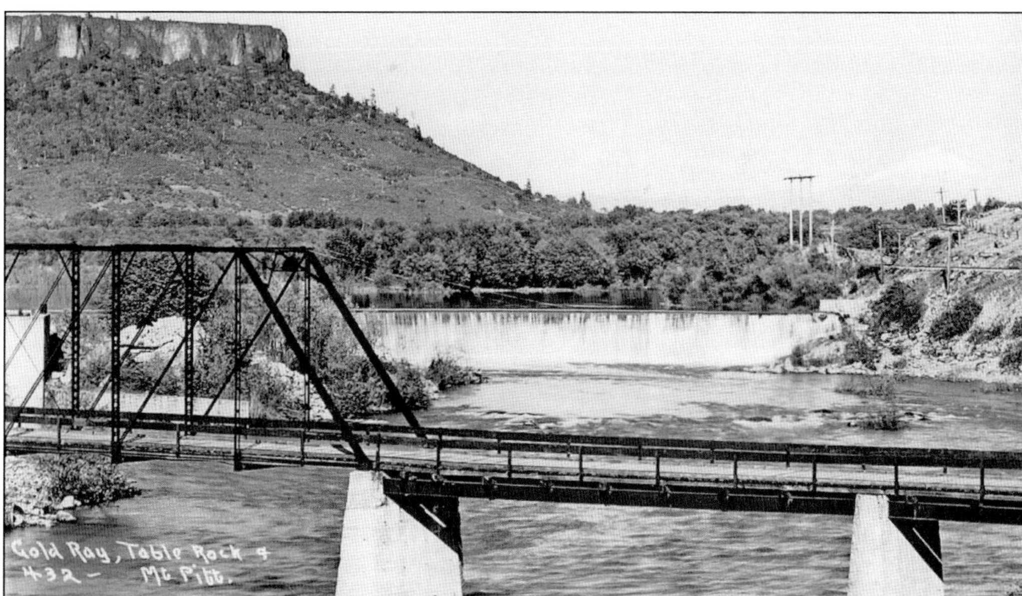

Table Mountain, Gold Ray Dam, and Mount McLoughlin fill the camera lens. Upper and Lower Table Rocks are prominent plateaus once inhabited by the Takelma tribe. Mount McLoughlin, also called Mount Pit, is the tallest volcano between Mount Shasta and Crater Lake. In 1900, Col. Frank Ray bought the Braden Mine and acquired rights to a power site to be constructed on the Rogue River. The facility was closed in 1972.

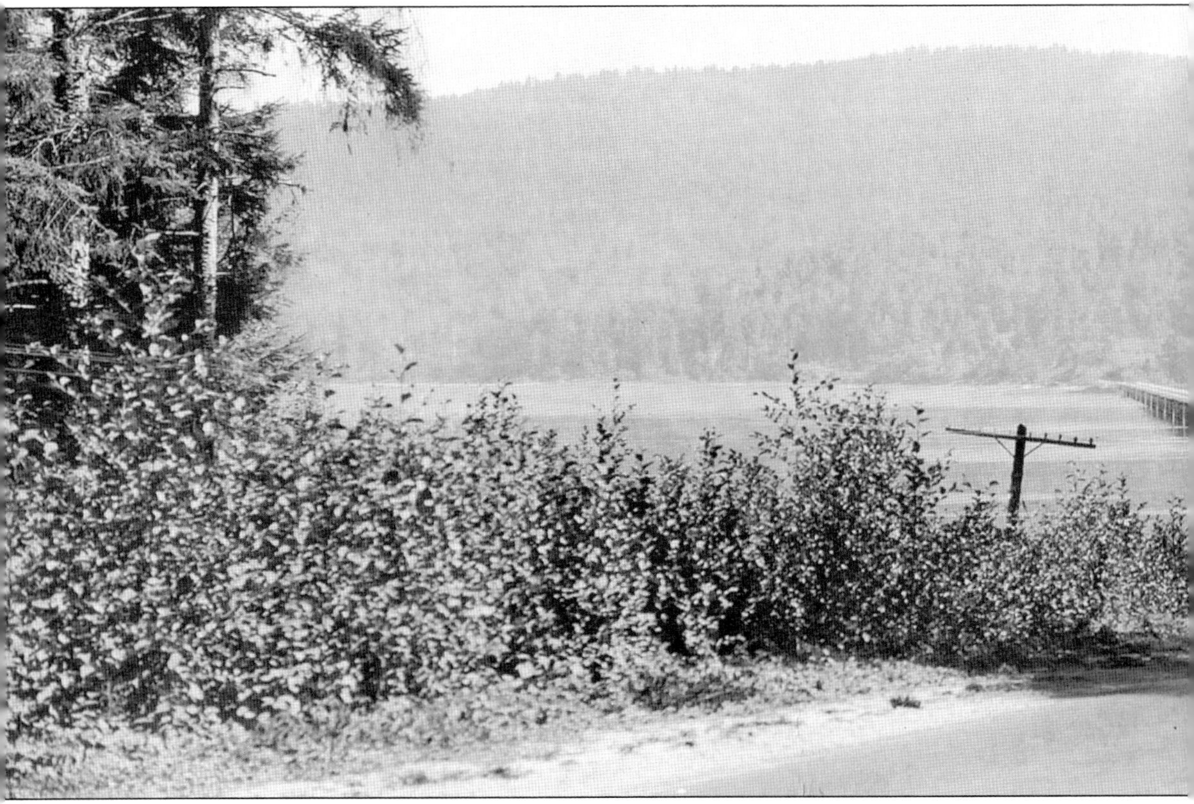

The Big Lagoon, located in Humboldt County, California, seen here, had to be crossed by travelers on the old Redwood Highway. Wind-driven shore currents helped shape the Big Lagoon; three streams—Tom Creek, Maple Creek, and Pitcher Creek—supply the majority of water entering the lagoon. The Redwood Highway constituted the northernmost portion of what is now known

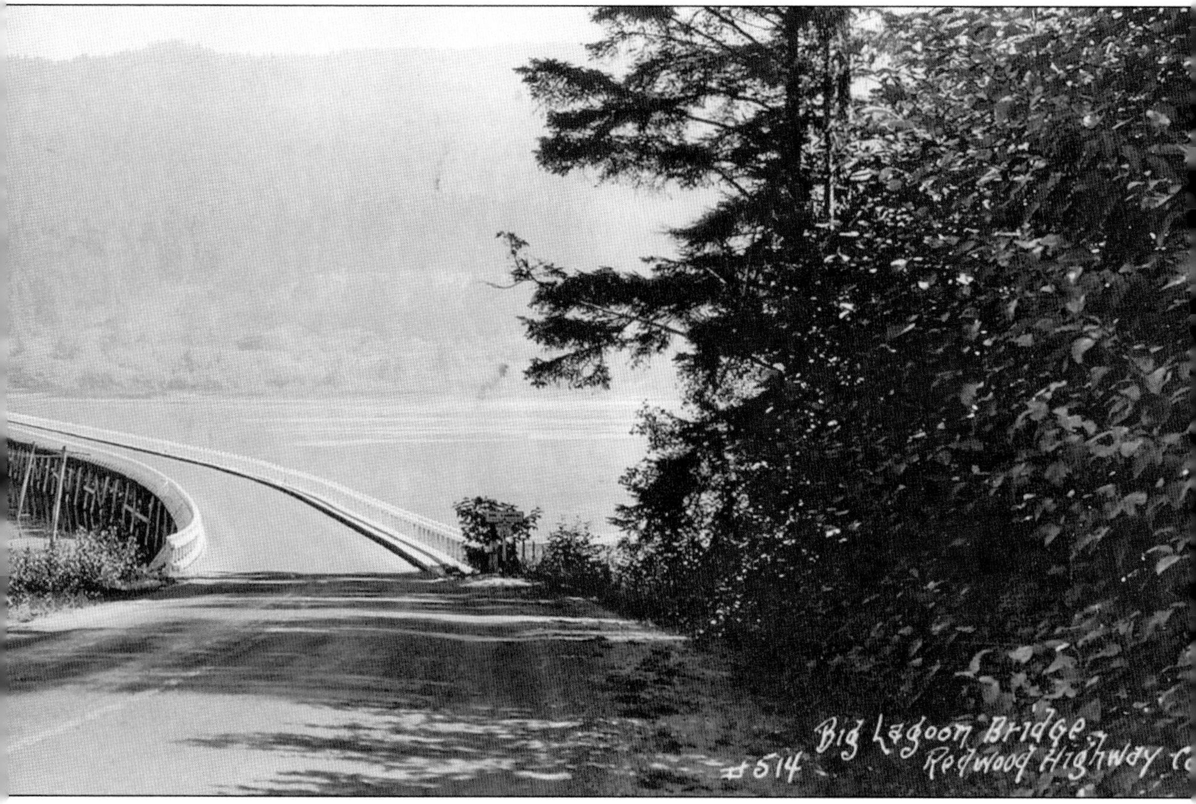

as Highway 101. Constructed in 1926, Highway 101 stretches 1,540 miles from Los Angeles to Olympia, Washington. Today, as in the 1920s, travelers driving the coastline highway have the opportunity to visit the coastal redwood forests, including Richardson's Grove State Park, Humboldt Redwoods State Park, and The Avenue of the Giants near Weott.

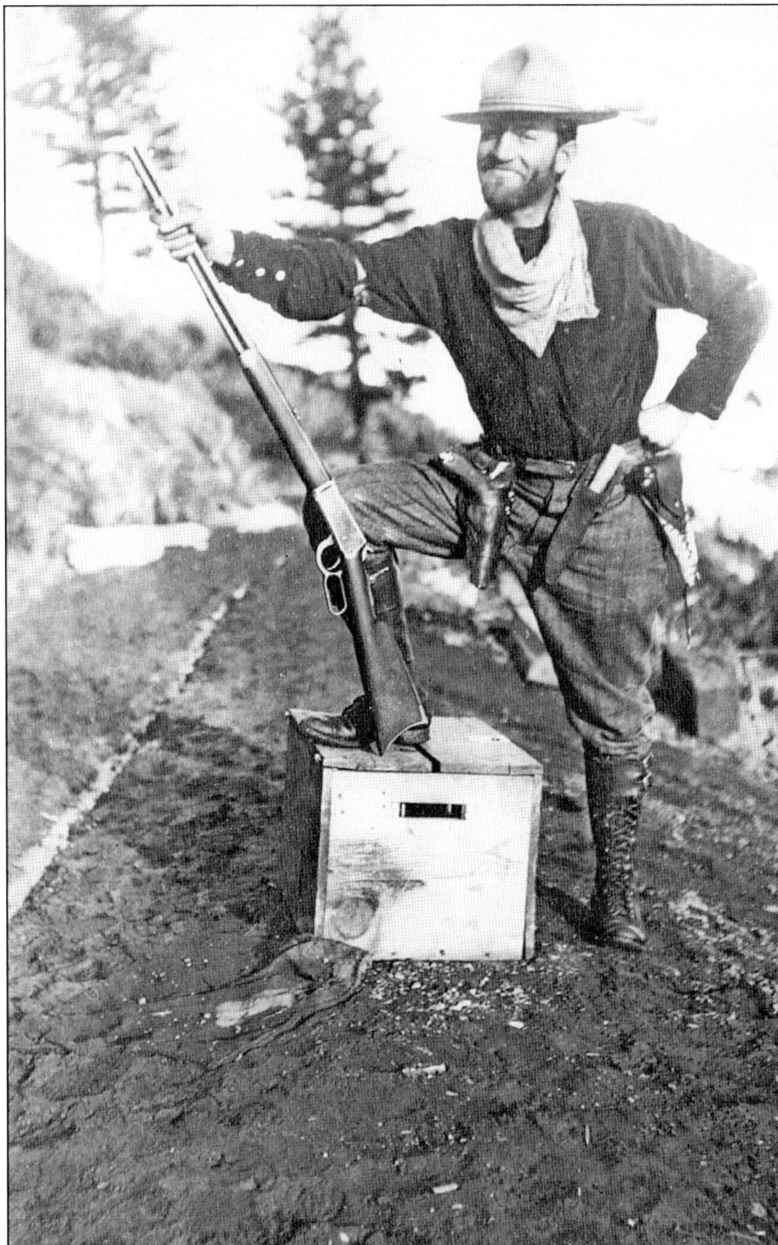

The Highland Mine was located in the Liberty mining district, 11 miles southeast of Etna, California. For many years, the Homestake and Highland Mines were chief producers and were considered two of the finer quartz mines in the region. P. Musick, who reportedly extracted $80,000 in gold, discovered the vein of gold at the Highland in 1899. The mine was then sold to the Belgium-Bohemian Mining Company of Belgium, and the superintendent was H.E. Mattern, seen here. The mine encompassed 100 acres, ran a 10-stamp mill, and sat at an elevation of 6,400 feet. It employed 26 men in 1916 and was said to have produced $350,000. Supplies had to come by way of pack trains. Other significant mines in the Salmon River country included the Black Bear Mine, owned by John Daggett, which reportedly produced $3 million in gold.

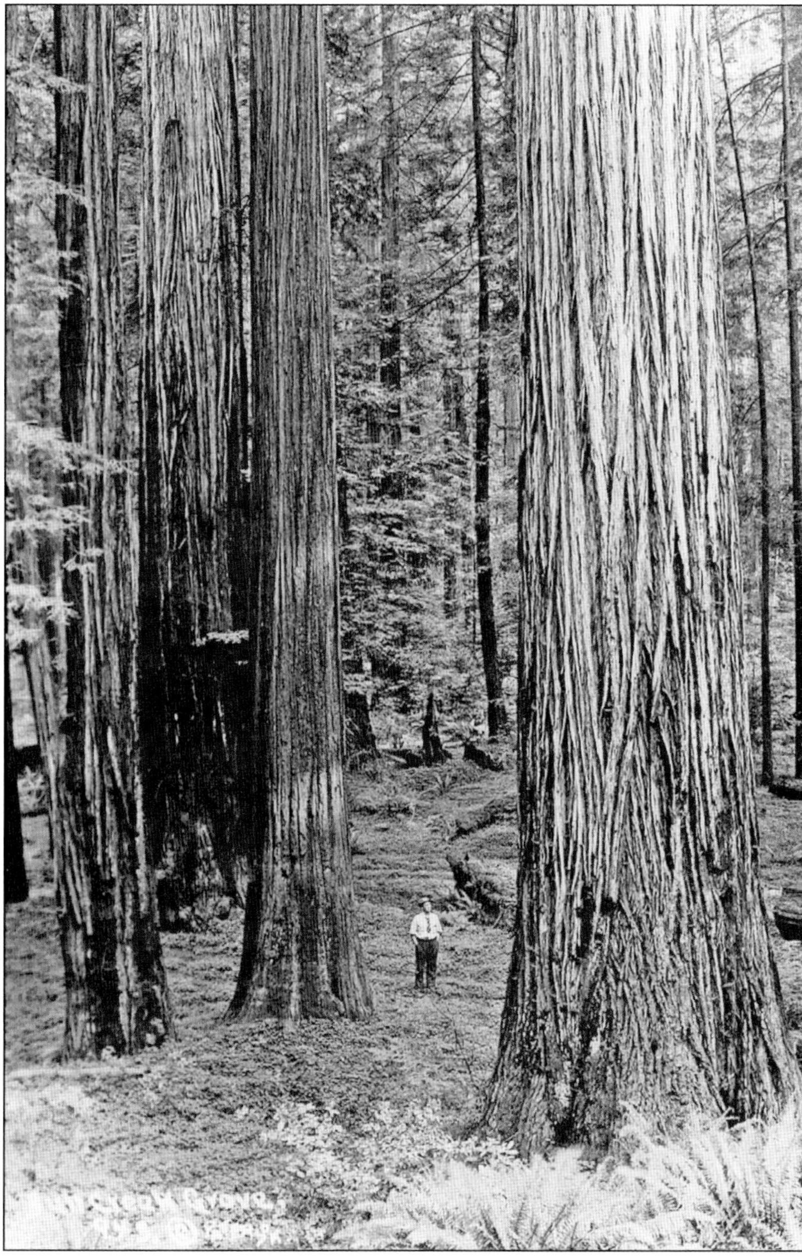

In 1917, conservationists Madison Grant, Henry Osborn, and John Merriam visited Bull Creek in California, now part of the Humboldt Redwoods State Park, and decided to establish the Save-the-Redwoods League. Upper and Lower Bull Creek Flat are home to what have been called the world's tallest trees. In 1921, with the addition of state funds, the league purchased its first grove, which is now part of Humboldt State Park. In 1930, John D. Rockefeller Jr. brought his family to Bull Creek Flat; his $2-million donation to the league in 1931 helped purchase 9,000 acres at Bull Creek. At the Big Tree area, visitors can still walk the half-mile loop. The full loop trail can only be walked in the summer and fall. Several special trees have been identified along this trail, including the Founders' Tree, which was dedicated to those who helped establish the Save-the-Redwoods League.

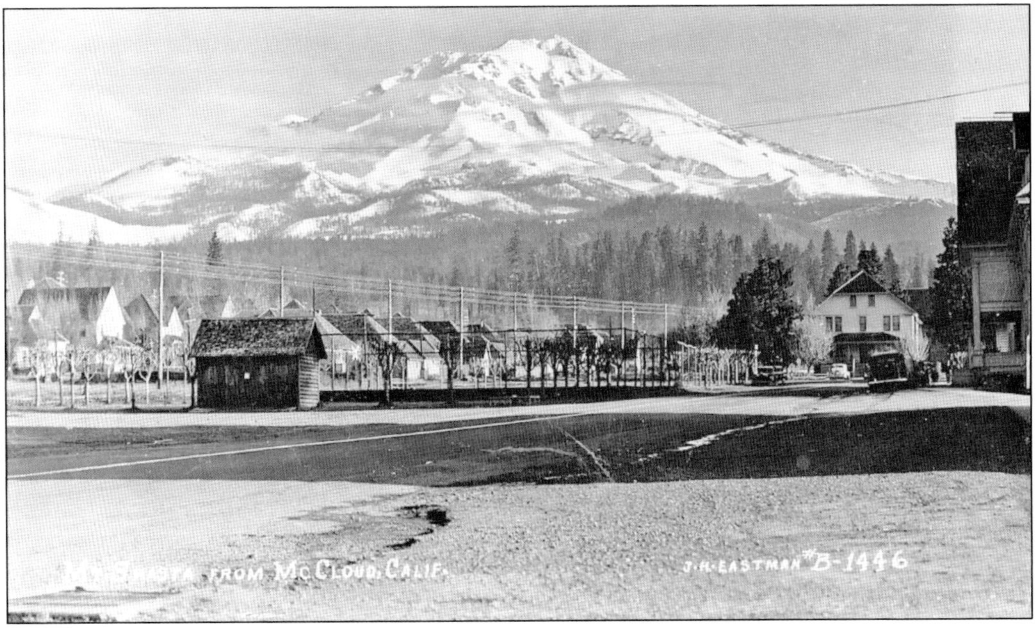

McCloud, California, is best known as a lumber town. In 1892, A. Friday George built the first mill but failed when he couldn't get lumber over the rugged terrain with oxen. In 1897, George W. Scott and William Van Arsdale founded the McCloud River Railroad Company. They also bought up several mills and established the McCloud River Lumber Company. Until 1963, McCloud was a company town.

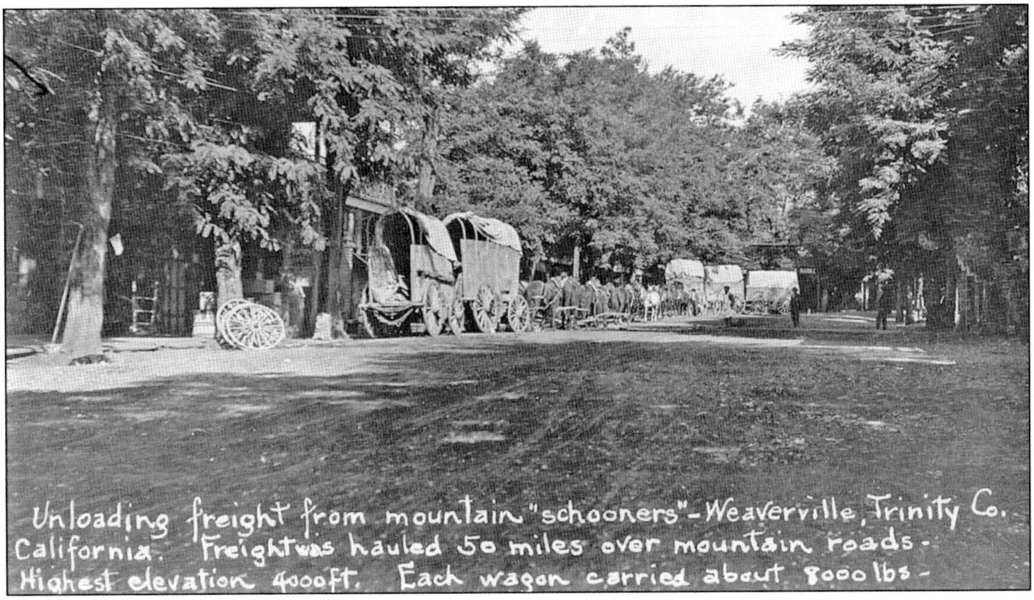

Here freight is being unloaded from "mountain schooners" at Weaverville, California. Hauling loads over treacherous roads at elevations of 4,000 feet, the lead wagon often carried three to four tons, while the second wagon carried less. Teamsters packed lanterns, kerosene, veterinary medicines, baling wire, shoeing tools, "mica" (axle grease, good for doctoring), laced leather, and a bedroll. Good horse care was critical; only after unloading and tending his horses did a teamster head to town.

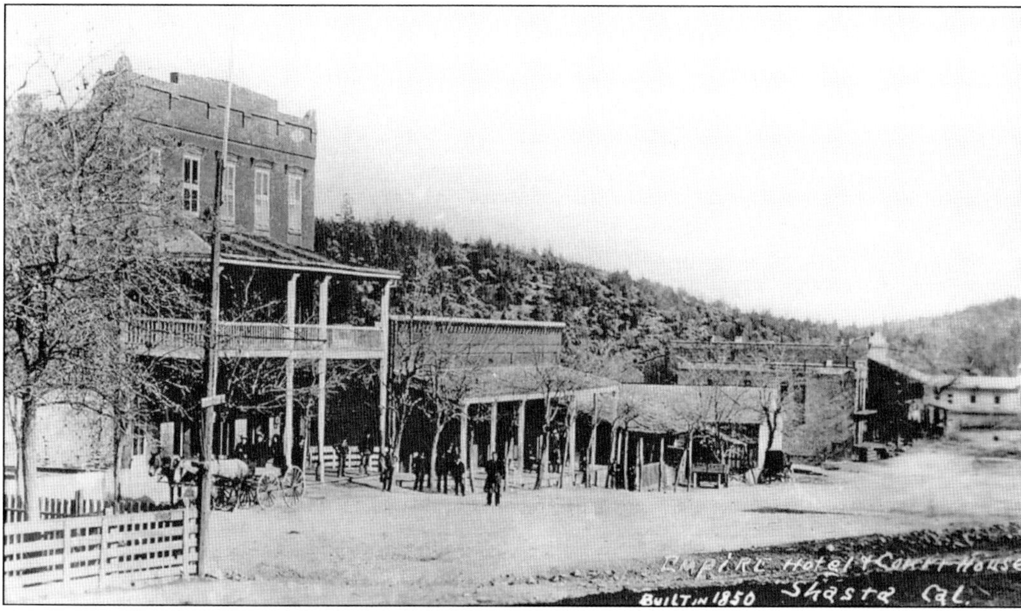

The Empire Hotel at Shasta, California, was the first Empire Hotel built in Shasta County. Destroyed by fire in 1853, it was rebuilt of brick in 1857. For its time, it was the finest hotel north of Sacramento and featured a number of first-class touches, including plastered walls and fine furnishings. In 1923 it was demolished and its bricks were used to build several buildings in downtown Redding.

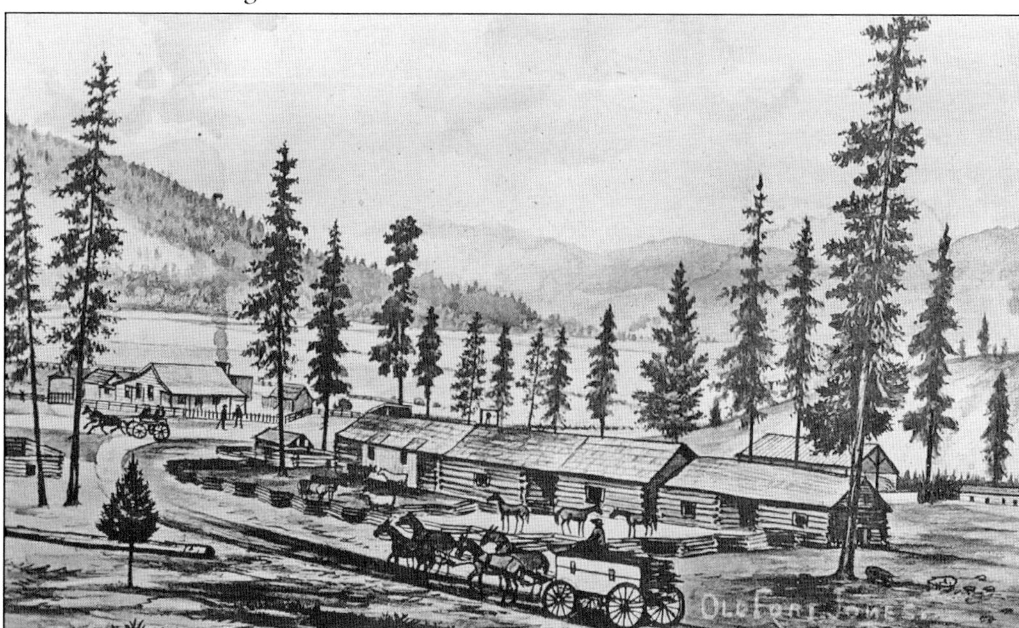

Named for Col. Roger Jones, adjutant general of the Army from 1825 to 1852, Fort Jones was garrisoned by Company E, 4th US Infantry in October 1852. Gen. George Crook, who later gained fame in the Civil War, was stationed here when he first left West Point. Gen. Ulysses S. Grant and Gen. Phillip Sheridan were also assigned duty at Fort Jones but never arrived. The garrison was evacuated in 1858.

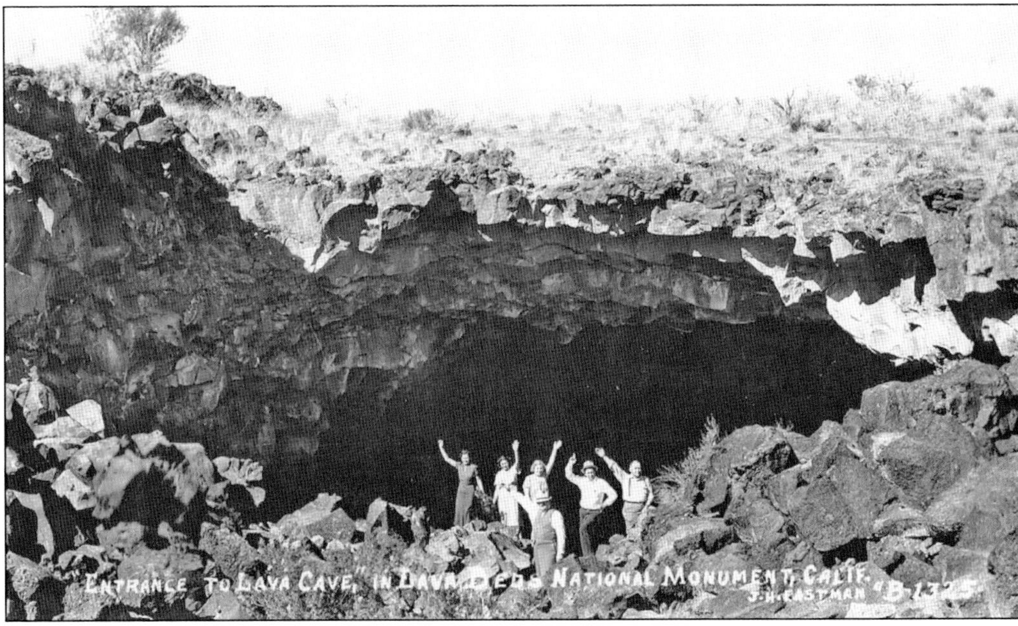

The entrance to the Lava Beds is located on the south shore of Tule Lake, California. The infamous 1872–1873 Modoc War was fought here after 50 Modoc warriors retreated into the natural fortress following the Battle of Lost River. The stronghold was created as molten lava cooled ages ago. It allowed the Modoc to defend their position against the US Army for five months. Today, it is called Captain Jack's Stronghold.

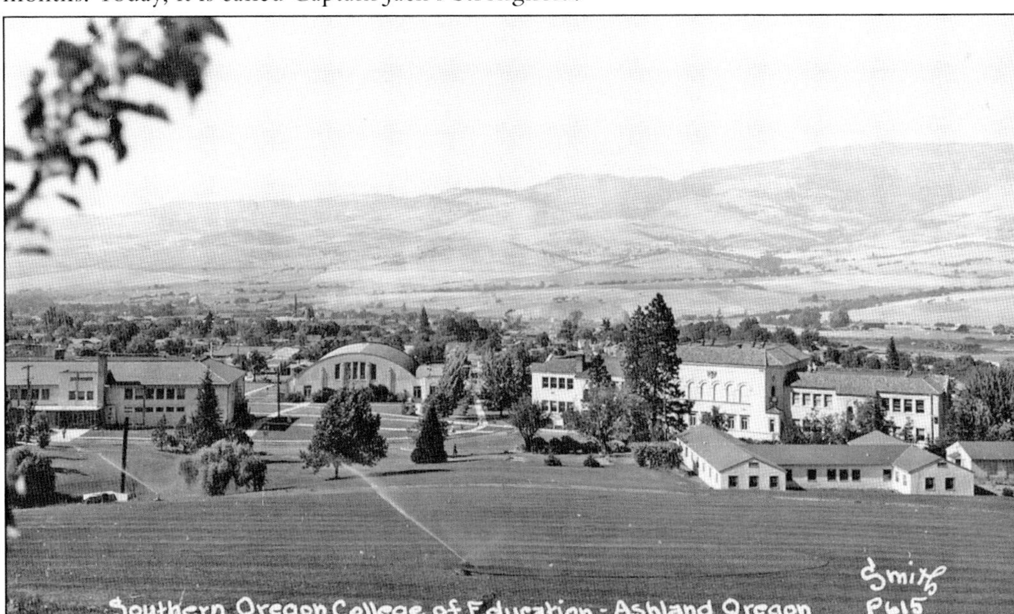

Southern Oregon University, in Ashland, Oregon, began as an academy in 1872 under the leadership of Rev. Henry Skidmore and the Methodist Episcopal Church. In 1887, the State of Oregon declared it a normal school—a school designed to train teachers. Without funding, however, the school closed. In spite of other openings and closings, SOU was officially reestablished in 1926.

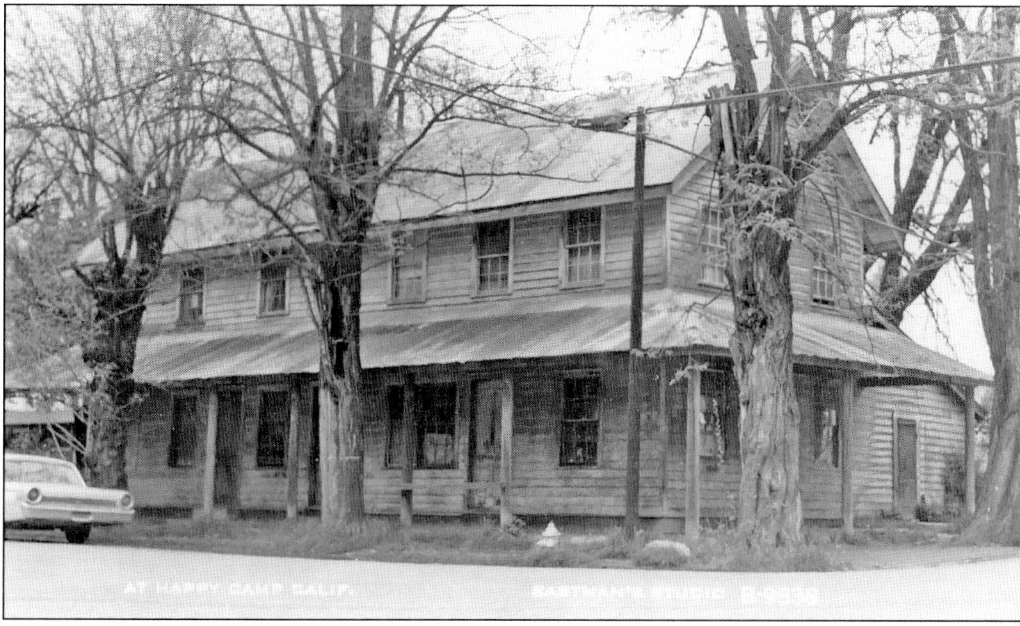

Cuddihy Hotel is at the corner of Second Avenue and Indian Creek Road in Happy Camp, California. Happy Camp is situated along Highway 96 and the Klamath River, almost completely enveloped by mountains. One of the earliest businesses established in the early 1850s was Henry Doolittle's American House, later called the Cuddihy Hotel. James Camp, another pioneer, patented claims that became the Classic Hill Mine.

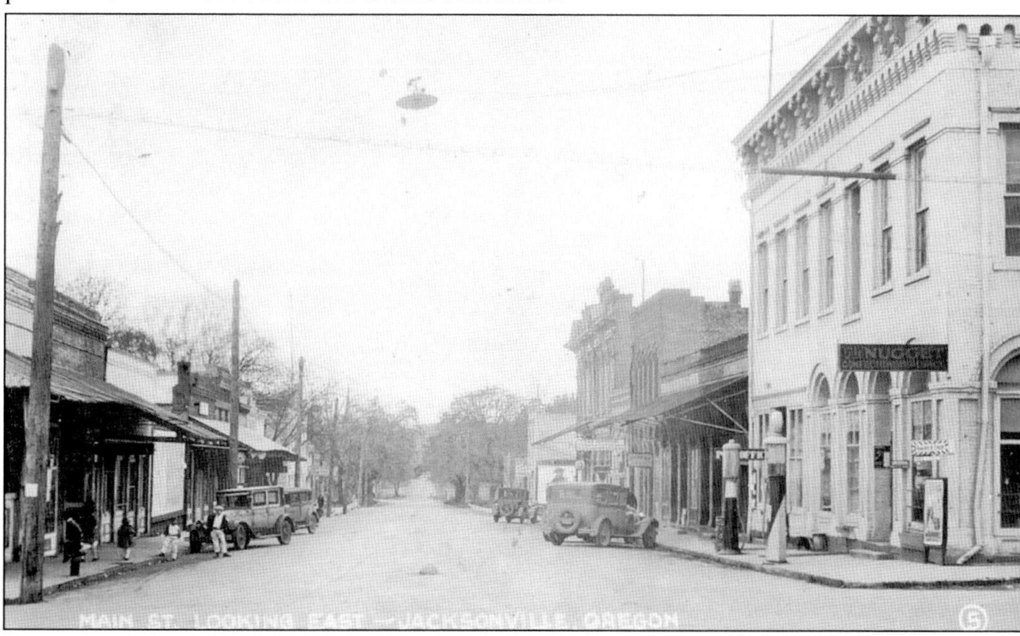

Jacksonville, Oregon, began as a makeshift mining camp and was first known as Table Rock City. By 1852, the community had boomed to a town of over 2,000. For decades, Jacksonville served as the commercial center of southern Oregon. In 1884, however, the all-important railroad was routed through nearby Medford. As a result, Jacksonville's population and popularity waned. Today, the town is a National Historic Landmark.

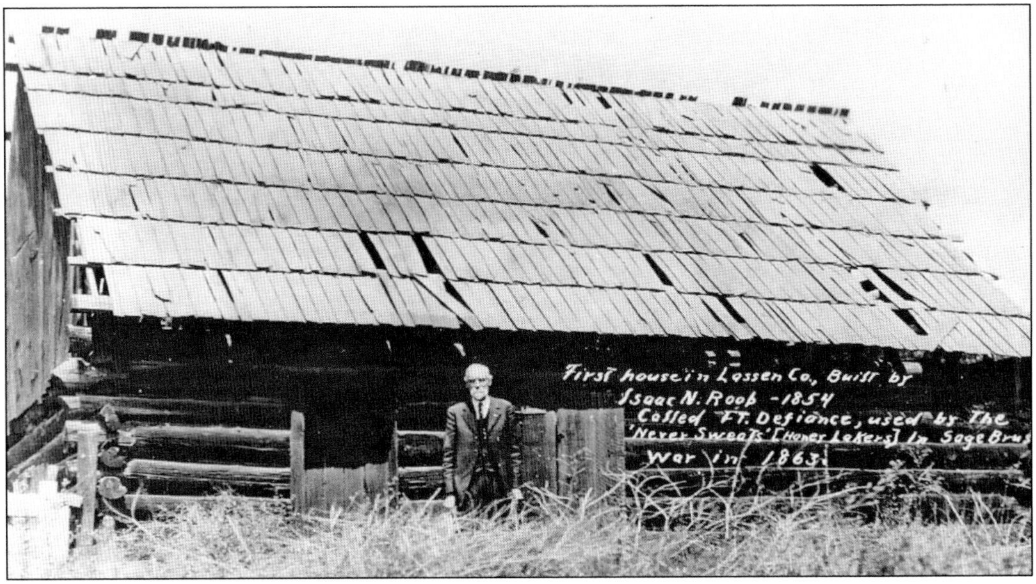

The first house built in Lassen County, California, was constructed in 1853. This log trading post, built by Isaac Roop, served early immigrants and became Susanville's first house and oldest structure. It was converted into a fortified blockade in 1854 when the area's independent and free-thinking citizens opposed Plumas County's sheriff and his tax officials in a two-day skirmish known as the Sagebrush War. The blockhouse was then renamed Fort Defiance.

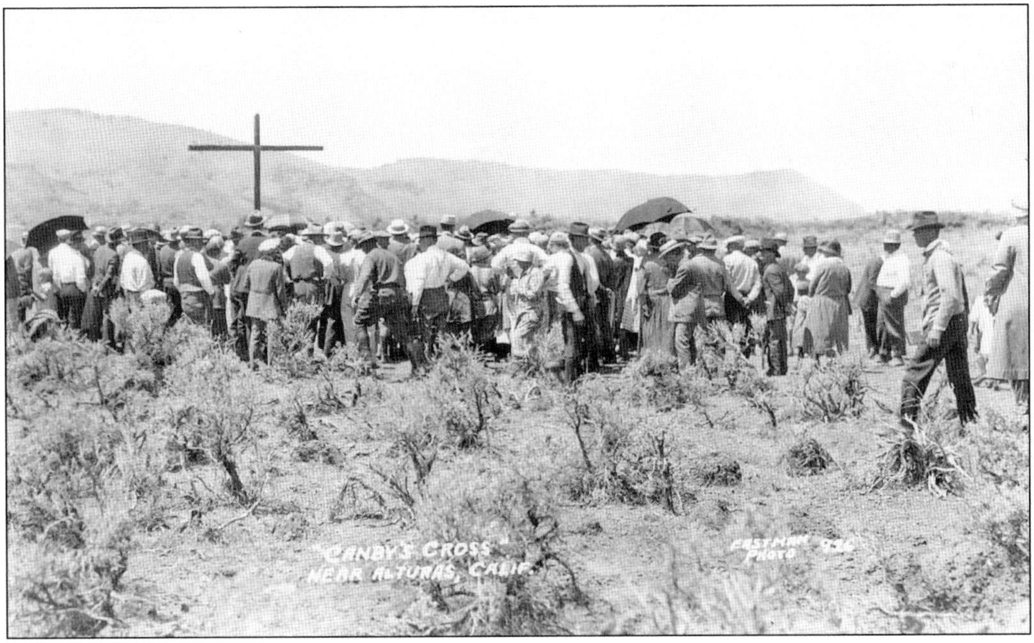

Canby's Cross stands near Tulelake/Alturas, California. The Modoc War, or Modoc Campaign, was fought in 1872–1873 between the Modoc and US Army. It was the last Indian war to occur in California or Oregon. Tule Lake was also the site of the largest Japanese internment camp during World War II; it opened on May 26, 1942, and closed on March 28, 1946. More than 18,000 persons of Japanese descent were interred at Tule Lake.

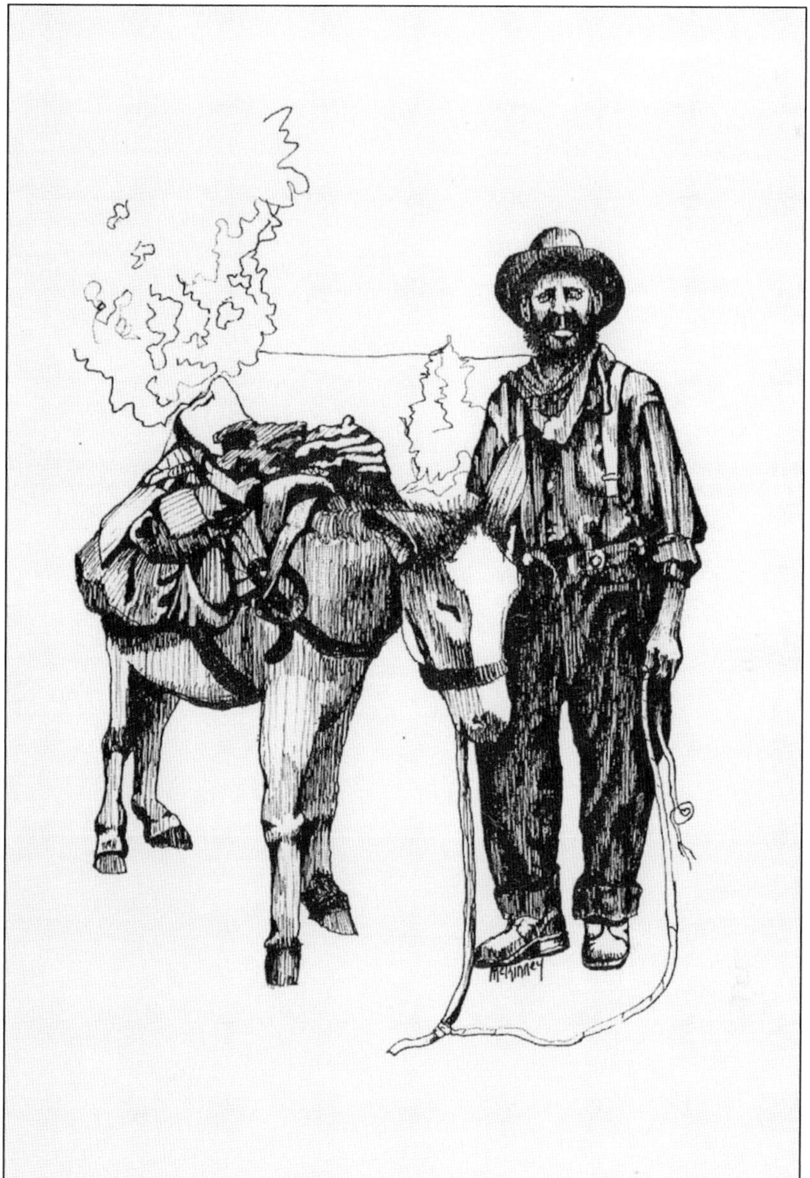

The first gold-seekers to move north followed waterways, in particular the Klamath River and its tributaries. Lindsay Applegate traveled south from Jacksonville, Oregon, in 1849 to mine Beaver Creek, the Klamath, and Scott River. Prospectors traveled from the Trinity River to the Salmon River. There they established a small settlement—the first—called Bestville in honor of Captain John Best, a sea captain, miner, and trader who discovered gold with the help of Squirrel Jim, a Shasta Indian who befriended many whites. Maj. Pierson Reading left the Sierra Mother Lode with nothing, but managed to pull out $80,000 along the Trinity. Gen. Joseph Lane, arriving from Oregon, discovered gold on the Shasta River in 1850 near where the town of Yreka now stands. John W. Scott led another group of miners into the region (his name was then given to a valley, a river, and a mountain pass). He and his men discovered gold at Scott Bar in July or August 1850. The richest and most extensive discovery north of the Trinity Range was near Yreka in March 1851 by Abraham Thompson.

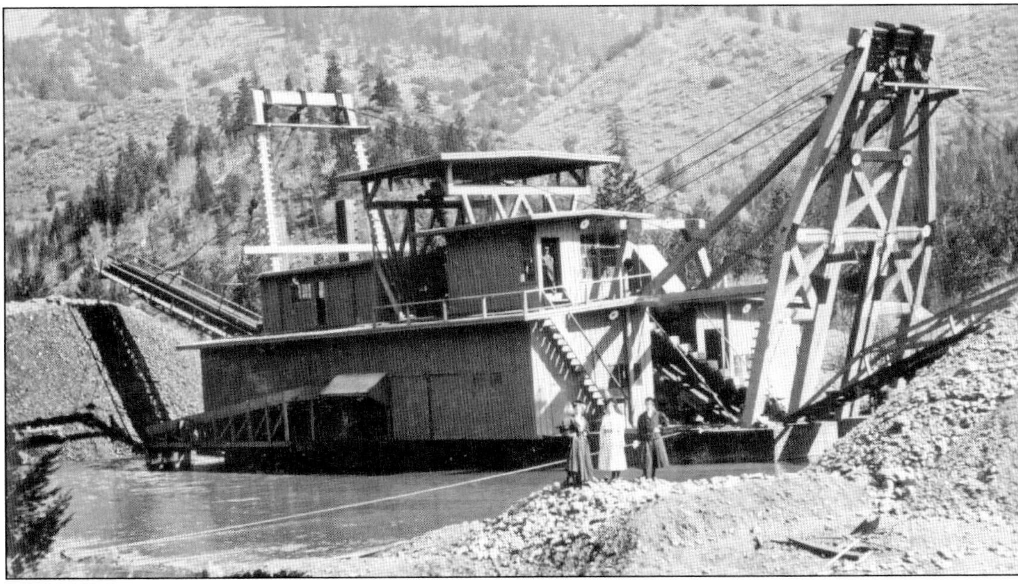

The Yuba Dredge was left abandoned near Callahan, California. Gold dredgers were introduced around the beginning of the 20th century. The Yuba Dredger Company built this one at the mouth of Sugar Creek. It plowed up to one mile of Callahan's Ranch, then turned downstream until it was stopped at the Wolford Ranch in the early 1940s, where the Wolford brothers refused to sell out. In all, it traveled little more than four miles.

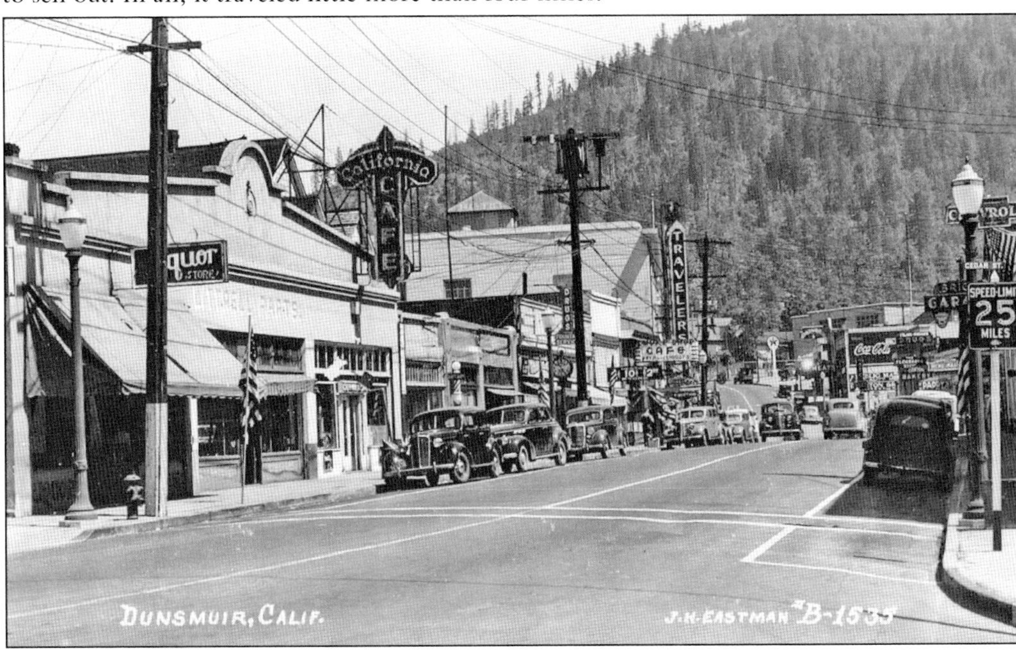

Dunsmuir, California, was a railroad town. The Central Pacific Railroad (later Southern Pacific) completed its line up the Sacramento Canyon in 1887, leading to the establishment of Dunsmuir. The settlement was first called Pusher. However, when a member of the wealthy Dunsmuir family from British Columbia agreed to send the town a fountain, it was renamed. Dunsmuir had invested heavily in the railroad company. The town has been listed in the National Register of Historic Places.

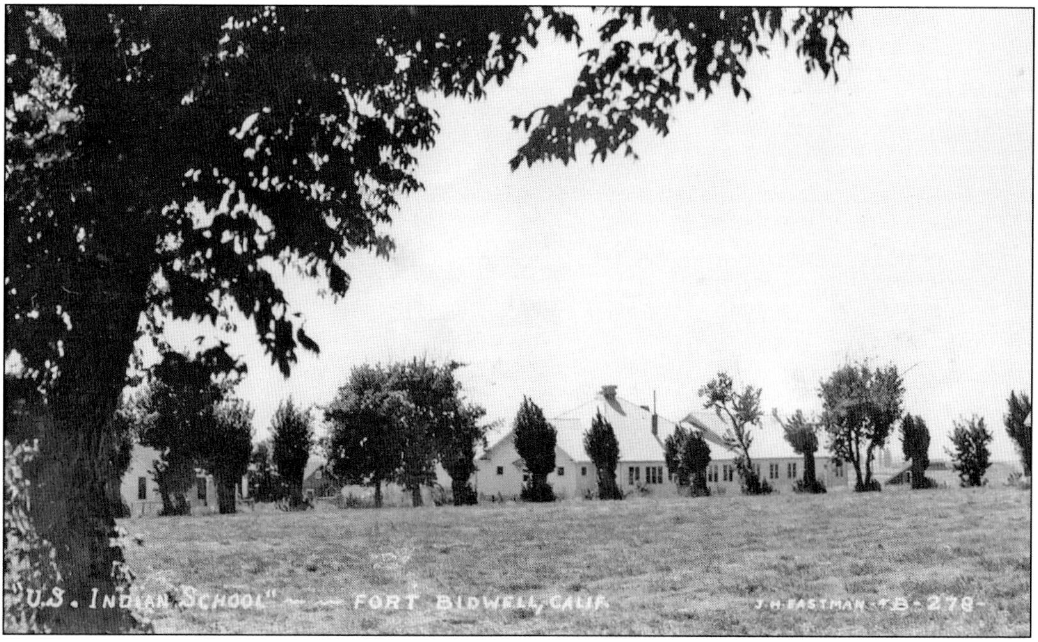

Fort Bidwell was established in 1865 after settlers from Red Bluff, California, petitioned Gen. John Bidwell to help protect miners and settlers traveling northeast into the mines of Idaho. A site was established at the base of the Warner Mountains at the north end of Surprise Valley, California. The fort acted as the base for campaigns against several tribes, including the Modoc, Nez Percé, and Snake Indians.

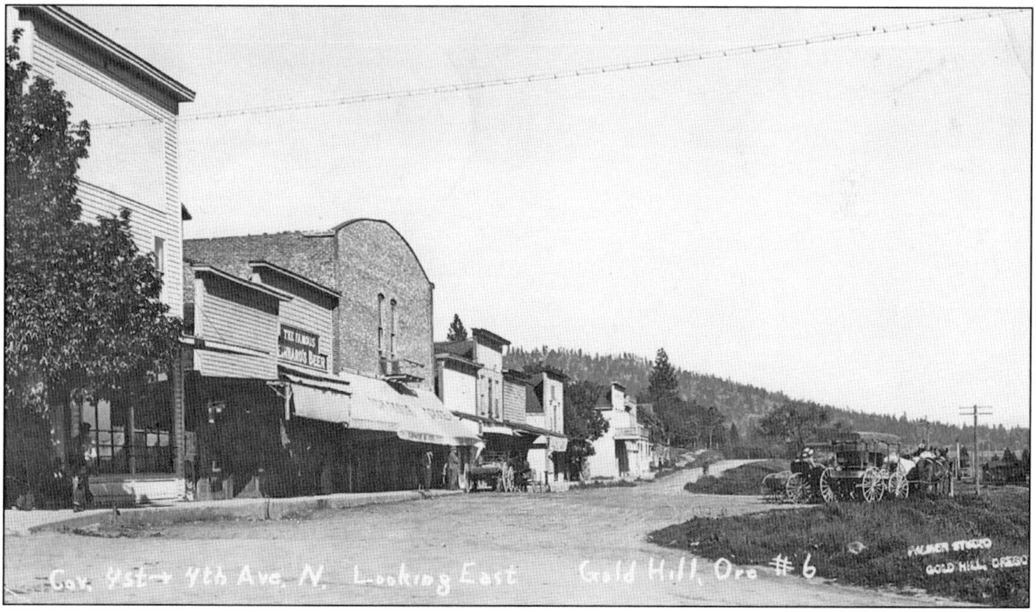

Gold Hill, Oregon, is located on a bend of the Rogue River and is famous for being the site of the Oregon Vortex. The town was founded in the 1850s by miners, particularly after gold on nearby Big Bar was discovered. In 1860, the first steam quartz stamp mill in southern Oregon was brought in, but it was not until the coming of the Oregon & California Railroad that Gold Hill grew substantially.

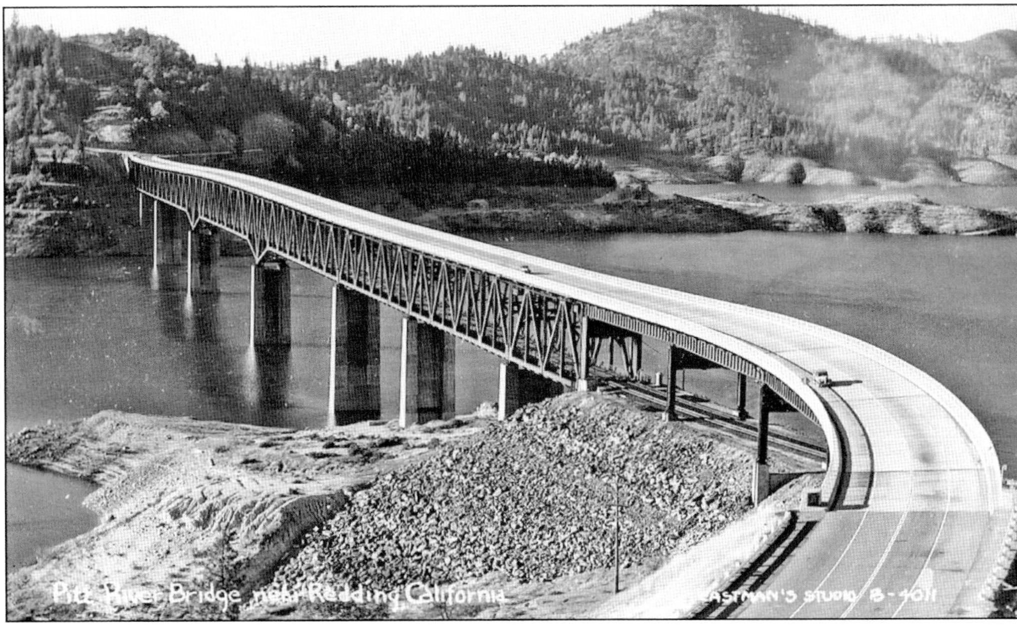

The Pit River Bridge, officially the Veterans of Foreign Wars Memorial Bridge, crosses the Pit (or Pitt) River arm of Shasta Lake 10 miles north of Redding, California. This double-decker steel bridge was completed in 1942. The lower deck carries the Union Pacific Railroad. The Pit River Bridge is the highest road-rail bridge in the world and the highest rail bridge ever built in the United States.

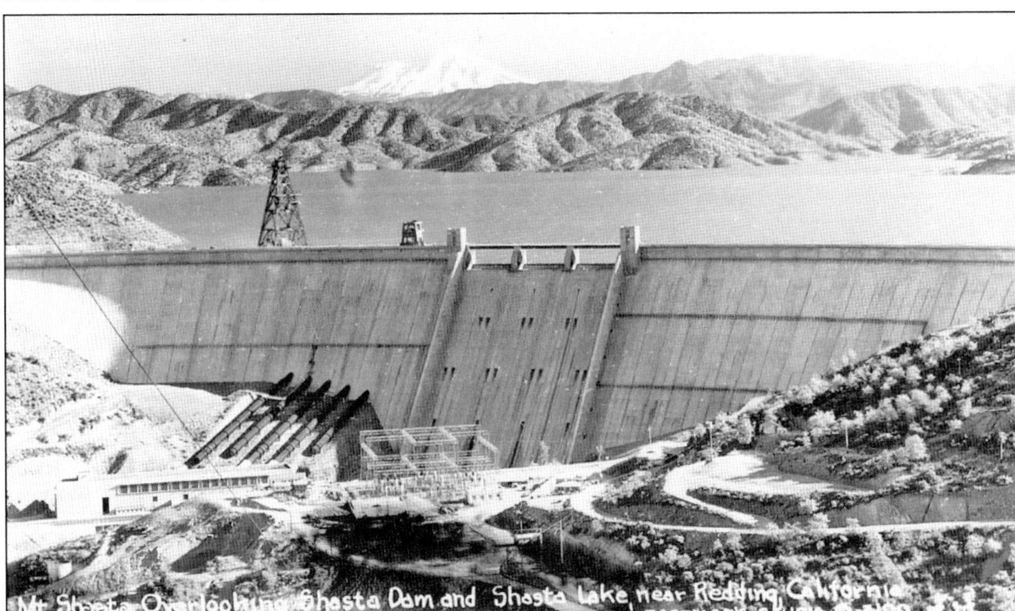

Mount Shasta overlooks Shasta Dam and Shasta Lake near Redding, California. The eighth highest dam in the United States, the 602-foot-high Shasta Dam was constructed near the junction of the Sacramento and Pit Rivers. The tallest dam in the United States is the Oroville Dam on the Feather River in California at 770 feet. Begun in 1961, the Oroville Dam was completed in 1968.

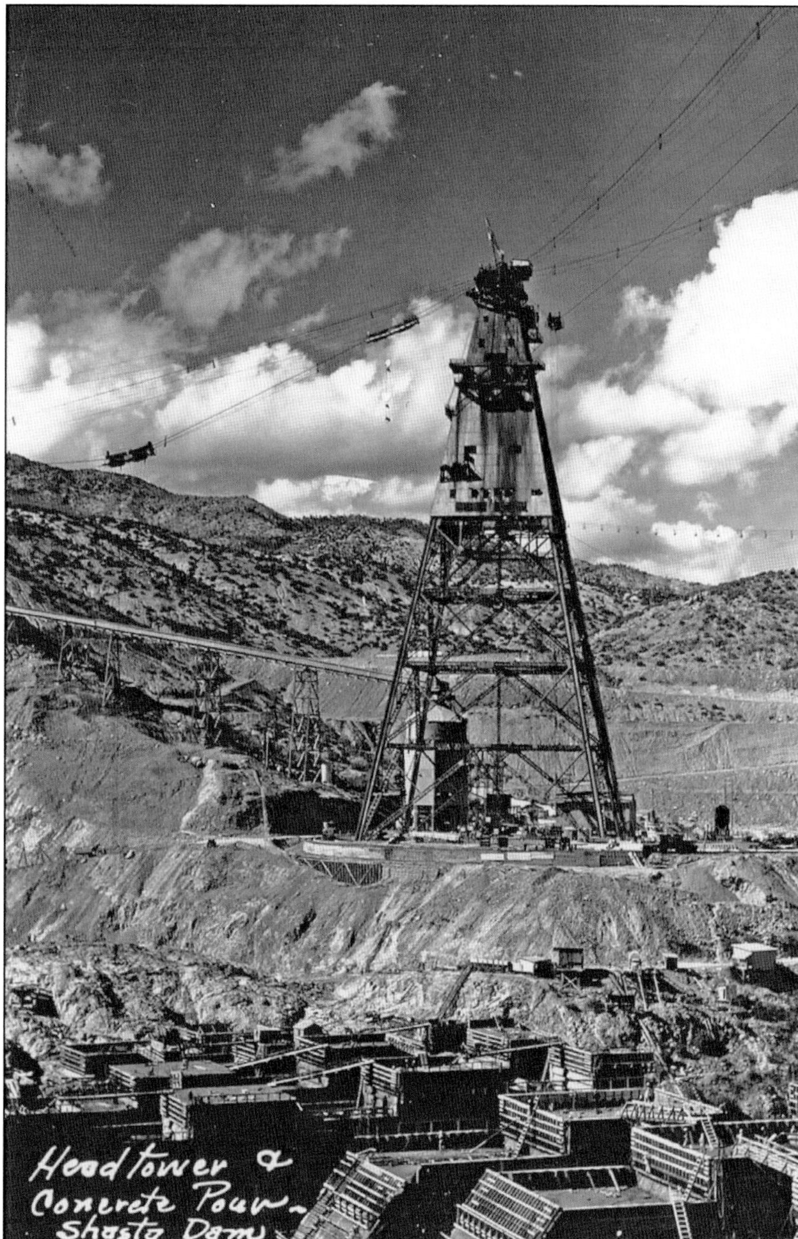

Work on Shasta Dam began in 1938, during the Great Depression. Men came from all over to get a job, many living in trucks or tents while waiting to be hired. Frank Crowe, who had supervised the construction of Hoover Dam, was selected to oversee the project. More than 4,500 men were hired to work 24 hours a day moving the millions of tons of granite and rock. A head tower was built that was connected to seven smaller towers by cables. Large buckets of freshly mixed concrete were moved via the cables to the crews working below. In the end, 15 million tons of concrete were poured into blocks laid out for the foundation. Construction on the abutments continued until 1943, and then work on the spillway began. Shasta Lake is the largest man-made lake in the United States. Lake Oroville in Butte County is the second; Trinity Lake in Trinity County is the third. All three lakes help feed the Central Valley of California.

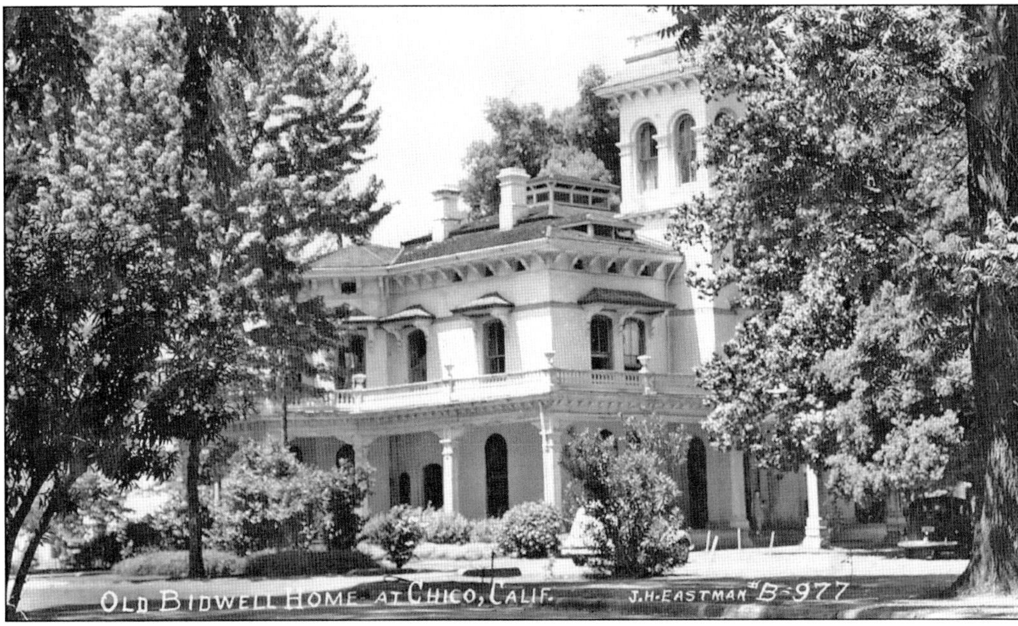

Bidwell Mansion, in Chico, California, was the home of Gen. John Bidwell and his wife, Annie. General Bidwell began work on his three-story home in 1865. The couple married in 1868 in Washington, DC, with Pres. Andrew Jackson and Ulysses Grant as family guests. The mansion boasted modern plumbing and gaslights and hosted visitors such as Susan B. Anthony and Gen. William Sherman. Today, it is a state historic park.

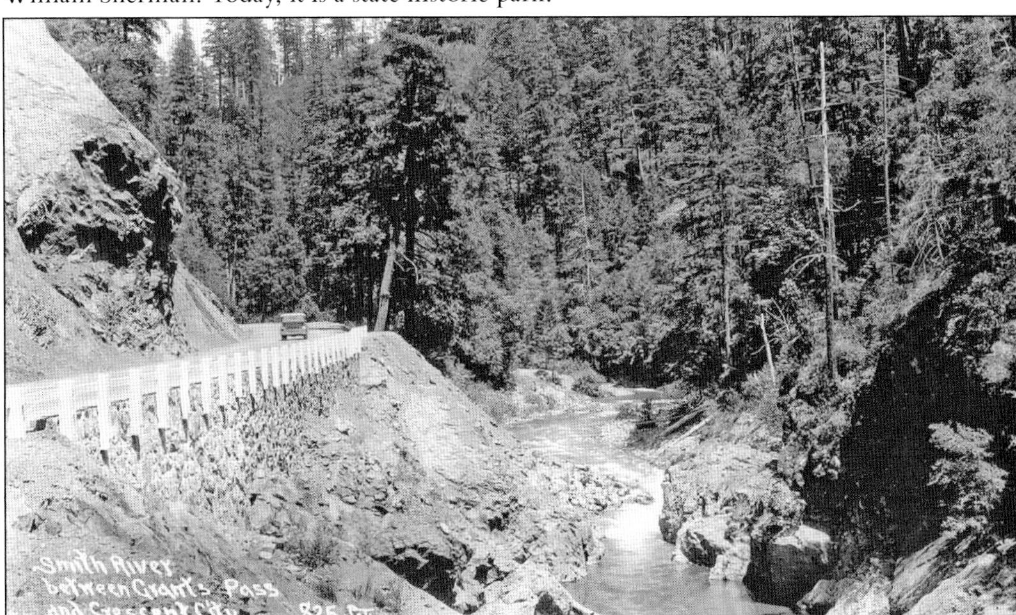

The Smith River Highway connects Grants Pass, Oregon, and Crescent City, California. Approximately 20 miles long, the river drains a rugged area of the Coast Ranges west of the Siskiyou Mountains and south of the Oregon border. The first noteworthy canning company here was the Occident & Orient Commercial Company, located at the mouth of the Smith River. Canning was done on a hot furnace and actually soldered, then cooked and readied for market.

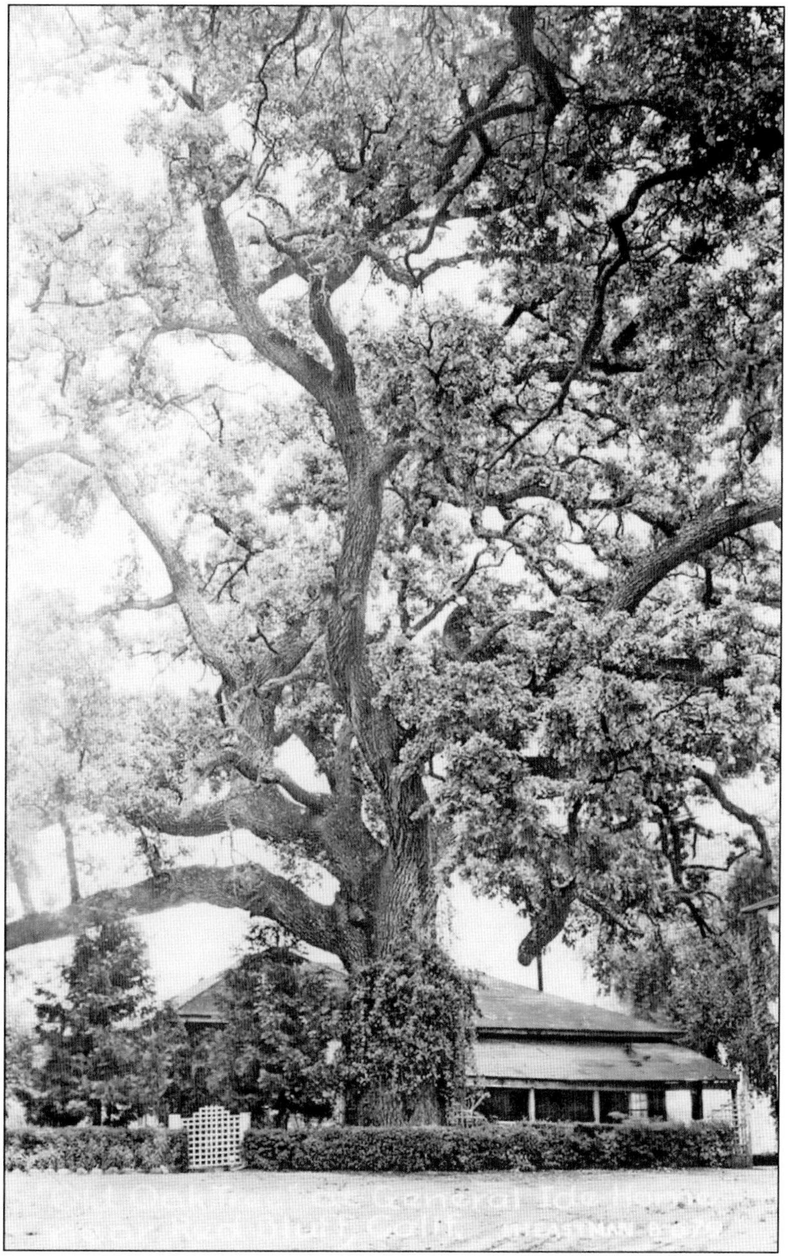

William B. Ide Adobe State Historic Park is located on the Sacramento River, a mile north of Red Bluff, California. Ide, a California pioneer, arrived at Sutter's Fort in 1845, than traveled north to work for Peter Lassen. In 1846, he took part in the Bear Flag Revolt, helping to capture the pueblo at Sonoma and the Mexican commander, Mariano Vallejo. Ide was responsible for writing the proclamation that declared California to be a republic no longer under the rule of Mexico. The new California bear flag was raised and Ide was selected as commander. The republic lasted only 25 days, and Ide served as its only president. He died in 1852 of smallpox at the age of 56. He is buried near Hamilton City, California. Contrary to public opinion, Ide never lived in the adobe that bears his name; he lived on property downriver. California purchased the adobe in the 1950s and dedicated it to Ide in 1960.

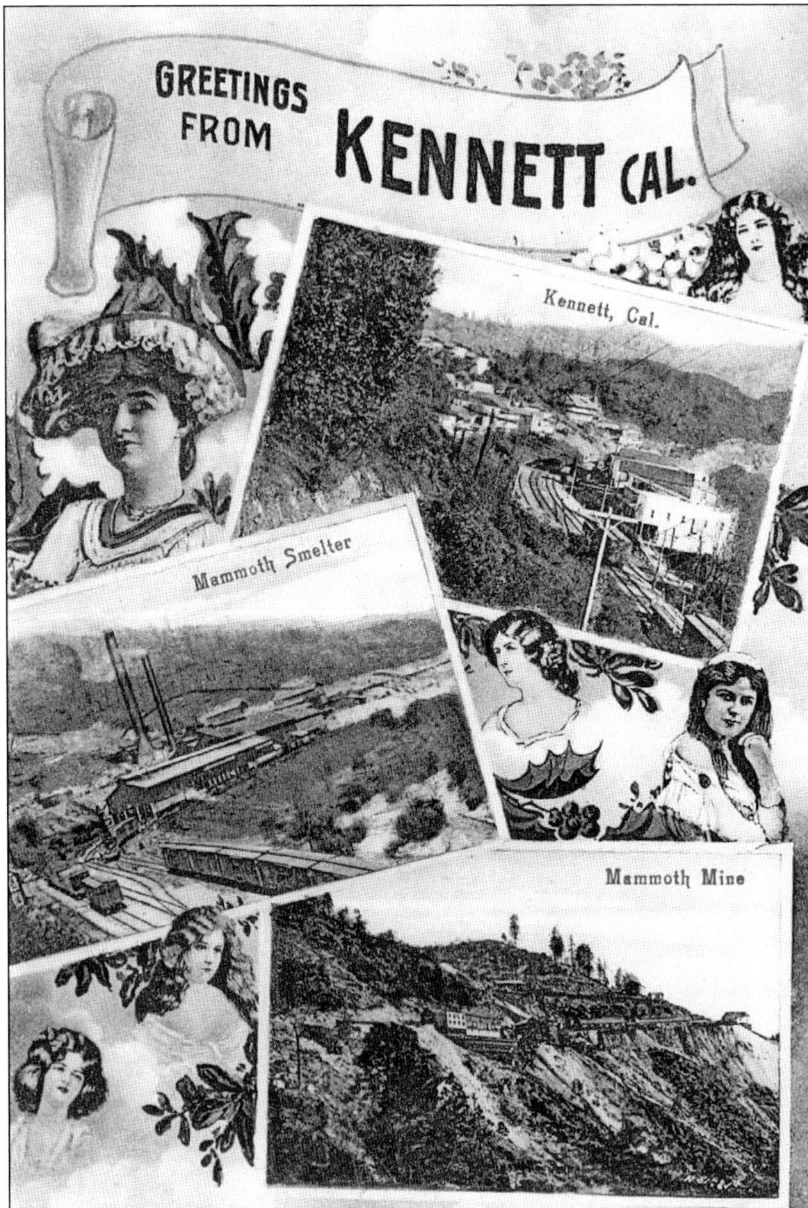

Prior to settlement, the region around Kennett was home to nine major groups of the Wintu people. In the 19th century, however, Kennett, California, became the home of the Mammoth Copper Mine and Mammoth Smelter. Along with the towns of Keswick, Ingot, Coram, and DeLaMar, Kennett came into being because of the burgeoning copper industry. Copper even replaced gold as the number one mineral in Shasta County in 1897, and in 1906–1907, Shasta County produced more copper than any other county in the nation. Unfortunately, processing copper ore caused severe environmental problems, and quantities of timber were required for the construction of mine tunnels as well as for the fires required to heat the ore. Local farmers gathered together and sued the mining companies over water and air pollution. Along with a falling market, most of the mines and smelters soon went out of business. Kennett, along with the other small towns in the area, was submerged under 400 feet of water when Shasta Lake was created.

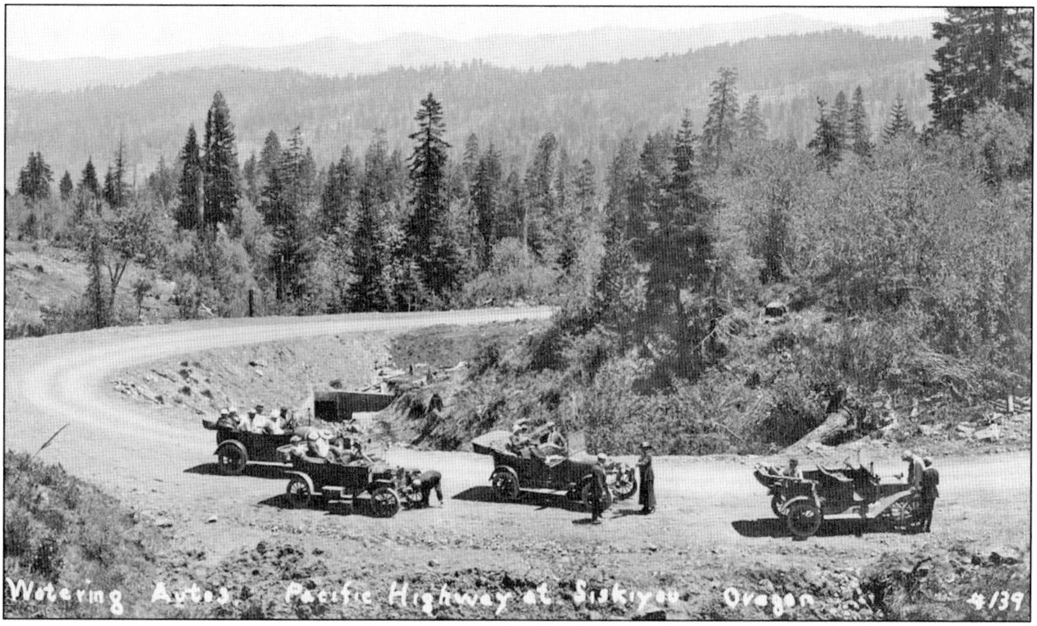

While the first pioneers used Pilot Rock as a landmark by which to navigate the Siskiyou Mountains, early highways snaked their way up and over into Oregon. Built in the mid-1910s, the Pacific Highway wound through the rugged Sacramento River canyon, Shasta Valley, and across the Klamath River, then over the Siskiyou Mountains into Oregon. Note the c. 1920s automobiles stopping to be "watered."

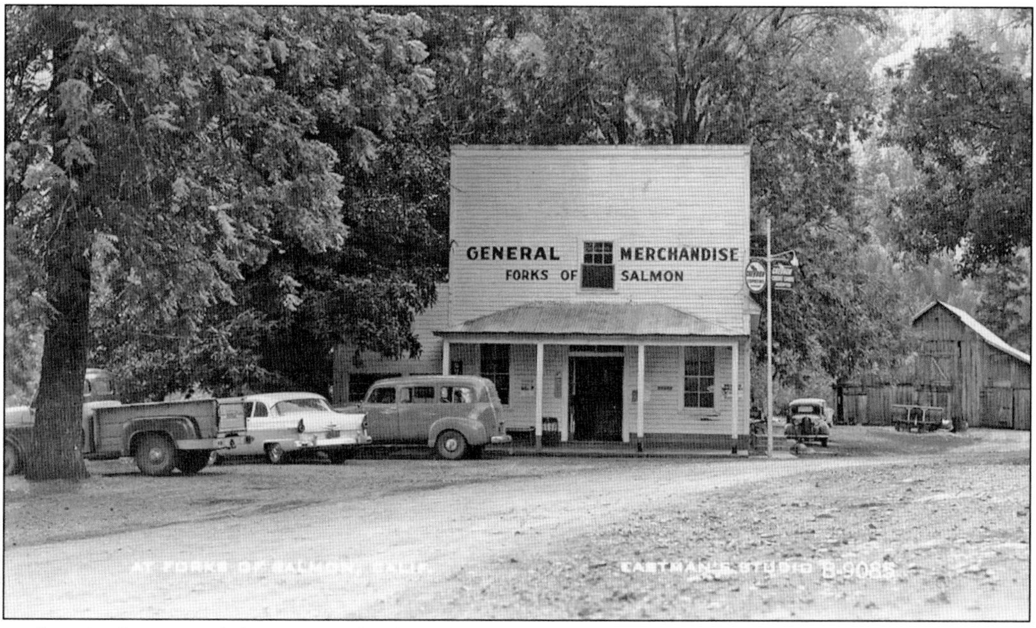

Forks of Salmon, California, was built at the confluence of the South and North Forks of Salmon River. Bennett's Store served a small settlement in 1849–1850, but miners soon flocked to the rugged region, establishing bustling communities up and down the river. After the beginning of the 20th century, the area's population began to wane, and the Forks became a remote outpost. (Courtesy of the Betty Jane Young Collection.)

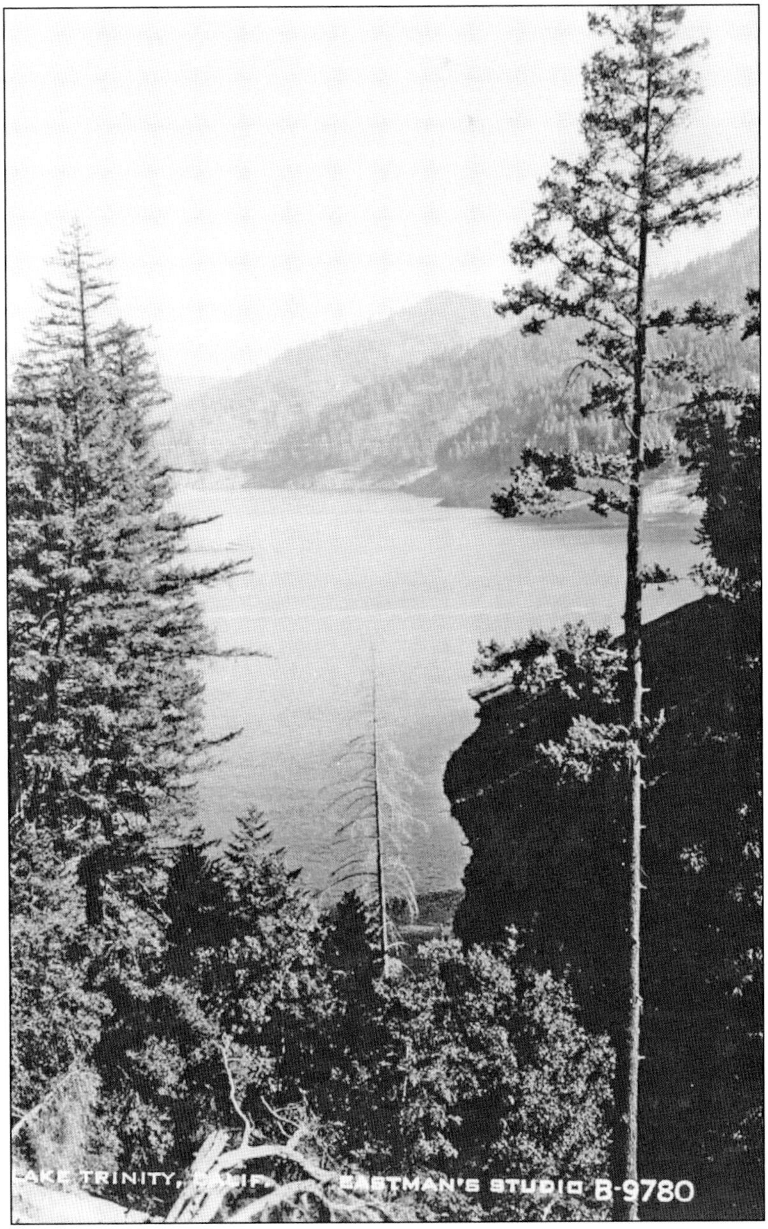

Trinity Lake, previously called Clair Engle Lake, is an artificial lake created by the Trinity Dam. Located north of Redding, California, off of Highway 299, Trinity Lake is more remote than Lake Shasta or Lake Oroville. It is surrounded by forestland and characterized by tree-lined shores. Built by the US Bureau of Reclamation in the 1950s–1960s as part of the Central Valley Project, it provides hydroelectric power as well as water for irrigation. The Trinity River, which is the longest tributary of the Klamath River, originates in northeastern Trinity County along the east side of the Scott Mountains and flows into Trinity Lake before moving into the smaller Lewiston Lake, formed by Lewiston Dam. Trinity Lake's capacity is 2,447,650 acre-feet, which makes it the third largest reservoir in the state. Trinity's earth-and-rock-fill dam is second only to Oroville Dam. After the death of California senator Clair Engle in 1964, the lake was renamed, but the name change did not last, and it was eventually renamed Trinity.

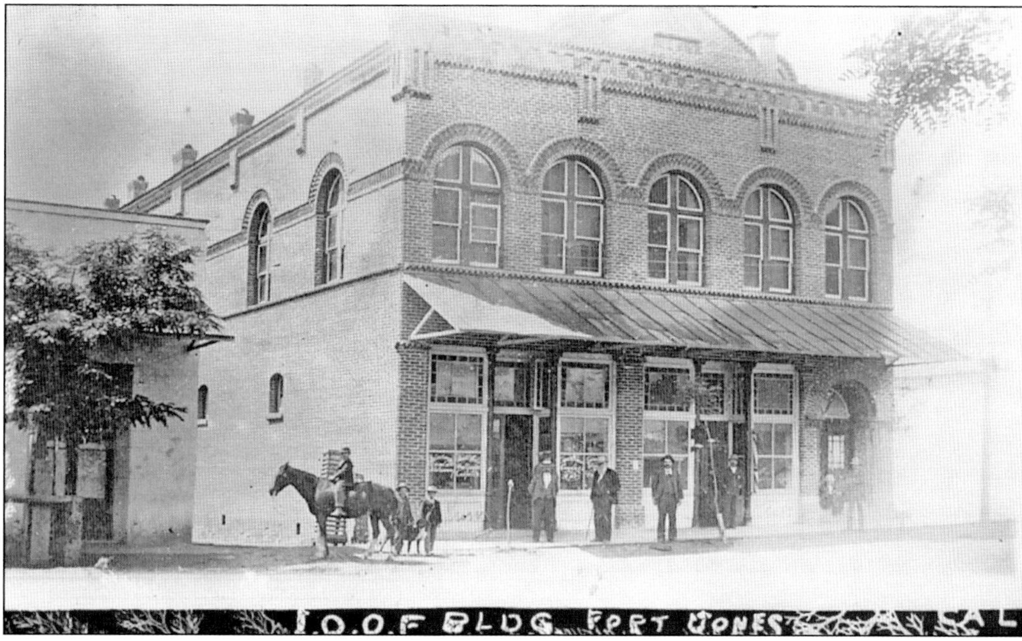

The origin of the Independent Order of Odd Fellows is not known, although the group has strong roots in America. The order in America supposedly started in 1806 with five men in New York City. They formed Shakespeare Lodge No. 1. On September 9, 1849, exactly one year before California was admitted to the Union, California Lodge No. 1 was established in San Francisco. Fort Jones was Lodge No. 115.

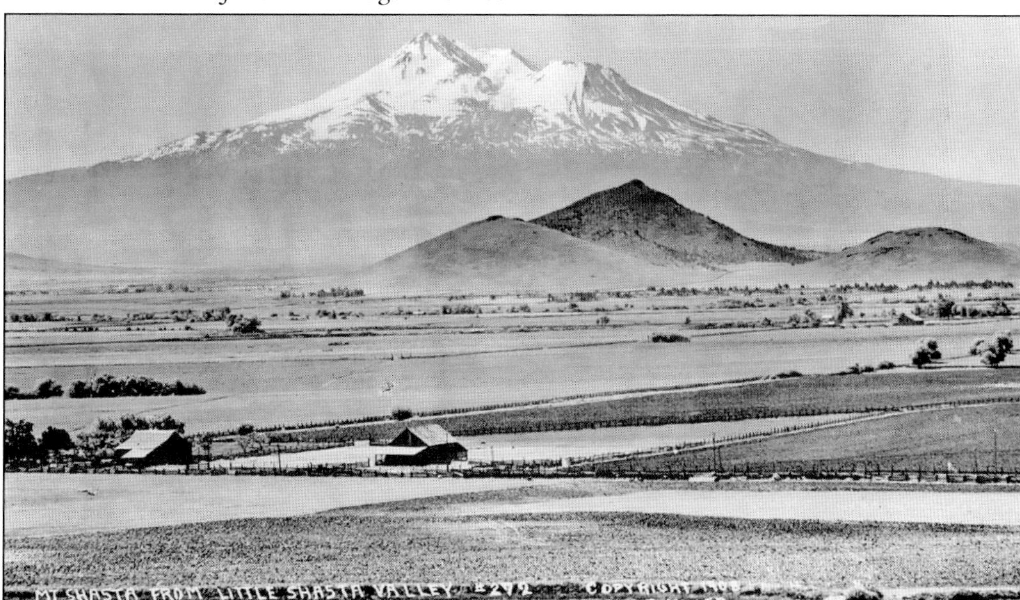

Mount Shasta looms over Little Shasta Valley, California, around 1908. Along the eastern edge of the Shasta Valley Basin lies a settlement known as Little Shasta. Settled in 1853 by John Rohrer, the area became a prosperous farming community. By the 1880s, there were two stores, a post office, a flourmill, two schools, and one church. Little Shasta Valley is bordered by Whaleback, Miller Mountain, and Goosenest Peak, but Mount Shasta fills the horizon.

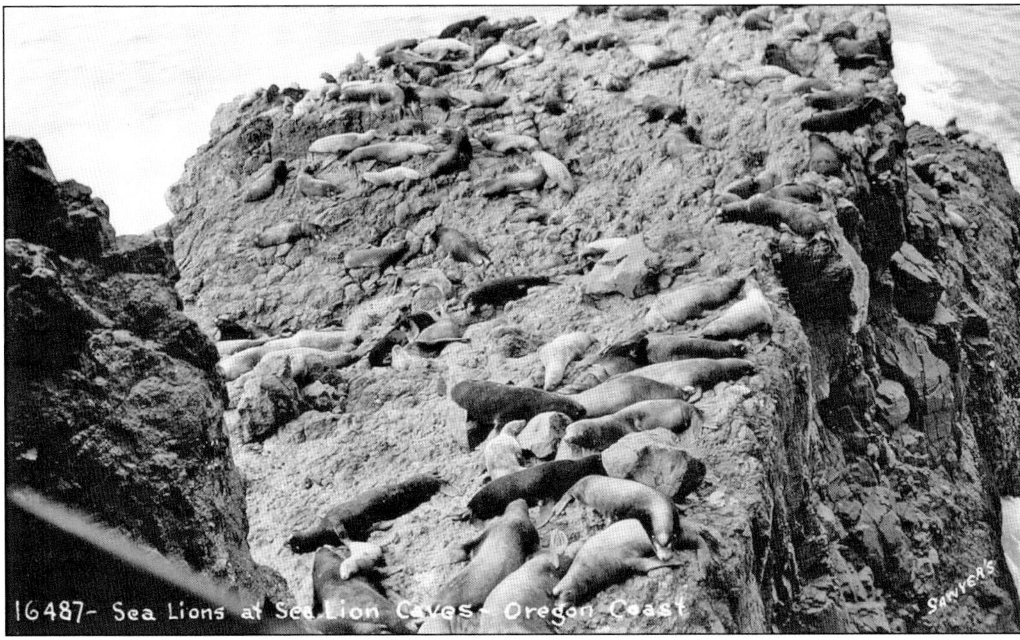

The Sea Lion Caves, north of Florence on the Oregon Coast, boast the largest sea cave in the world. Capt. William Cox was the first non-native to see the caves. In 1926, three men, R.E. Clanton, J.G. Houghton, and J.E. Jacobson, purchased the property, and in 1928, they dropped a rope ladder down to a footbridge that led to the entrance. They had to work on the cliff trail by hand and could only work in April and May, while the sea lions were outside the cavernous grotto. The caves opened to the public in 1932. Sea birds can also be seen in early April during mating season.

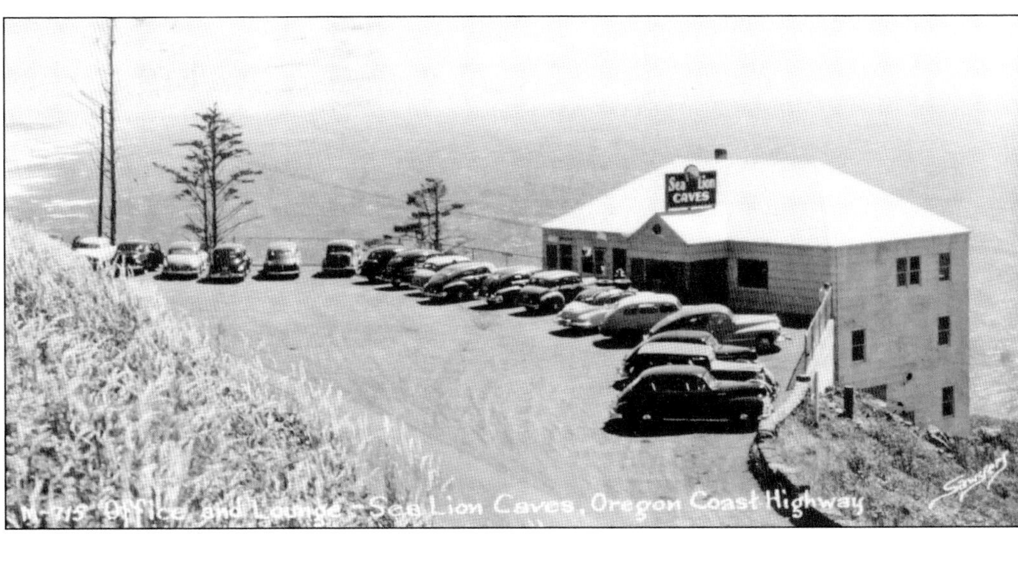

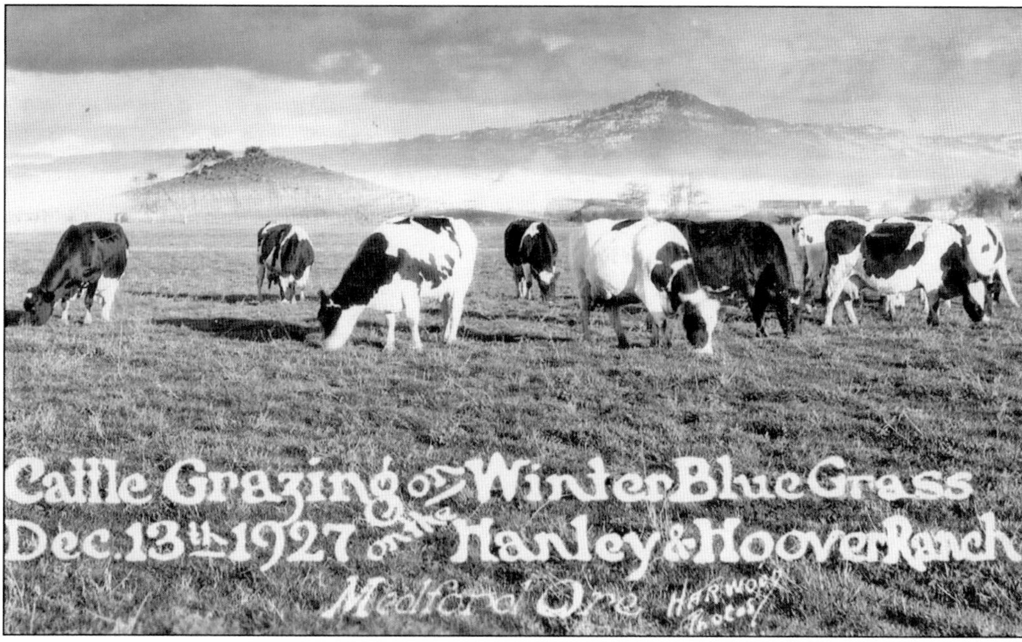

Michael and Martha Hanley purchased "Hanley" Farm in 1857. Alice Hanley inherited it in 1889. A strong woman, Alice worked to improve conditions for farm women and even ran for Oregon state representative. She never married; her three nieces—Claire, Martha and Mary—then managed the farm until their deaths. Claire and Mary helped establish the Southern Oregon Historical Society. Mary, the last to live at Hanley, donated the farm to the society in 1982.

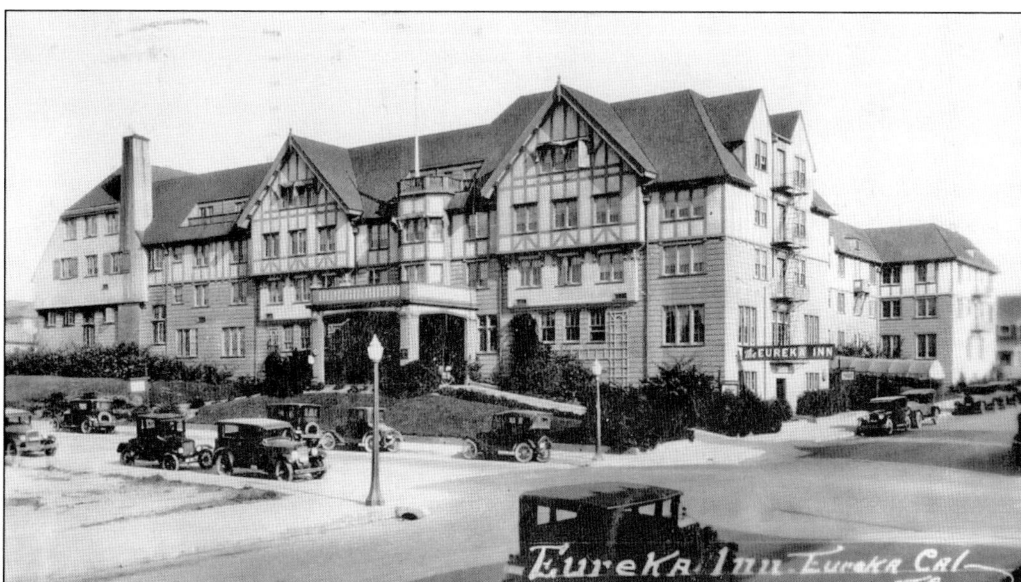

The Eureka Inn, in Eureka, California, was built in 1922. Listed in 1982 in the National Register of Historic Places, the four-story Elizabethan Tudor Revival structure fills an entire city block. The hotel was shut down for a number of years but reopened in 2010 under new ownership; however, much renovation is still being done. The hotel's original opening coincided with the construction of the Redwood Highway in 1922.

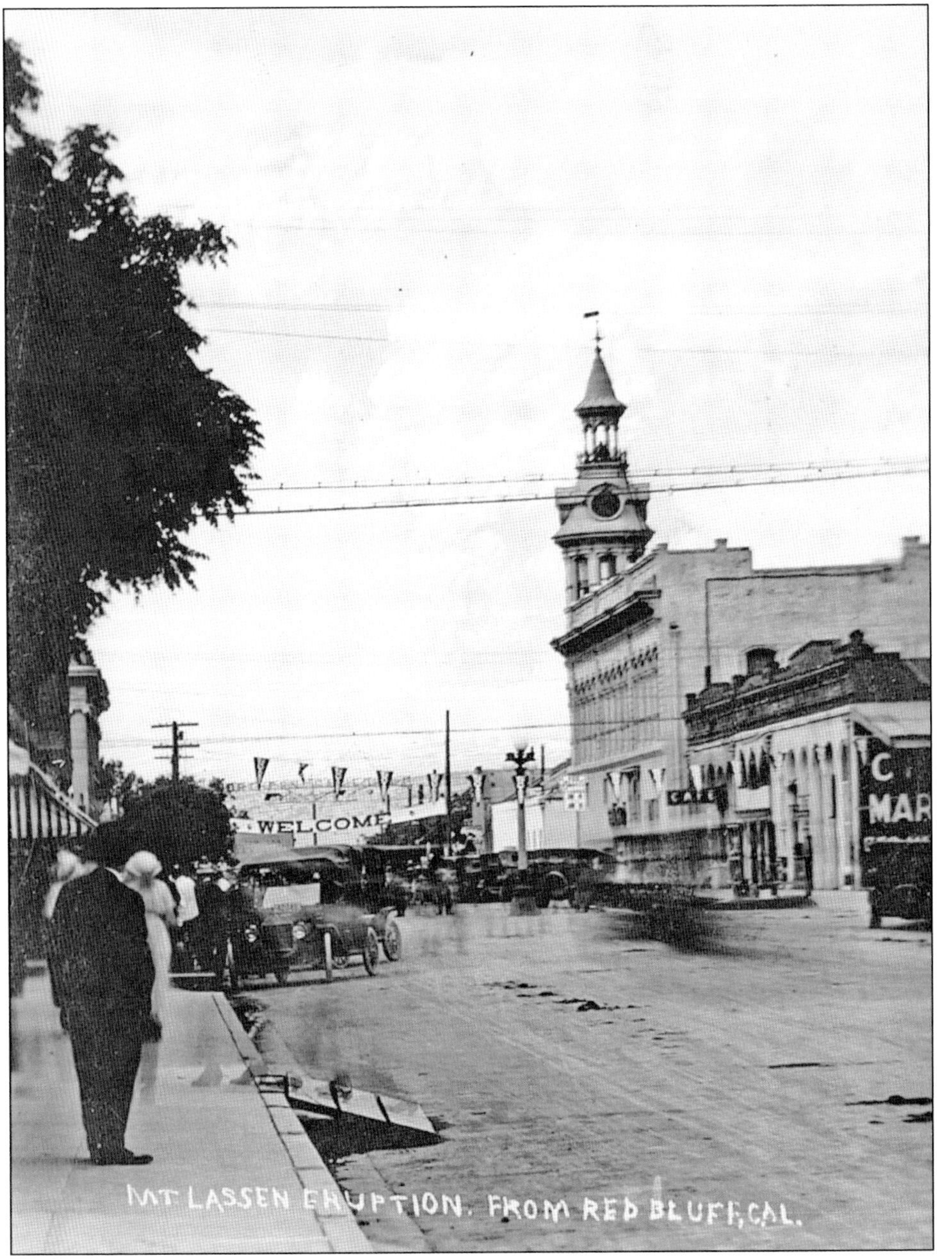

On May 22, 1915, a violent eruption at Lassen Peak devastated nearby areas and dropped ash down as far as 200 miles away. The explosion was the most powerful in a series of eruptions that occurred between 1914 and 1917. Lassen Peak, the southernmost active volcano in the Cascade Range, is actually the largest of a group of 30 or more volcanic domes within Lassen Volcanic National Park. The 1915 eruption and the eruption of Mount St. Helens in 1980 were the only two volcanic eruptions in the continental United States in the 20th century. B.F. Loomis documented the eruption, and he also worked to promote the park's creation, which was officially established in 1916. His extensive group of photographs is on display at the park's Loomis Museum. In August 2016, Lassen Volcanic National Park will celebrate its 100th anniversary, making it one of the oldest national parks in the United States.

Two

SUMMER

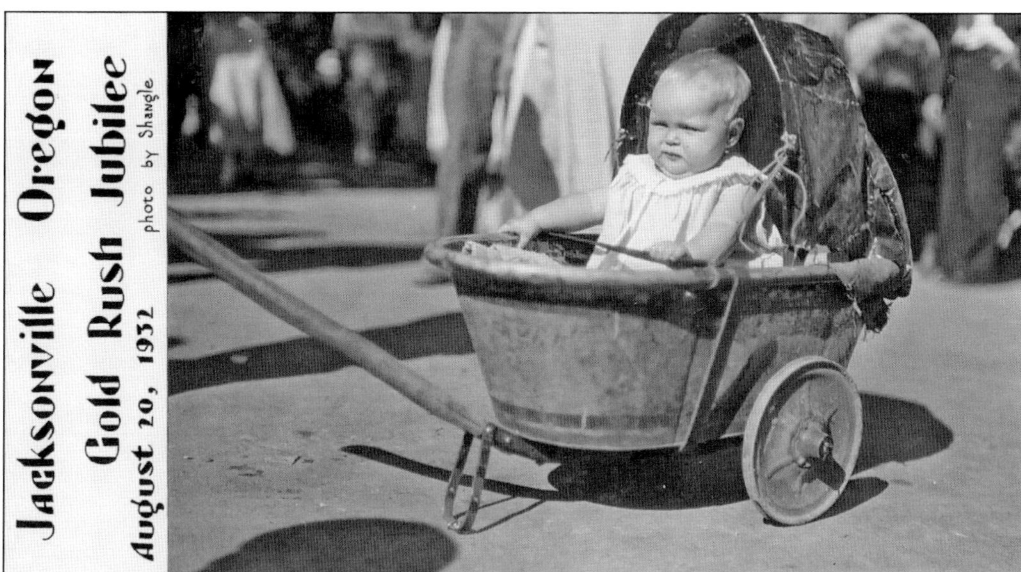

All was still, the air was light; the grass grows—Grow, grass of God; the bird sings.
—Fyodor Dostoyevsky

The Gold Rush Jubilee in Jacksonville, Oregon, on August 20, 1932, commemorated the heyday of the 19th century. Jacksonville, which included over 100 historic buildings, many made from locally fired bricks, was designated a National Historic District in 1966. Celebrations and tours bring visitors to town every year; trolleys take tourists down quaint streets, and audio downloads are available, full of historic anecdotes.

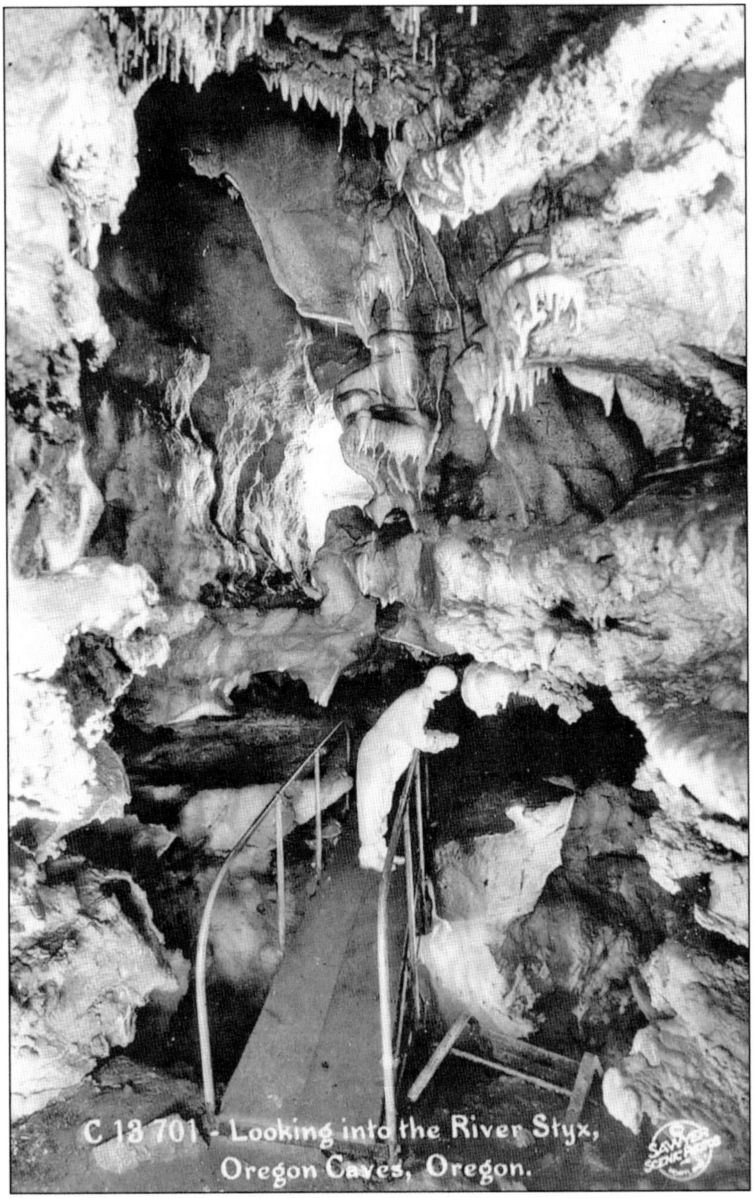

Outside the Oregon Caves, the stream flowing by is known as Cave Creek. Inside the caverns, Cave Creek becomes the River Styx. As recorded by journalist Larry Bingham of the *Oregonian* in 2008, "Inside, where the water has carved formations that make you feel like you're walking through the belly of the whale, Cave Creek becomes the River Styx, named for the border between the Earth and the Underworld in Greek mythology." The river meanders through the park's six-story chateau, between the open dining room and gift shop, then back outside where it eventually flows into the Illinois and Rogue Rivers. Temperatures within the near-dark caves along the River Styx hover right above 40 degrees, and to reach the caves, visitors must climb 500 steps. While in the past visitors often broke off stalactites, turning the surfaces black, today's visitors are prohibited from touching anything or even bringing in anything except a camera. Even the lint from visitors' clothes is now captured in nets stretched out under the walkways and stairs.

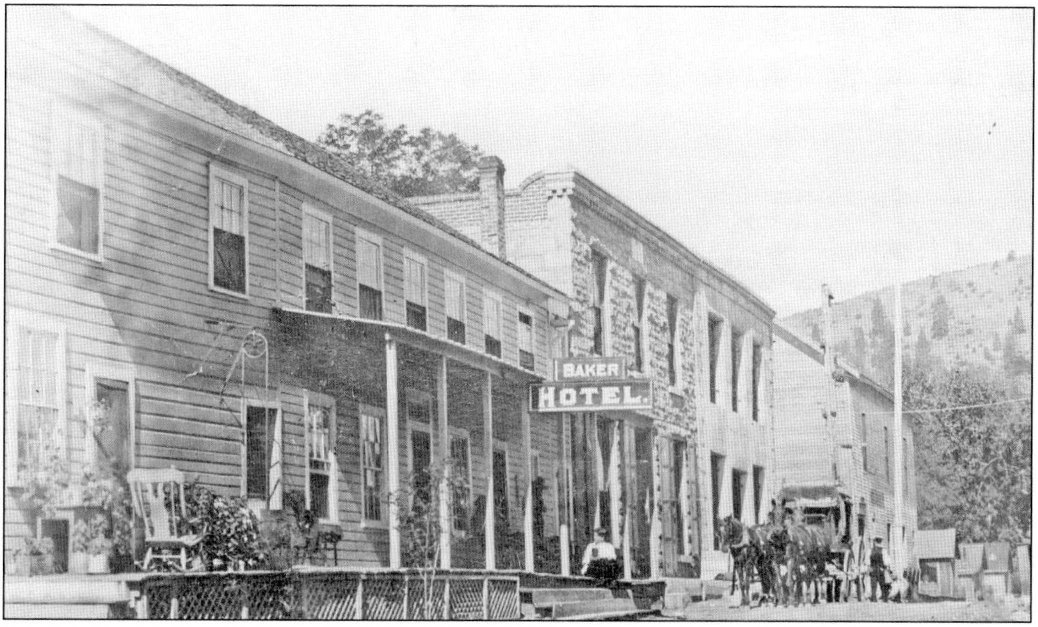

Callahan's Baker Hotel no longer exists; the Callahan Emporium, a general store, and the bar next door replaced it long ago. The Callahan Ranch Hotel, across the road, however, is being restored. Once a booming gold rush town, Callahan, California, located 30 miles west of Mount Shasta on Highway 3, is little more than a handful of homes and vintage storefronts, but its quaint ambiance attracts visitors.

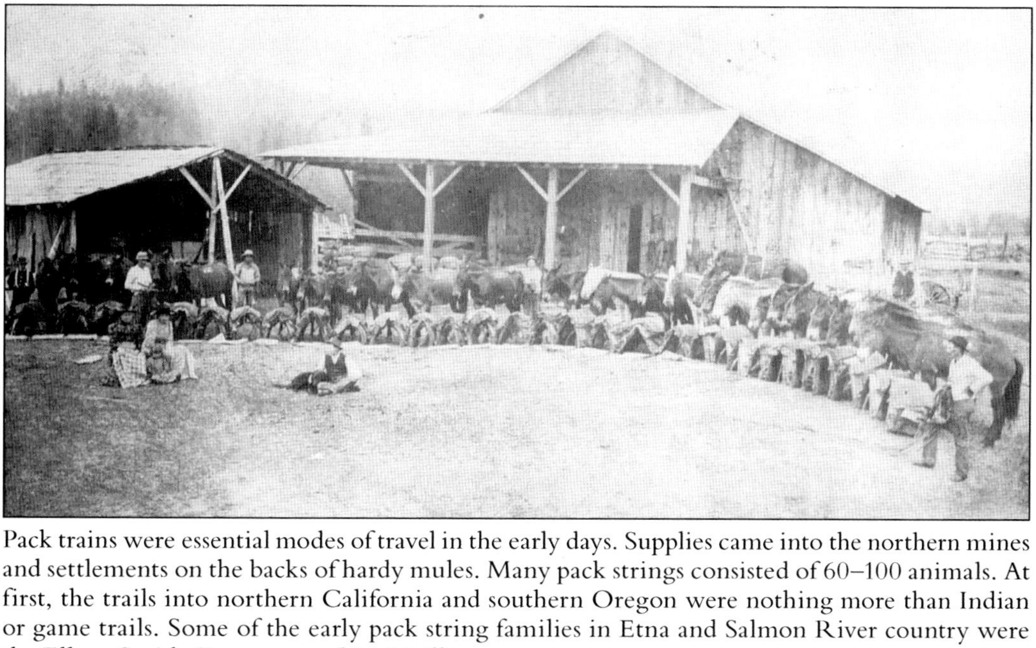

Pack trains were essential modes of travel in the early days. Supplies came into the northern mines and settlements on the backs of hardy mules. Many pack strings consisted of 60–100 animals. At first, the trails into northern California and southern Oregon were nothing more than Indian or game trails. Some of the early pack string families in Etna and Salmon River country were the Ellers, Smith-Bennetts, and McNeills.

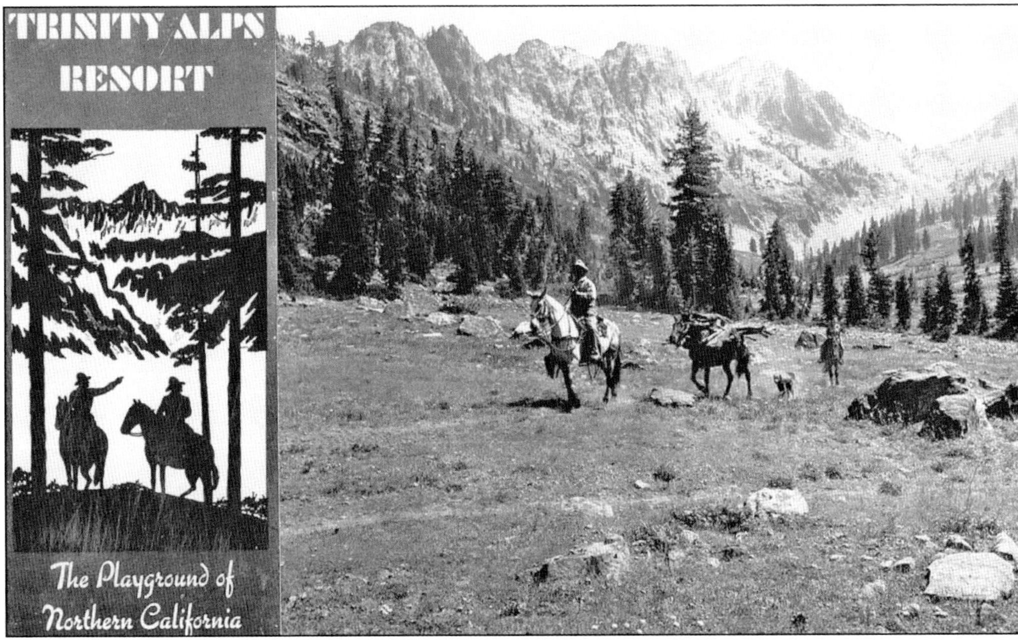

The Trinity Alps, which form the heart of Trinity County, lie between the Pacific Coast Ranges to the west and the Cascade Range to the east. Rugged and alpine, they differ from the Sierras and the Coastal Ranges. Elevations in the Trinity Alps range from 1,350 feet to 9,001 feet at Thompson Peak. The Trinity Alps Wilderness Area covers 517,000 acres, which makes it the second largest wilderness in California.

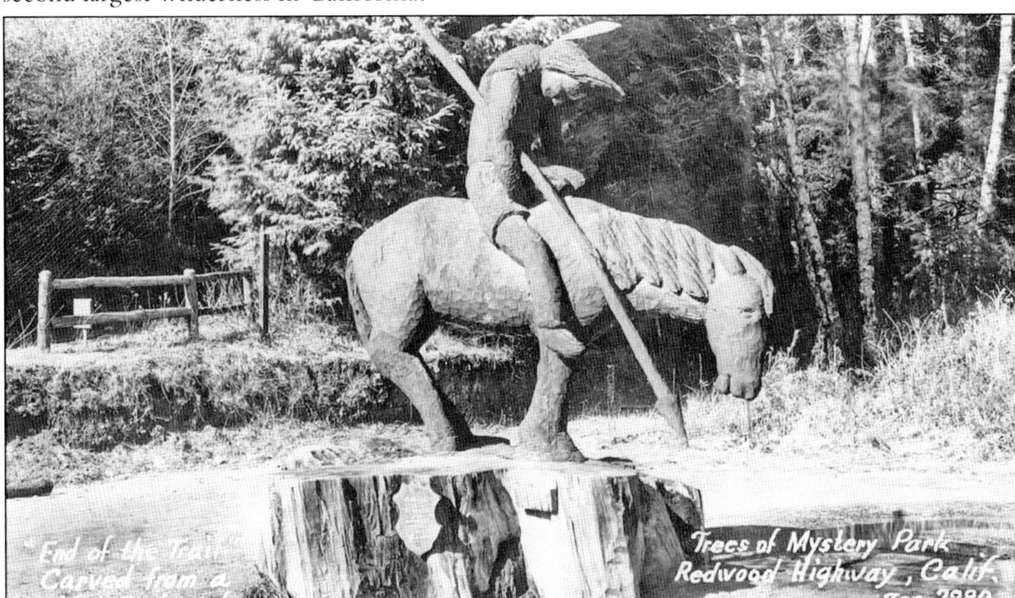

End of the Trail is a redwood statue at Trees of Mystery in Klamath, California. The Trees of Mystery is a roadside redwood attraction adjacent to Highway 101, the Coastal Highway. Surrounded by Redwood National and State Parks, Trees of Mystery contains a number of unique tree formations. Among the best known are the 49-foot statue of Paul Bunyan and the 35-foot Babe the Blue Ox, both of which are visible from Highway 101.

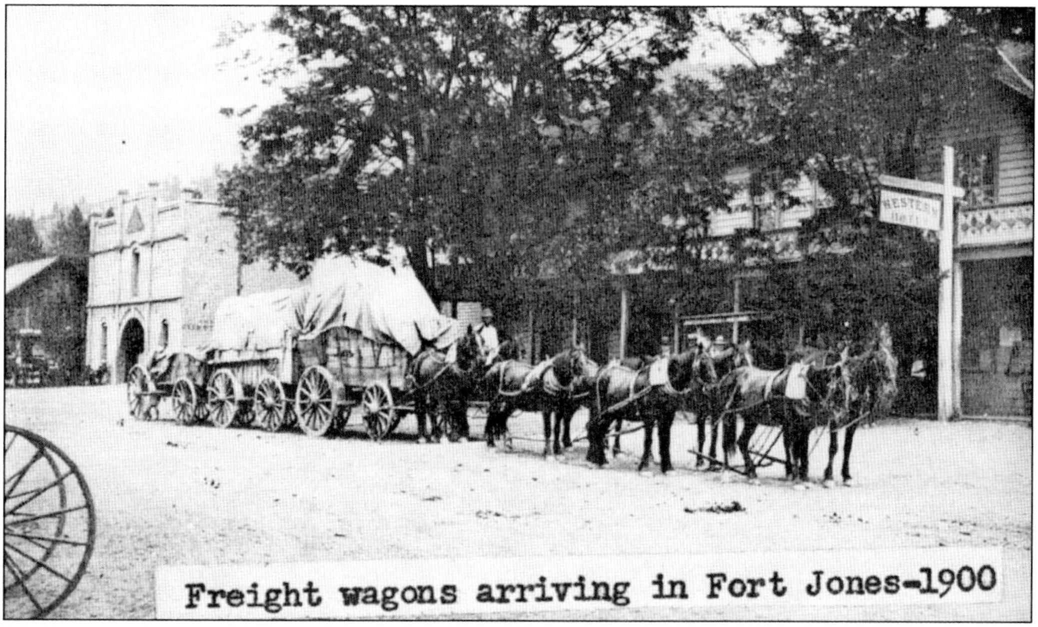

Fort Jones, California, was first called Scottsburg, then Scottsville. In 1852, it became Wheelock after the man who built the first trading post. In 1854, it became Ottitiewa, the name of the nearby Shasta tribe. Finally, in 1860, the name became Fort Jones. In spite of its many name changes, Fort Jones was an important hub for incoming and outgoing freight wagons as well as for local trade.

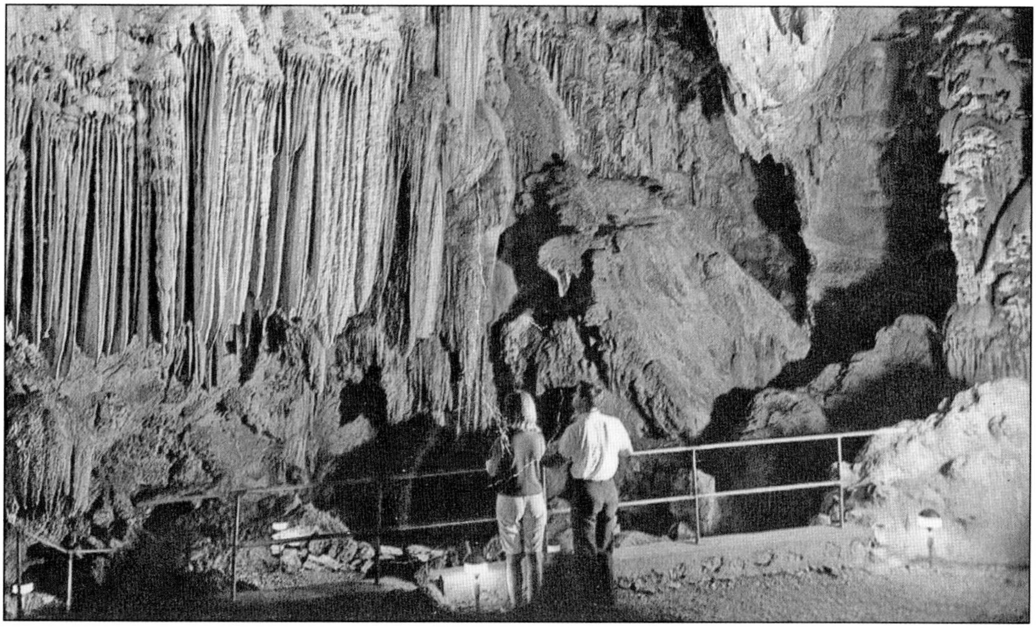

The Shasta Caverns are located on Lake Shasta near Redding, California, and are one of three identified limestone caverns in Shasta County. Well known to the local Wintu tribe, the cave was officially discovered by J.A. Richardson. His inscription, dated November 3, 1878, is evidence of that "discovery." The caverns opened to the public in 1964. To reach the caverns, visitors must take a ferry across Shasta Lake.

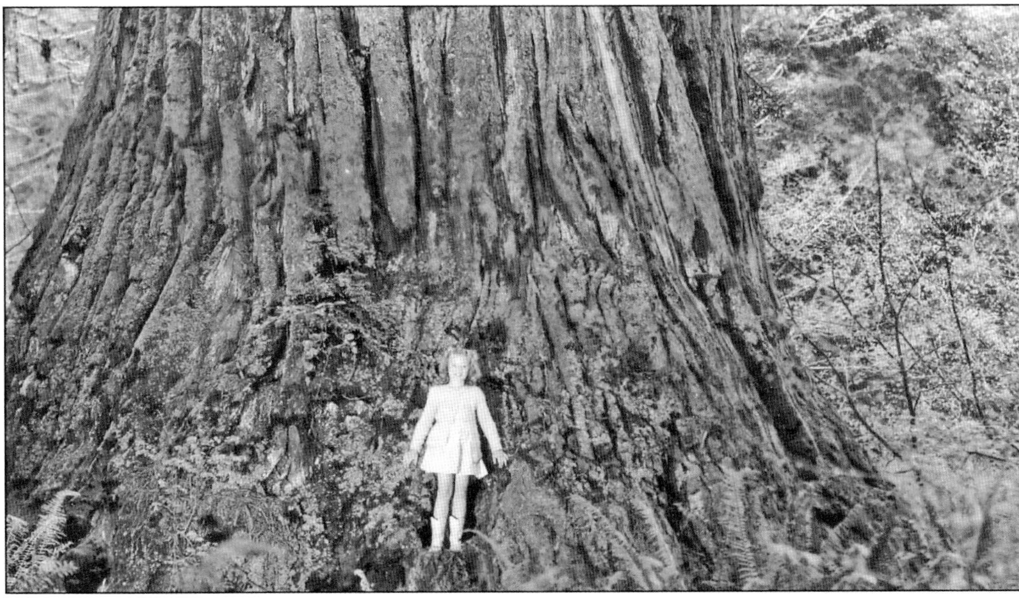

In 1922, the Save-the-Redwoods League was concerned about the potential destruction that would occur with any proposed highway construction as it moved through the coastal redwoods. In an effort to preserve at least a portion of the affected forest, the league persuaded the state to acquire 120 acres of redwood groves. In 1925, the government authorized the construction of US Highway 101, the nation's westernmost federal highway.

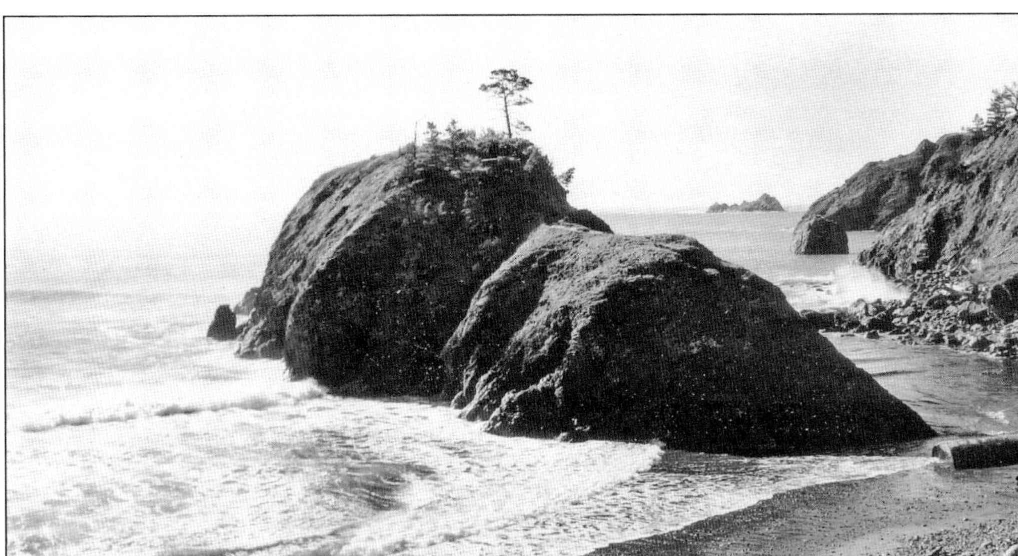

A group of settlers led by Capt. William Tichenor was attacked at Port Orford in 1851. Tichenor, needing to get supplies, left nine men behind. Unfortunately, more than 100 members of the local Quatomah tribe attacked them as they took refuge on what is now called Battle Rock. After two weeks, a larger band attacked them again. The chief of the tribe was killed, and the settlers fled north.

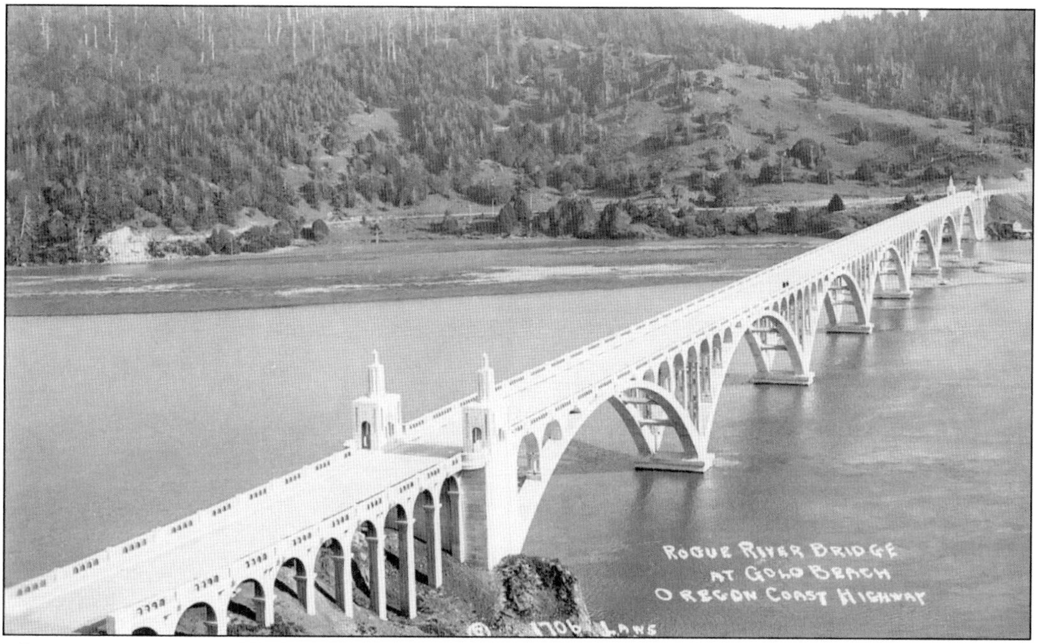

The Isaac Lee Patterson Bridge, or Rogue River Bridge, is a concrete arch bridge that spans the Rogue River. The 1,898-foot bridge was designed by Conde Balcom McCullough in the 1930s. It was dedicated in May 1932 and named for Oregon's governor. It was listed in the National Register of Historic Places in 2005 and is still considered one of Oregon's most interesting bridges.

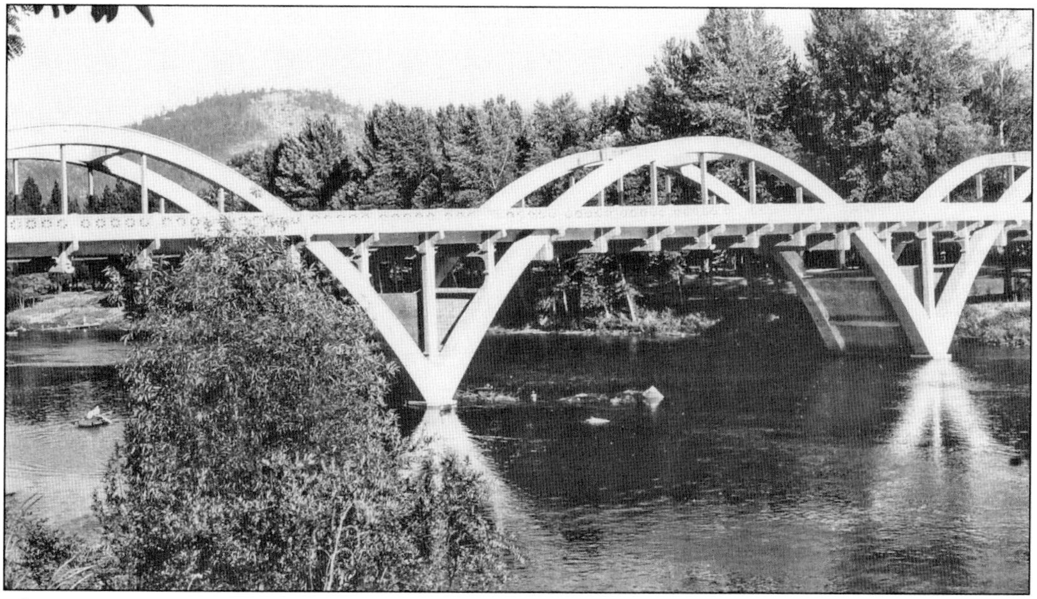

The Caveman Bridge, located in Grants Pass, Oregon, was completed in 1931. It replaced the 1909 three-span steel bridge, which was then moved downriver to replace the ferry at the mouth of Pickett Creek. Conde B. McCullough designed the Caveman Bridge, as well as the Rogue River Bridge, the Coquille River Bridge, the Myrtle Creek Bridge, the Grave Creek Covered Bridge, and hundreds of other bridges in Oregon.

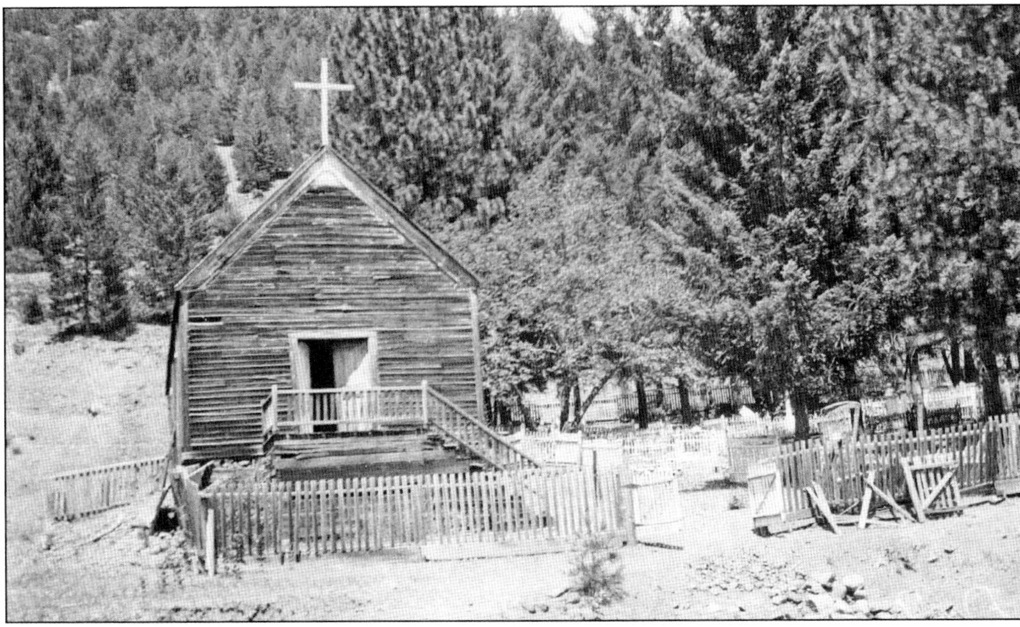

An Austrian Benedictine monk, Fr. Florian S. Schwenninger, oversaw the construction of the Sawyers Bar Church in Salmon River, California, in 1855. It is the oldest Catholic church in northern California and one of few locations in the Klamath National Forest listed in the National Register of Historic Places. Father Florian brought with him a painting of Christ's crucifixion that hung above the altar for many years. (Courtesy of the Betty Jane Young Collection.)

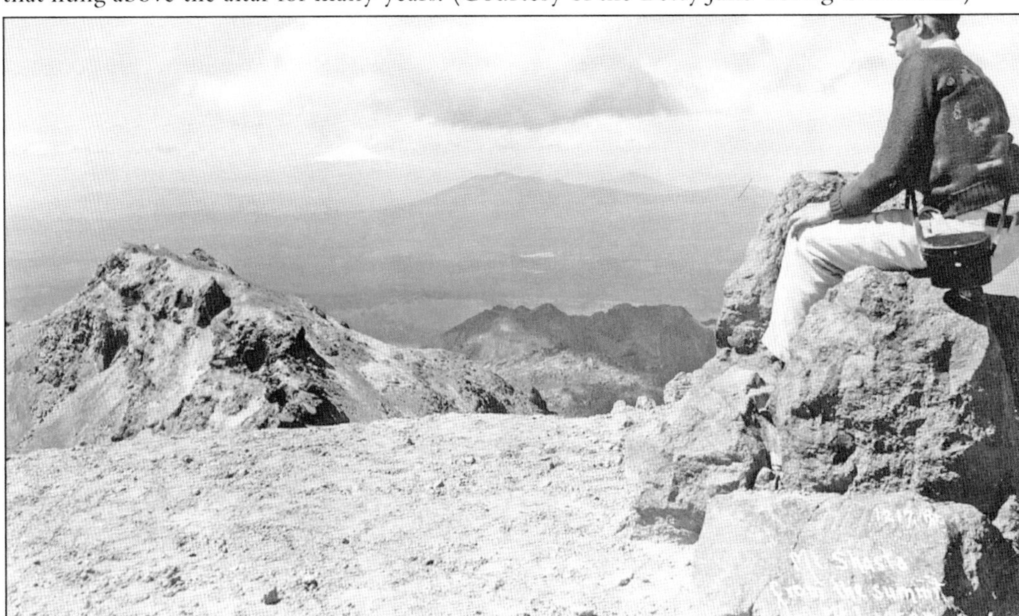

Mount Shasta and Mount Lassen are both peaks within the Cascade Volcanic Arc, which stretches from British Columbia to northern California. Lassen is one of the largest lava domes on earth and receives more precipitation than any other place within the Cascade Range south of the Three Sisters in Oregon. Mount Lassen rises to 10,462 feet, while Mount Shasta stands at 14,179 feet.

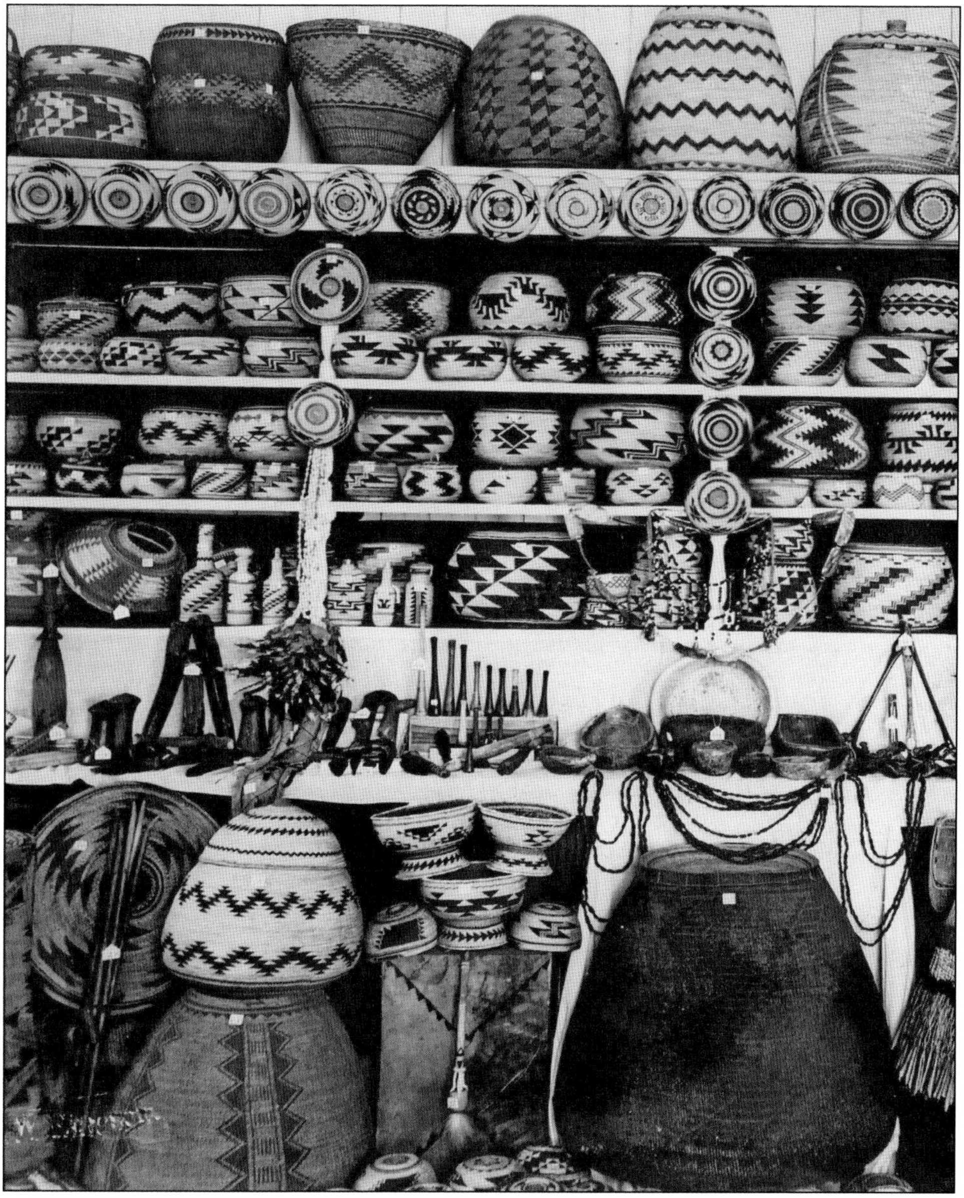

The Shasta homeland stretched across northern California and southern Oregon and entailed most of what is now known as Siskiyou County, in addition to parts of Jackson, Josephine, and Klamath Counties. It represented an area approximately 200 miles wide and 200 miles long with almost 20 million acres. The Shasta occupied the Klamath River from Keno to Happy Camp, all of Scott Valley and Quartz Valley, the north half of Shasta Valley, and parts of Salmon River. They constructed permanent winter villages with houses made of cedar planks set down in the ground; each home had a basement. In spring, the bands would build brush houses at the mouths of various creeks. The Karuk settled principally along the Klamath River. They called the Salmon River *Quoratem* and where the Salmon River meets the Klamath *Kut-ah-min*, which is the center of the Karuk world. Today the Karuk tribe is one of the largest in California. The tribal headquarters are located in Happy Camp, California. Both tribes are known for their exquisite baskets, which incorporate traditional patterns.

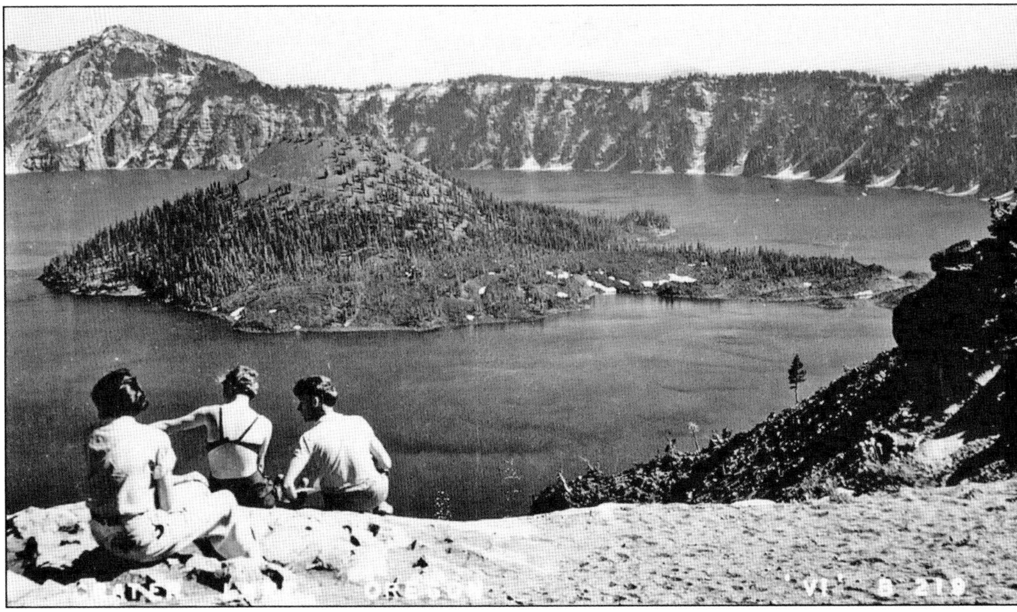

Crater Lake in Oregon is a caldera created by the eruption of the ancient volcano Mount Mazama. It was a place of mystery to the Klamath Indians. John Wesley Hillman, Henry Lippel, and Isaac Skeeters, in search of the mythical Lost Cabin gold mine, stumbled upon it in 1853. Skeeters called it Deep Blue Lake. It was newspaper editor Jim Sutton who named it Crater Lake for the crater located on Wizard Island.

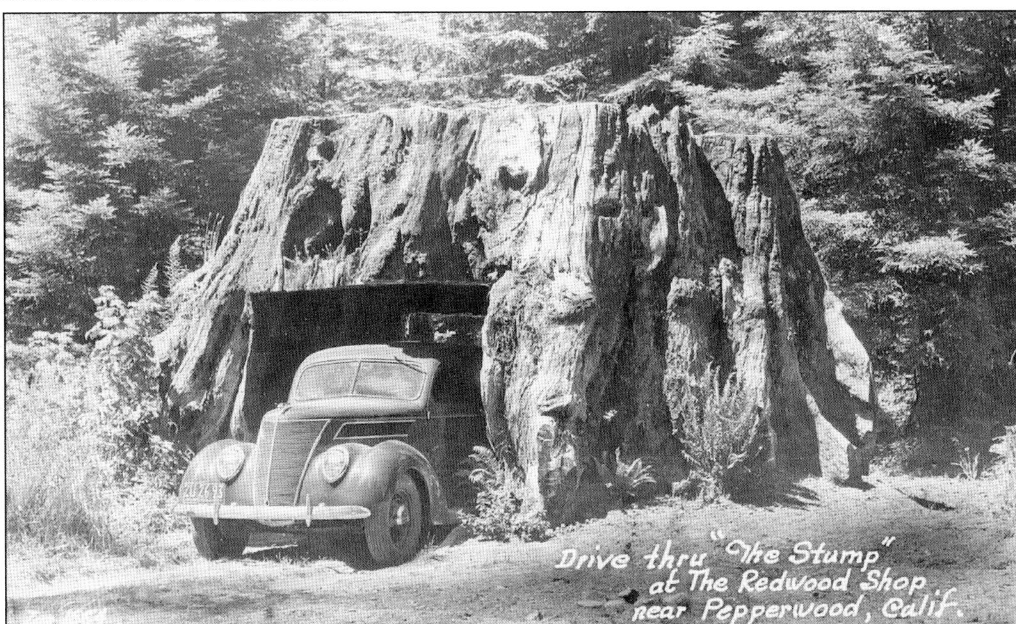

One of the redwood wonders is "the Stump" at the Redwood Shop near Pepperwood, California, pictured here around 1941. The diameter of this redwood tree was 23 feet. Pepperwood is located in Humboldt County, 320 miles north of San Francisco, and is the northernmost community along The Avenue of the Giants. The avenue, now maintained as State Highway 254, winds along the Eel River and connects several small towns, including Pepperwood.

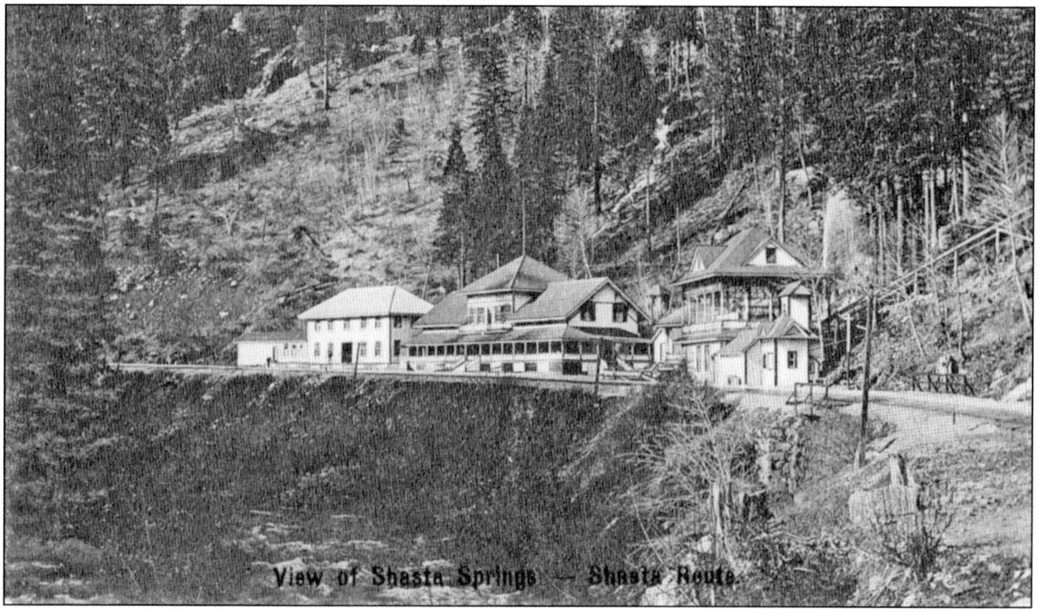

Shasta Springs Resort, located along the Sacramento River near Dunsmuir, California, was one of several resorts that popularized mineral baths. In 1886, George W. Scott discovered mineral springs on his property. Before long, the location was expanded and became a summer resort promoted by Southern Pacific Railroad, which offered passengers a ride on the "Road to a Thousand Wonders." The resort's popularity waned after the 1920s.

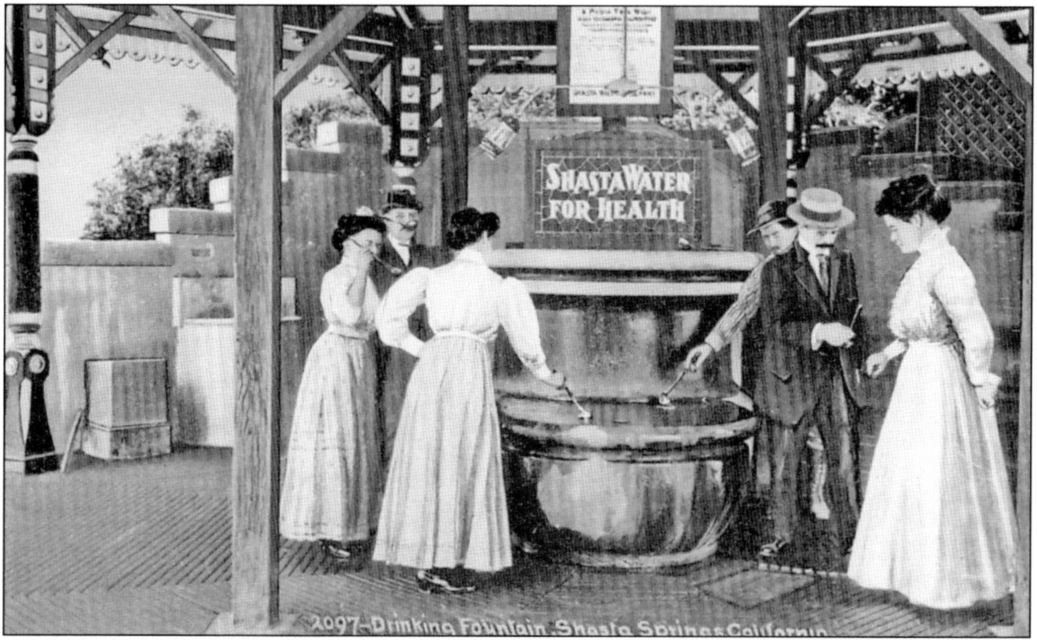

The 1887 completion of the railroad along the line of the Siskiyou Trail brought a dramatic increase in tourism, lumbering, and population into southern Siskiyou County, California. George W. Scott, who tapped into some mineral springs and built a popular resort, also formed a corporation with several San Francisco–area merchants to market his healing mineral water. This was the beginning of the Shasta Water Company.

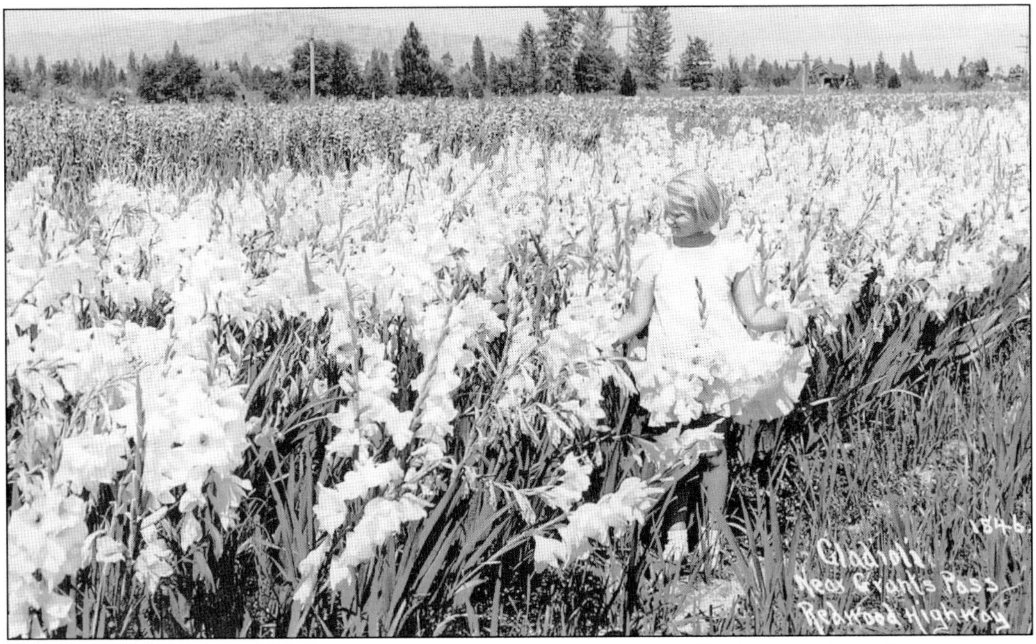

In June, the gladiola fields of Grants Pass and southern Oregon fill the air with color and scent. Today's gladioli, often called sword lilies, are more magnificent and hardy than the old-time varieties. Over 260 species exist in this genus of the iris family *(Iridaceae).* Although Grants Pass and Douglas County are heavily timbered, agricultural crops, including field crops and vineyards, have grown in importance.

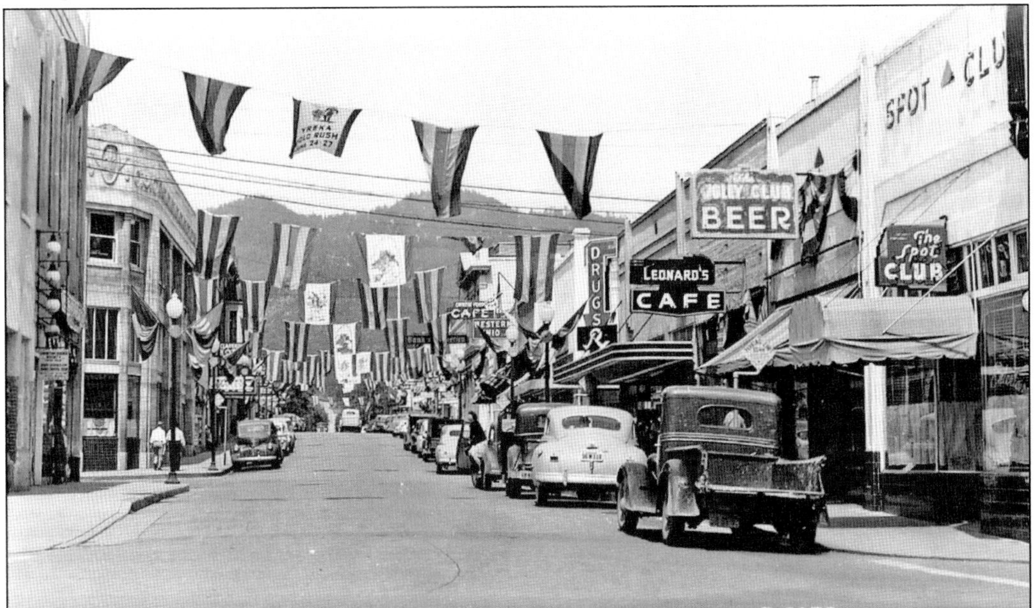

Yreka Gold Rush Days in Yreka, California, is held every year on the first day of summer. It is a two-day street fair that commemorates the anniversary of the founding of Yreka. Gold Rush Days also features reenactments of the Old West by groups such as the Cowboy Action Shooters. Flags line historic Miner Street in this photograph, taken around the late 1940s.

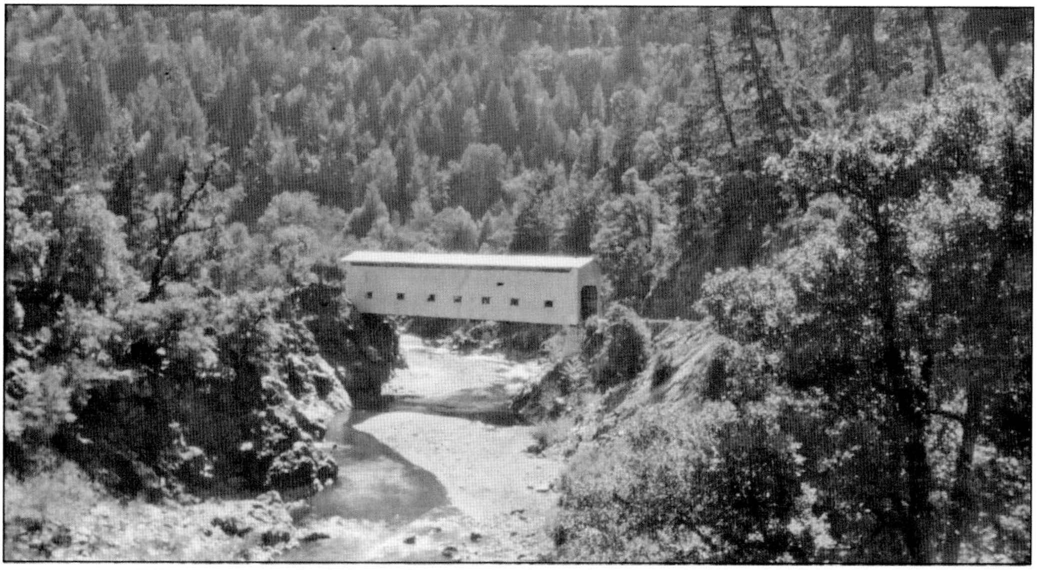

This covered bridge crosses Crapo Creek, a tributary of Salmon River, in California. Crapo Creek is located 12 miles east of Sawyers Bar. Historically, Crapo Mine, three miles southwest of the Forks of Salmon, was an important gold mine. The mine comprised 39 acres and was owned by the Bennett Company. Production records show that most of the bars ran 400 to 1,000 ounces of gold per acre.

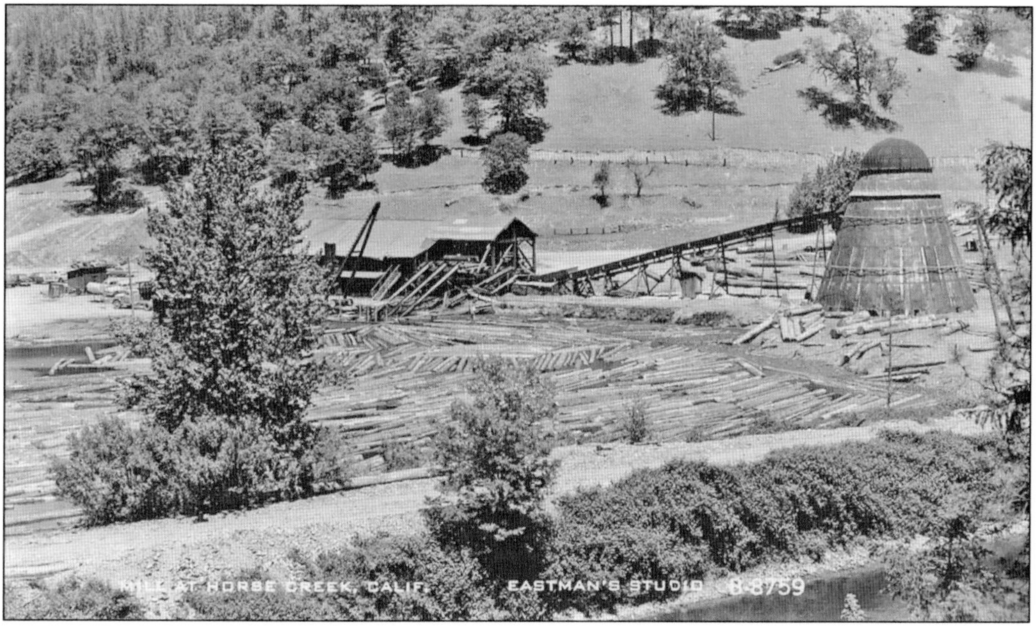

Horse Creek, California, is an unincorporated community on the Jefferson State Byway (Highway 96), 19 miles west-northwest of Yreka. In 1890, Robert Rainey homesteaded Horse Creek. A large sawmill supplied the region with lumber. There were a number of mills throughout the area, including ones at Ditch Creek, Ash Creek, Barkhouse, Beaver Creek, Hamburg, and Happy Camp. (Courtesy of Hazel Davis Gendron.)

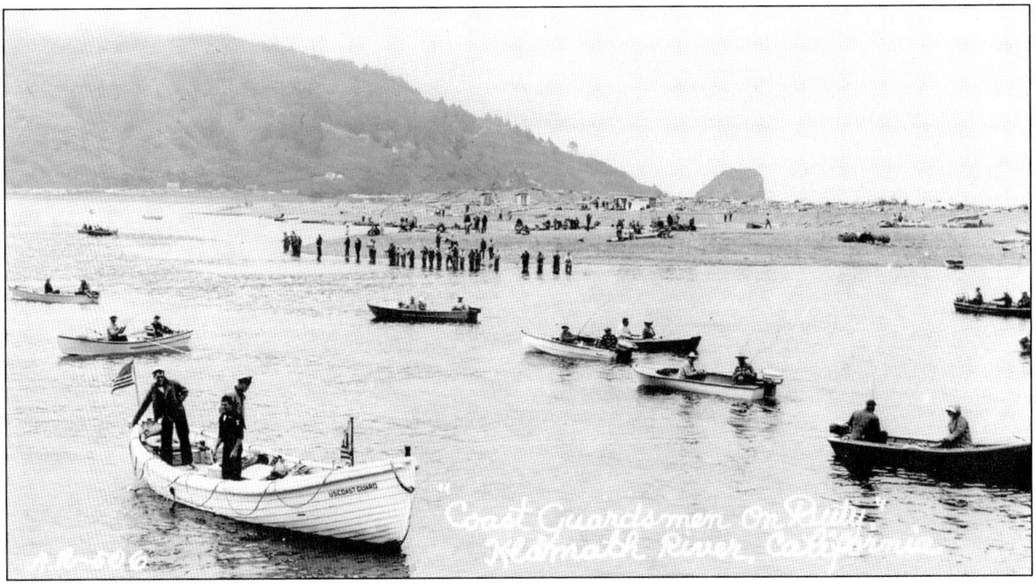

Fishing boats wait eagerly at the mouth of the Klamath River in California. The Klamath River (*Ishkeesh* to the Karuk) flows over 260 miles through southern Oregon and northern California to the Pacific Ocean, draining a watershed of nearly 16,000 square miles. It is the second largest river in California. The river has been a major source of food for several tribes, including the Karuk and Yurok. After fur trappers from the Hudson Bay Company arrived, some time in the 1820s–1830s, a trail was established that followed the Klamath River into the Sacramento Valley. The river became a hotbed for miners during the 1850s–1860s. Today, the Klamath remains an important river for the area's tribes as well as a popular recreational river for fishermen, kayakers, and others.

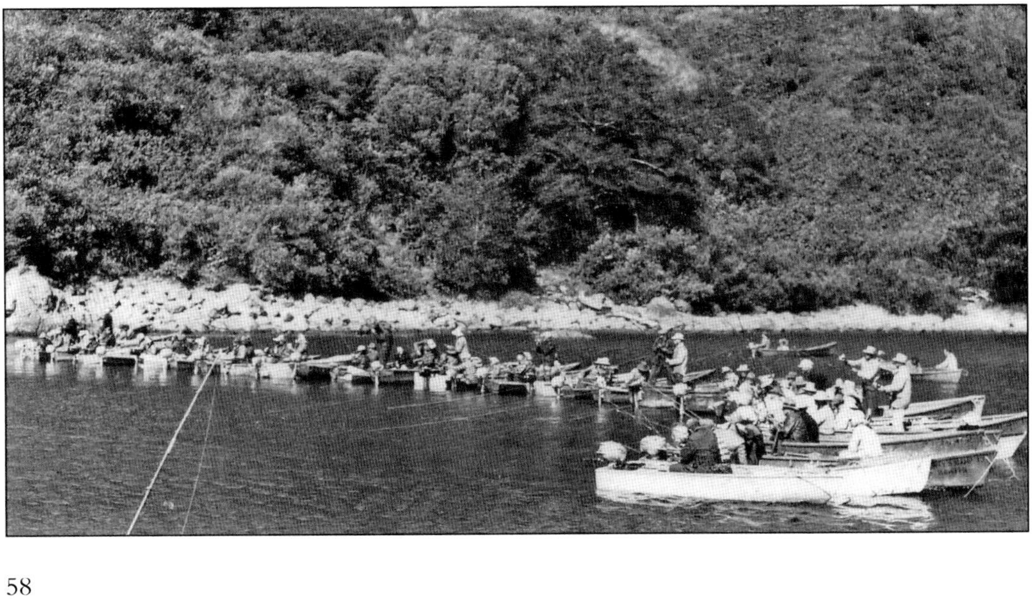

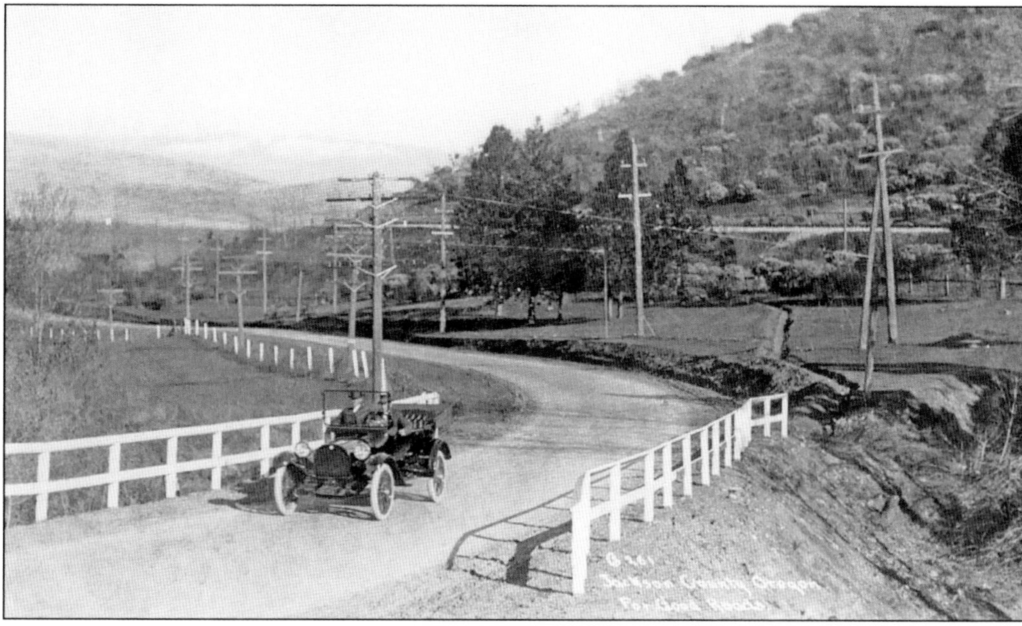

Driving through Jackson County, Oregon, is as popular today as it was around 1920. The county, named for Pres. Andrew Jackson, was established in 1852 and encompasses 2,802 square miles, with 11 cities and 34 unincorporated communities for a population of nearly 205,000. Medford has been the county seat since 1927, taking over after the railroad bypassed Jacksonville, the first county seat.

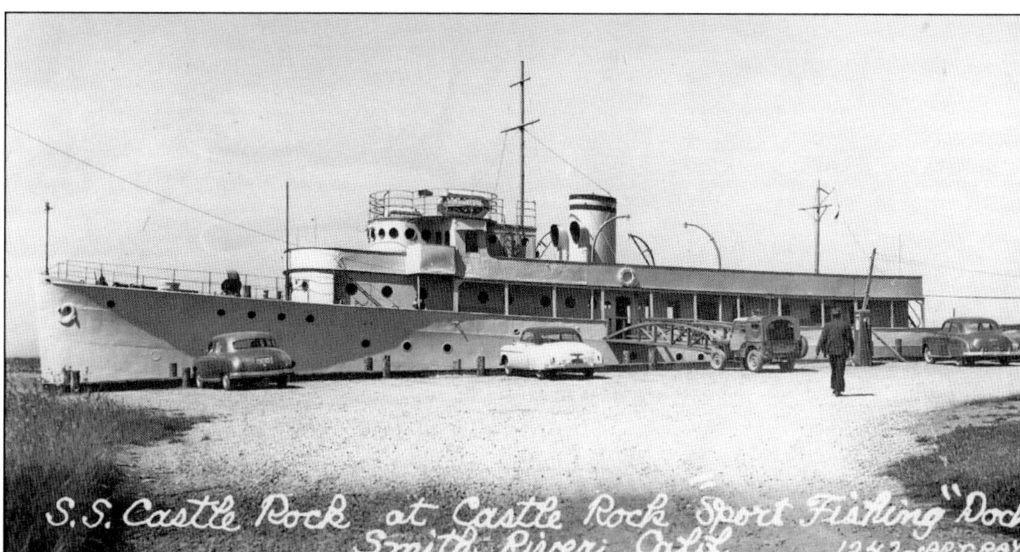

The SS *Castle Rock* was once a US Navy patrol ship and, before that, a privately owned yacht. After the attack on Pearl Harbor in 1941, the beautiful yacht was appropriated by the Navy and assigned patrol off the California coast. After the war, she sat neglected until 1949, when Joe Sierka, who owned a run-down fishing village at Smith River, California, gave her a new home.

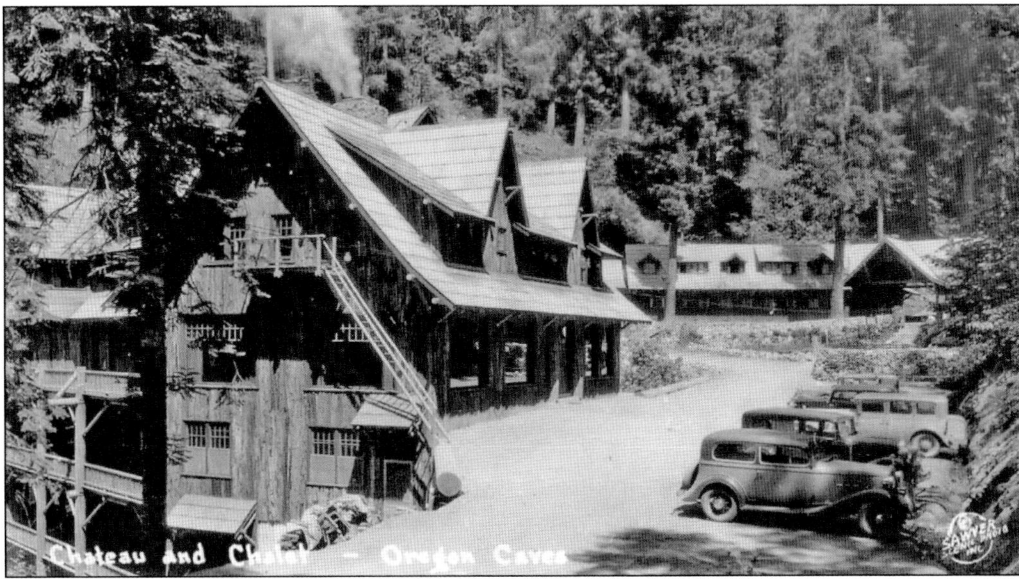

The rustic Oregon Caves Chateau is a six-story hotel open from May to October. Off to the side is the entrance to the Oregon Caves National Monument. A local nonprofit group, the Illinois Valley Community Development Organization, manages the lodge. The chateau is one of the national park system's Great Lodges and a National Historic Landmark. It features 23 guest rooms.

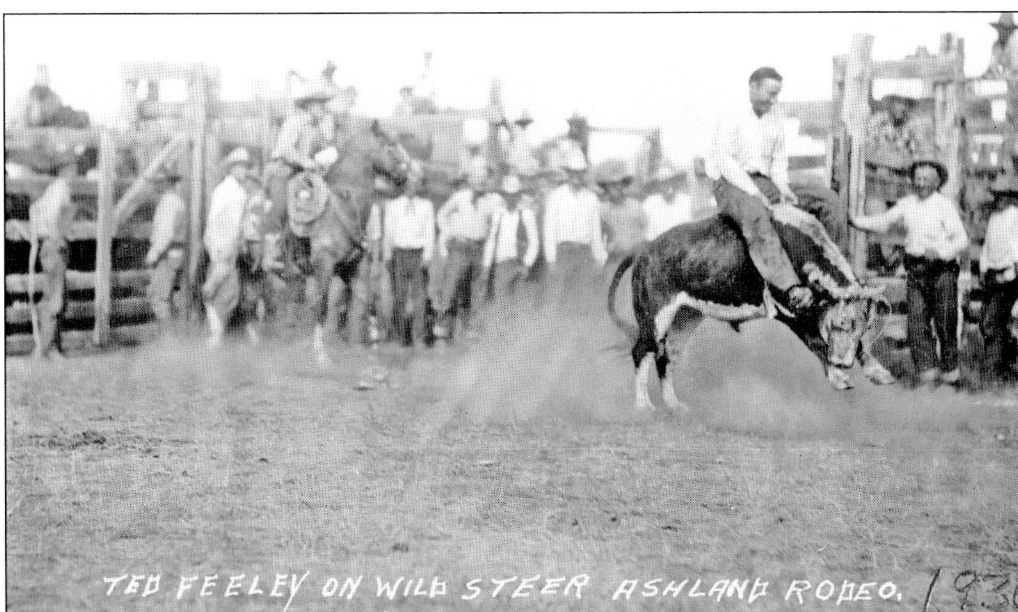

In 1916, Lithia Park sponsored a rodeo, the Rogue River Round-Up. Thousands crowded the stands, and 80 contestants vied for purses ranging from $10 to a $150 saddle. In 1917, notable contestants included John Spain, who bulldogged steers with one arm and his teeth, and Josephine Sherry, the most renowned woman trick rider. Most Ashland rodeo roundups were part of Fourth of July celebrations. Here, Ted Feely rides a steer around 1930.

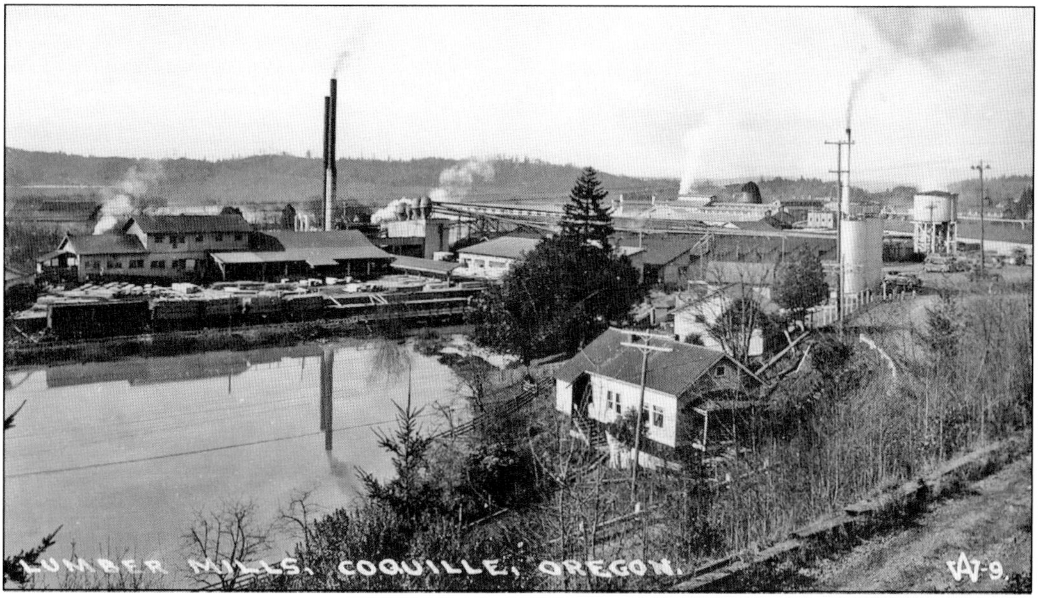

Coquille is the county seat of Coos County, Oregon. It was incorporated in 1885. Its name comes from the Coquille Indian language. Coquille is bordered by the Coquille River, which drains part of the Coast Range into the Pacific Ocean at Bandon. Logging has dominated Oregon's history. With the 1849 California Gold Rush, the lumber market boomed, and sawmills sprang up all over Oregon. The first sawmill was located at the Columbia River in 1851, near Lewis and Clark's Fort Clatsop. The first sawmill on the southern coast was built at Port Orford in 1854; a third was opened up on the Coquille River. Coquille's primary economic base has been the timber industry.

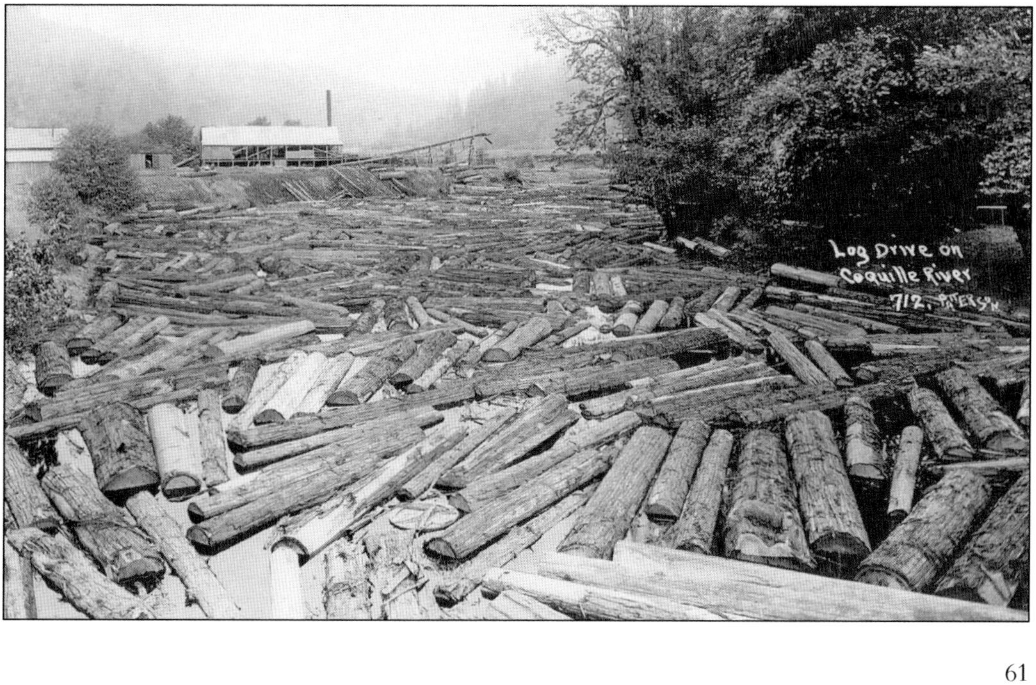

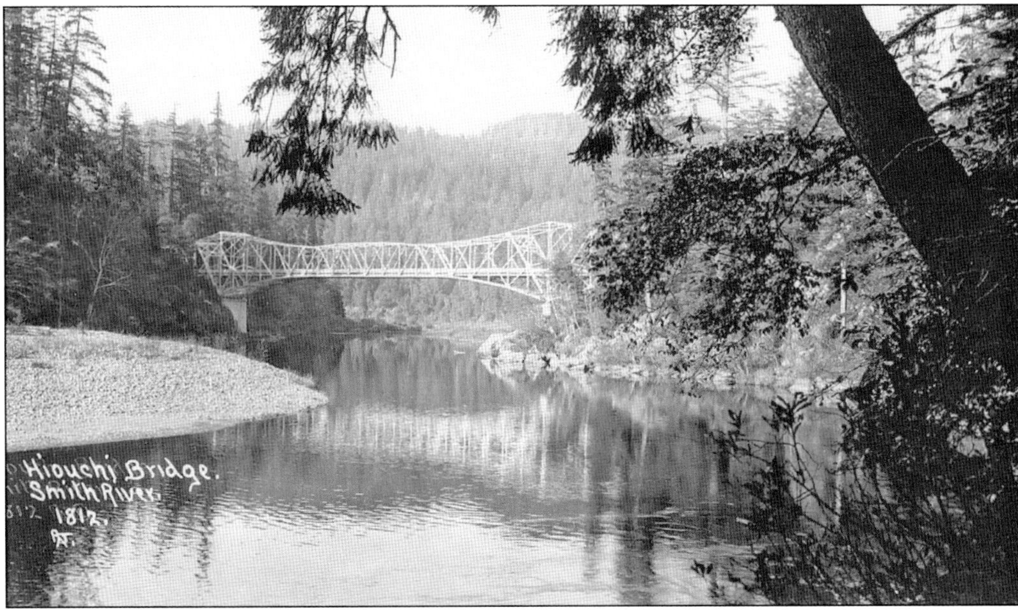

The Smith River, located in Del Norte County, California, is approximately 20 miles long. *Hiochi* is an Indian word that means "blue water," and the Hiouchi Bridge was a rare California example of a cantilevered highway truss bridge, popular during the late 1920s and 1930s. It was built in 1929, but after being damaged by a truck, it was demolished in 1989. It spanned 615 feet across the river.

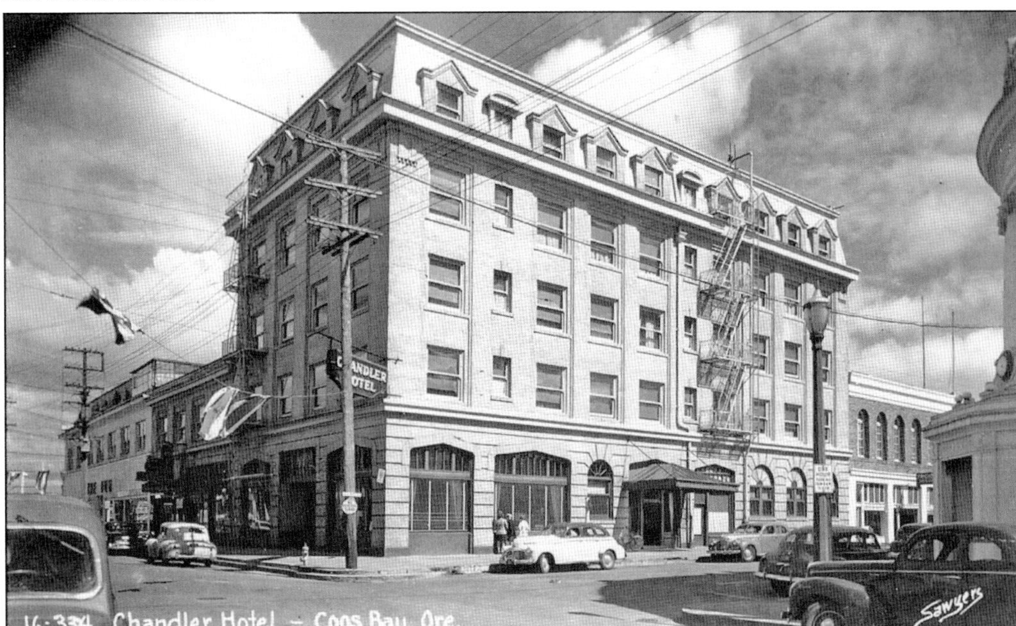

The Chandler Hotel was a landmark in Coos Bay, Oregon. In 1909, the Coos Bay Hotel Company, composed of prominent businessmen, built a $75,000, first-class, five-story hotel. Bricklayers laid thousands of bricks fired at a kiln on Coos River. The company spent thousands of dollars for furnishings. For decades, the Chandler was one of the best hotels in Oregon. It was listed in the National Register of Historic Places in 1984.

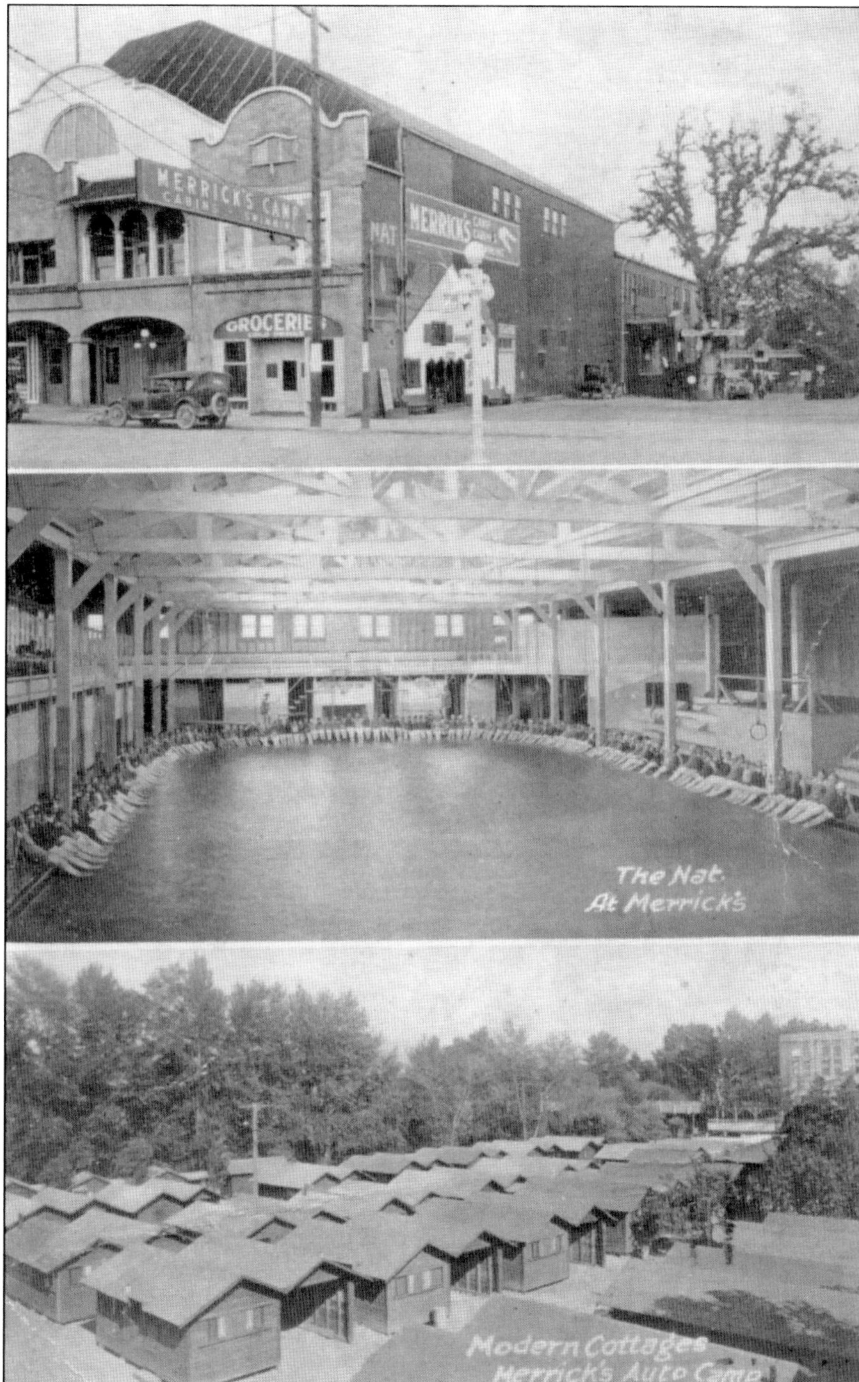

Merrick's Auto Camp in Medford, Oregon, was a unique place. In 1909, ten teams of horses pulling fresnos broke ground for Merrick's Natatorium. It was the largest building of its kind in southern Oregon and featured an enormous swimming pool with 50,000 gallons of water. Skirted bathing suits, bloomers, and stockings were rented to the ladies who came to swim. In winter, the pool was converted into a roller rink.

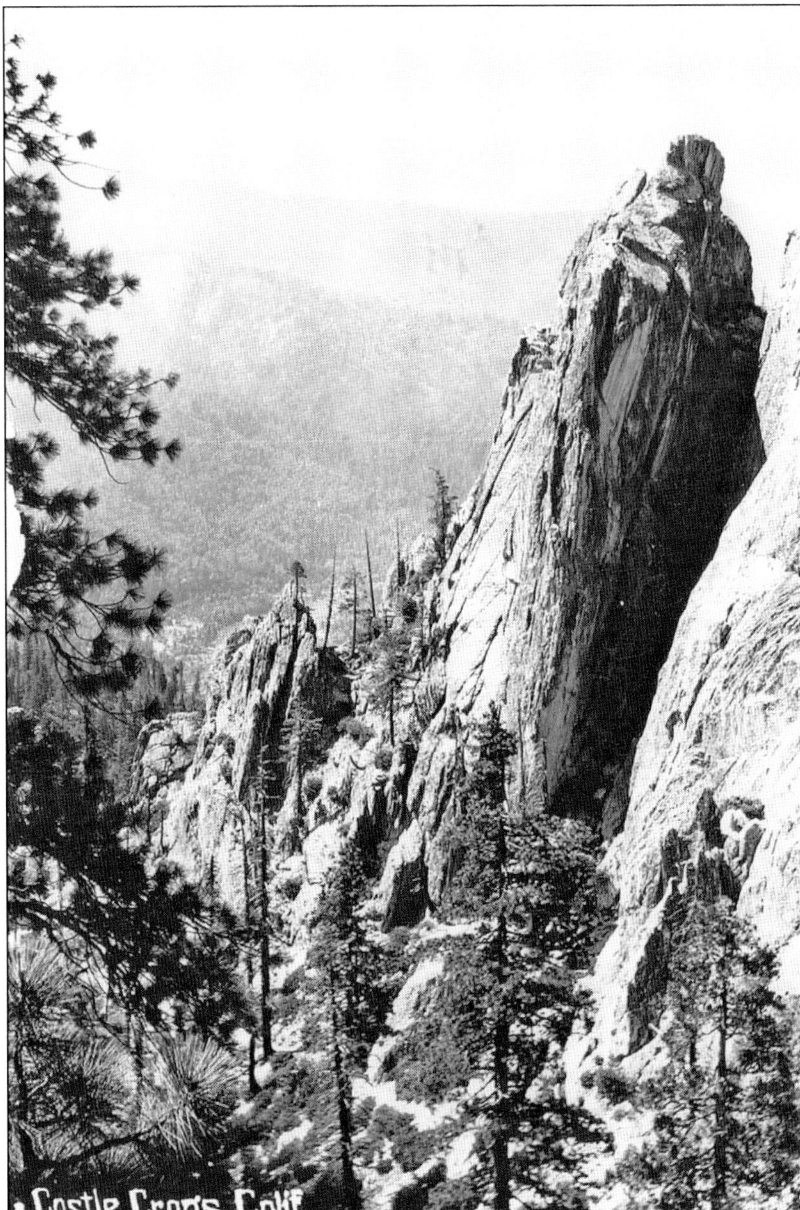

The Castle Crags Wilderness Area is located within the Shasta-Trinity National Forest, about 40 miles north of Redding, California. The crags range in elevation from 2,500 feet to 7,300 feet. Originally the Wintu, who have resided in the area for generations, called the crags the "Abode of the Devil." Mineral springs at the base of the crags were first used by traders and trappers, then later by visitors to the various health resorts that dotted the Upper Sacramento River Canyon. During the Depression, a Civilian Conservation Corps (CCC) camp was built north of town. When Castle Crags State Park was created in 1933, the 200 CCC workers built most of the roads, trails, campgrounds, and buildings. The Wilderness Act of 1984, signed into law by President Reagan, set aside the crags as a designated wilderness. For visitors today, the Castle Dome Trail is a strenuous hiking trail. In addition, 19 miles of the Pacific Crest Trail pass through the crags.

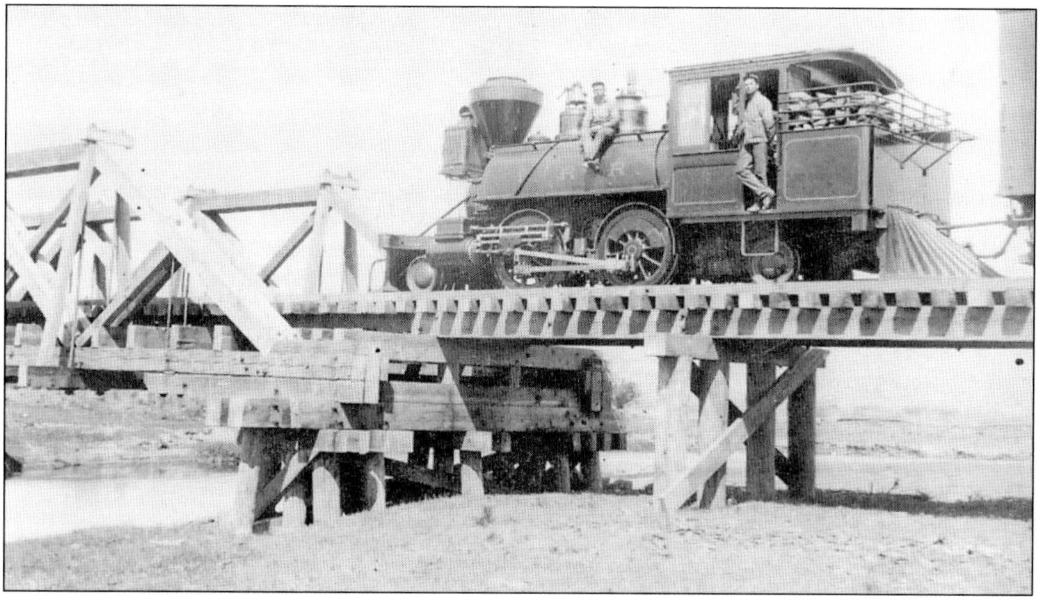

By the mid-1880s, the railroad entered Siskiyou County, California, and in August 1886, completed its track up through the Sacramento River Canyon. The Yreka Railroad Company incorporated in May 1888, serving area miners and settlers. In 1889, Yreka became a stop on the Southern Pacific line. Ultimately, Southern Pacific Railroad acquired the Central Pacific and Oregon-California Railroad Companies, but the small, independent Yreka Western Railroad, incorporated in 1933, ran a local run for many years.

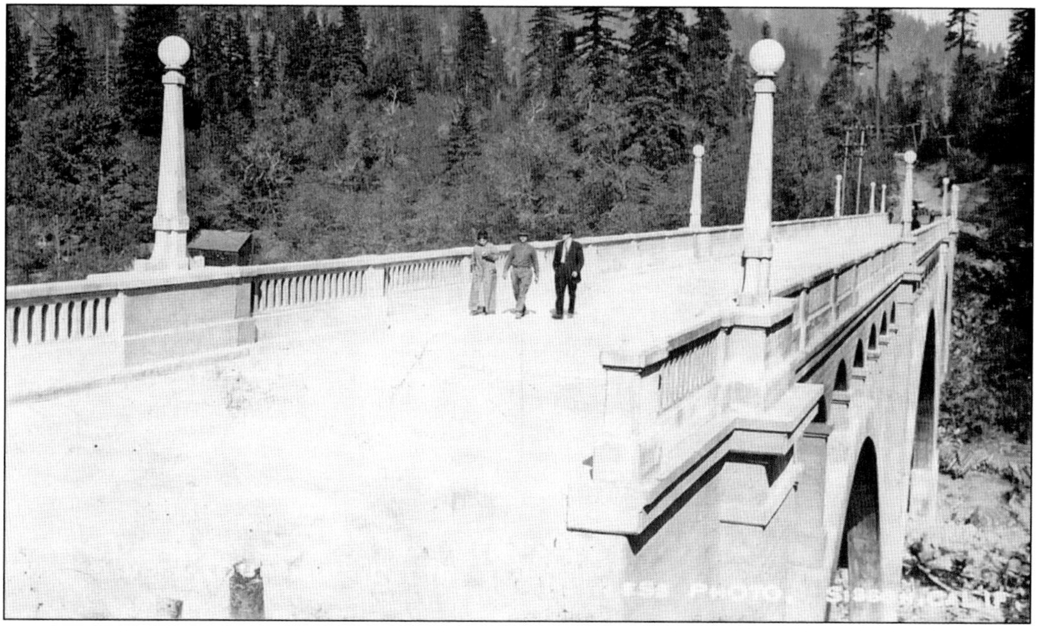

The Pacific Highway ran north through Redding, California, and followed the original Siskiyou Trail and early wagon roads. It remained virtually the same from 1862 to 1916. In 1916 and again in 1927, it was modernized under the new California Division of Highways. Not until 1952 was it actually revamped. During construction of Interstate 5 in the 1960s, the narrowed Sacramento River Canyon proved to be a bottleneck, and much excavation was required.

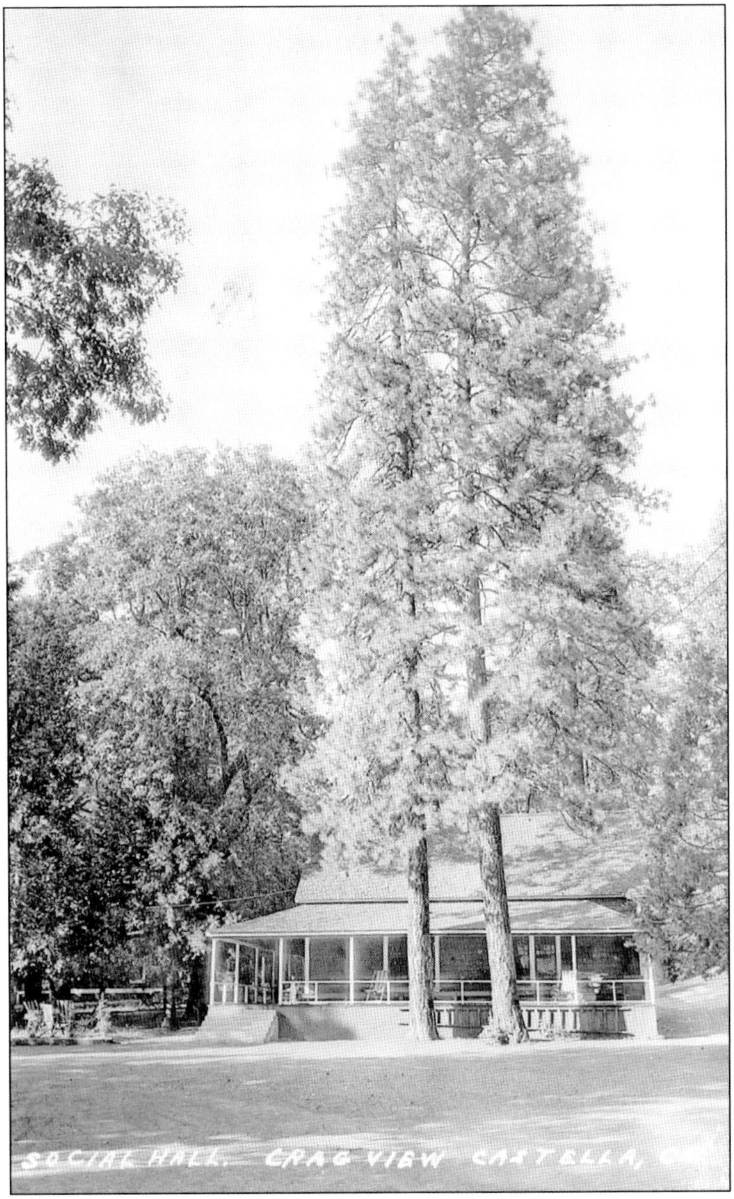

Castella, California, is located along Interstate 5 in northern Shasta County, along the Upper Sacramento River Canyon. Originally called Castle Rock, it was renamed by William Mullen in the 1880s. One of the first residents of the area was George Washington Bailey, who came seeking the healing power of mineral springs found near the river. Bailey built an inn along the California to Oregon Trail at Lower Soda Springs. His business grew into a resort, and in 1883, he built a second hotel, Castle Rock Springs. He eventually sold this property to a company that sold bottled spring water; Castle Rock Natural Springs Company won a number of awards. During Prohibition, Castella again found itself booming. Local still operators pooled their alcohol, then hired drivers to haul the illegal booze to cities to the south. Castella also supported a number of bootleg joints. Mike Padula built his across from the local Southern Pacific depot. It quickly became a favorite hangout for newspaper mogul William Randolph Hearst and his celebrity friends.

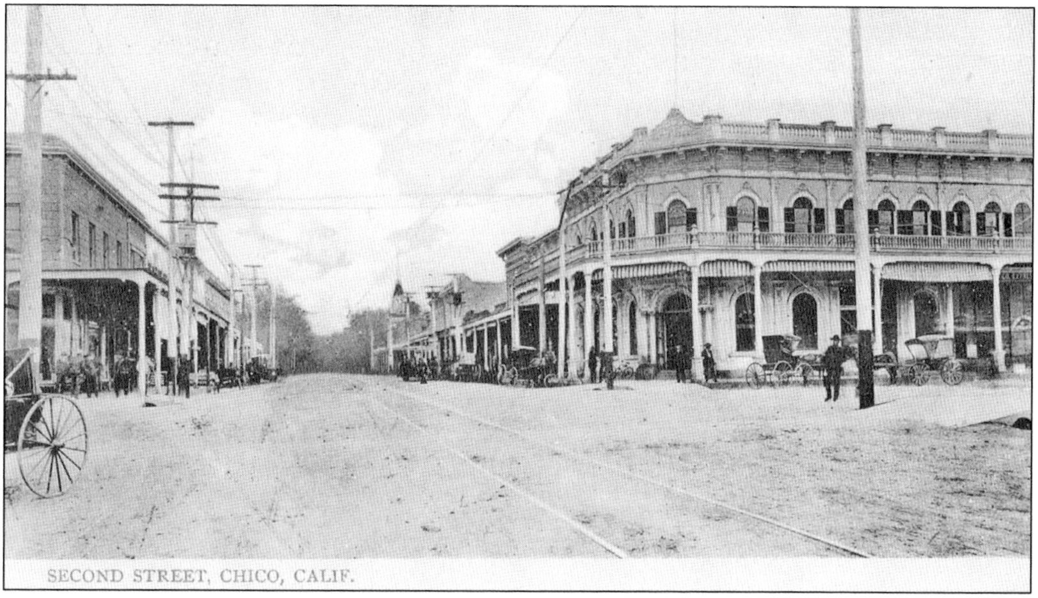

Chico, California, was founded in 1860 by Gen. John Bidwell. Bidwell arrived in California in 1841 and worked for a time for John Sutter. Ten years later, he purchased property known as Rancho Arroyo Chico. In 1887, a state normal school was established; it later became California State University, Chico. In 1917, a parade through downtown Chico was held that started Chico's celebrated Pioneer Day parade tradition.

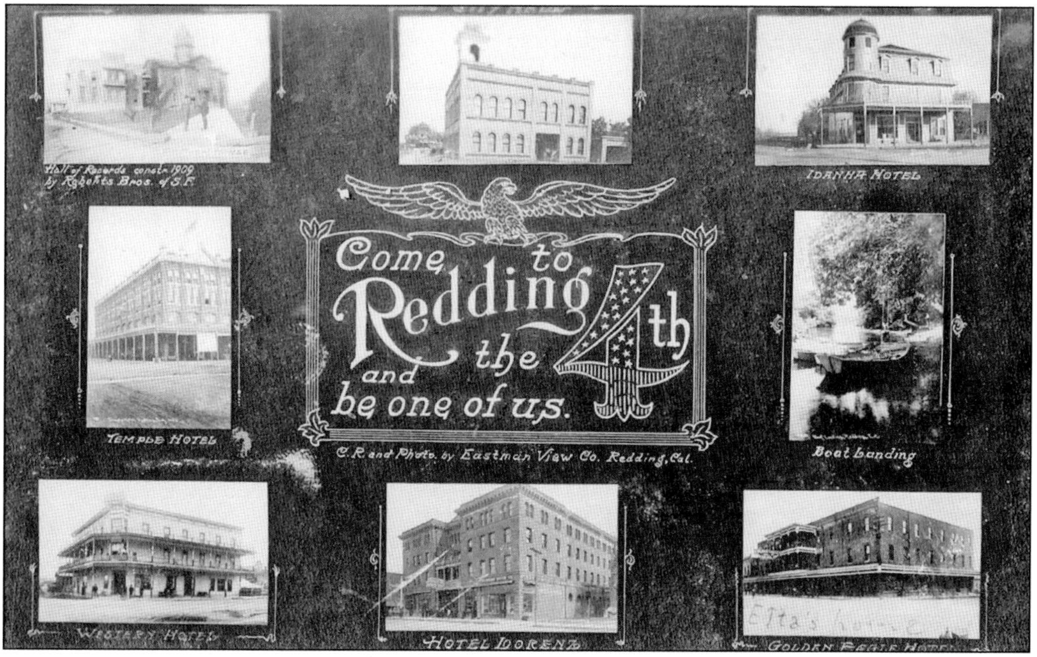

Redding, California, located along the Sacramento River, is the county seat of Shasta County. In its early days, Redding connected the Central Valley and the mountainous regions to the north. This c. 1920 card invites the reader to "Come to Redding the 4th and be one of us." Pictures feature some of Redding's landmarks, including the Golden Eagle Hotel and the gracious Lorenz Hotel, the first building in Redding to have an elevator.

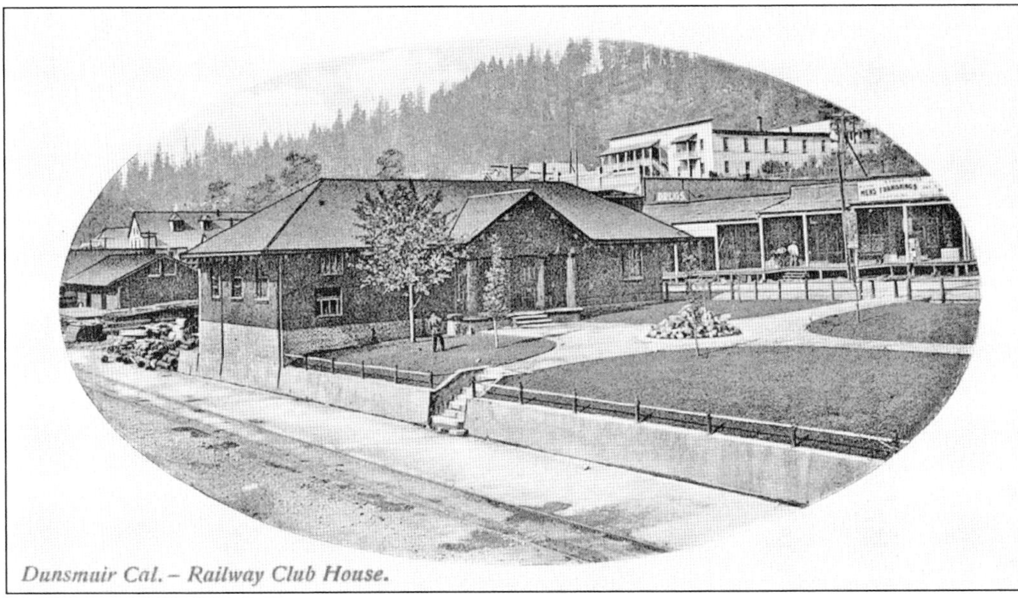

Dunsmuir Cal. – Railway Club House.

A sketch of Dunsmuir's clubhouse reveals the importance of the railroad. Dunsmuir, California, became a railroad hub and was, for many years, the most prosperous and largest of the communities in southern Siskiyou County. The construction of the railroad through the rugged Sacramento River Canyon proved to be the most dangerous section of any California line built by California's "Big Four" (Leland Stanford, Collis P. Huntington, Mark Hopkins, and Charles Crocker).

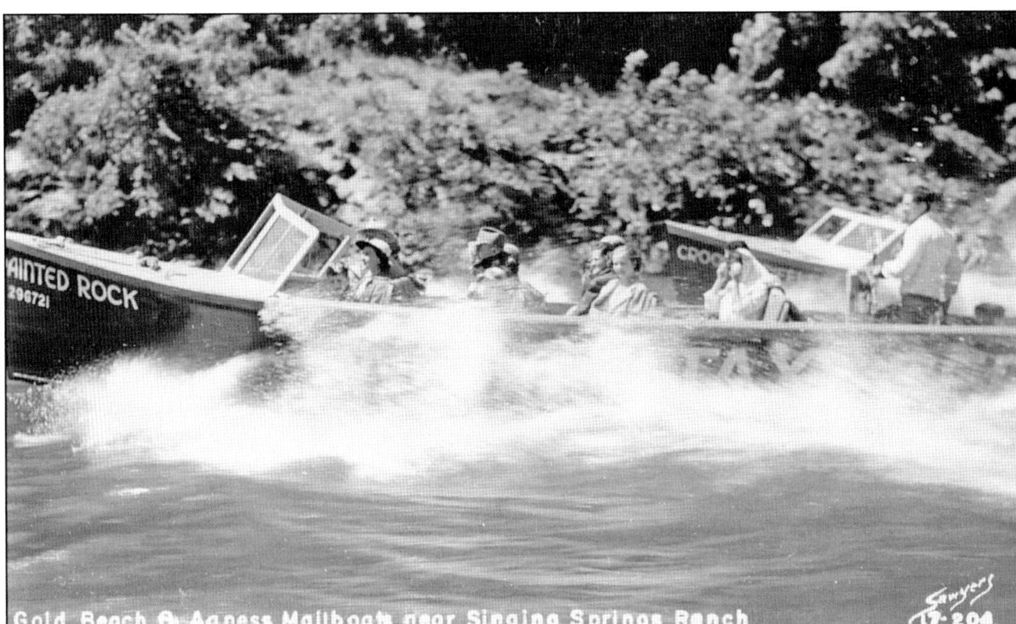

Gold Beach & Agness Mailboats near Singing Springs Ranch

Agness, Oregon, is served by one of only two rural mail boat routes still running in the United States. Agness is located 32 miles upriver from the mouth of the Rogue River and was originally settled in 1895. The post office, established in 1897, was named for the first postmaster's daughter, Agnes, but her name was unfortunately misspelled. Today, visitors still enjoy riding the mail boats, which move up and down the Rogue daily.

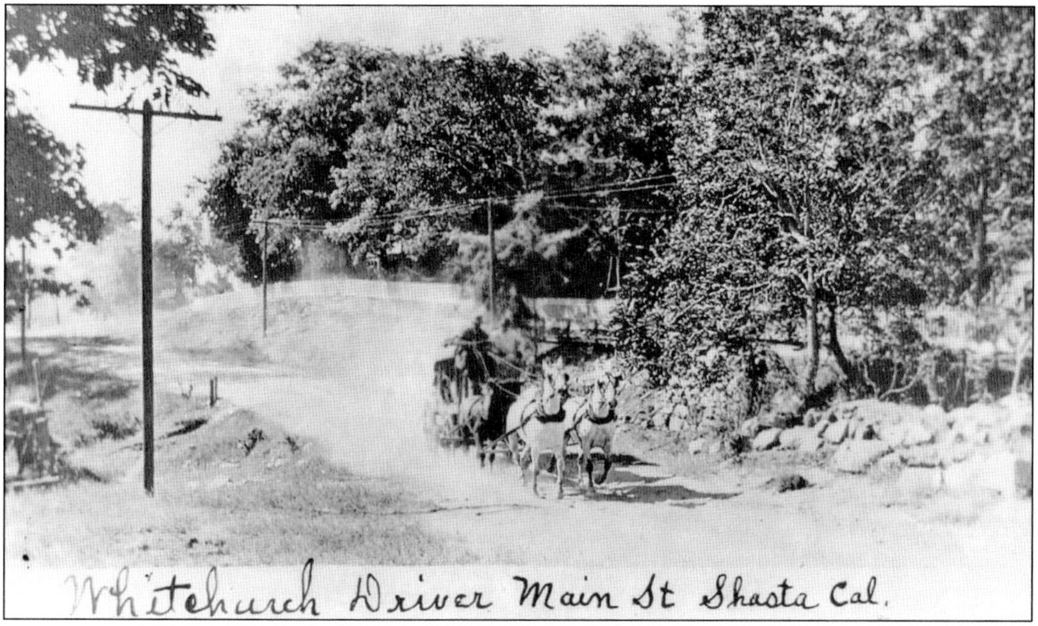

Six miles west of Redding, California, on Highway 299, is the remnant of Shasta. A state park today, Shasta contained the longest row of brick buildings erected in the 1850s. Because of its location, it was called the "Queen City" and the gateway to the rich northern mines. It was also a supply depot for mule trains, stages, and freight trains. The stage driver is identified as a Mr. Whitechurch.

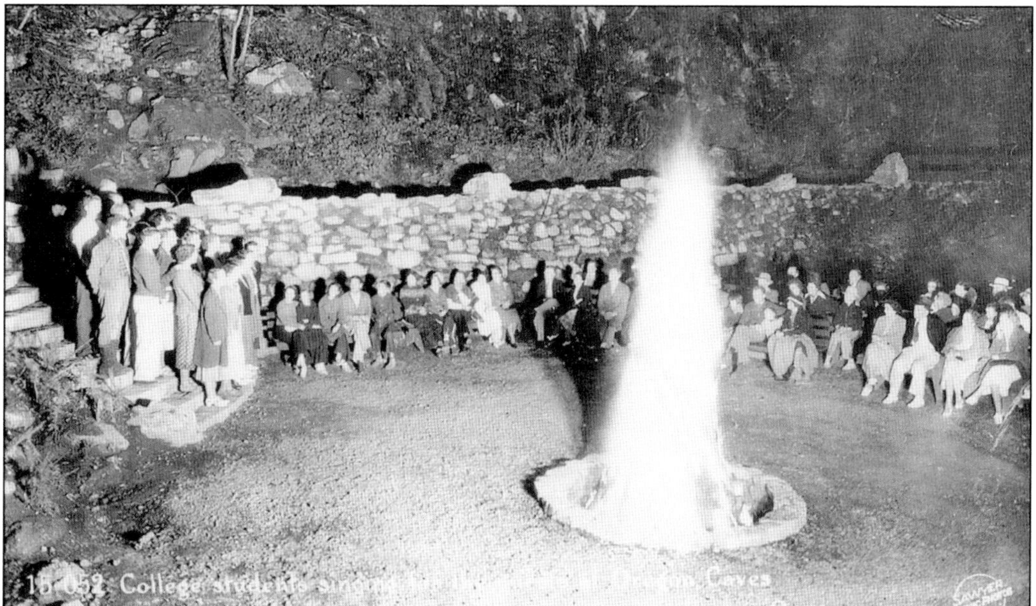

College students entertained guests visiting the Oregon Caves Monument. A popular attraction, the Chateau is still available for weddings, tours, or educational events. For those who don't stay at the lodge, there is camping at Cave Creek and Grayback. There are also four trails that take hikers around the monument. Other attractions include the stream that moves through the dining room as well as the arts and crafts style of the lodge.

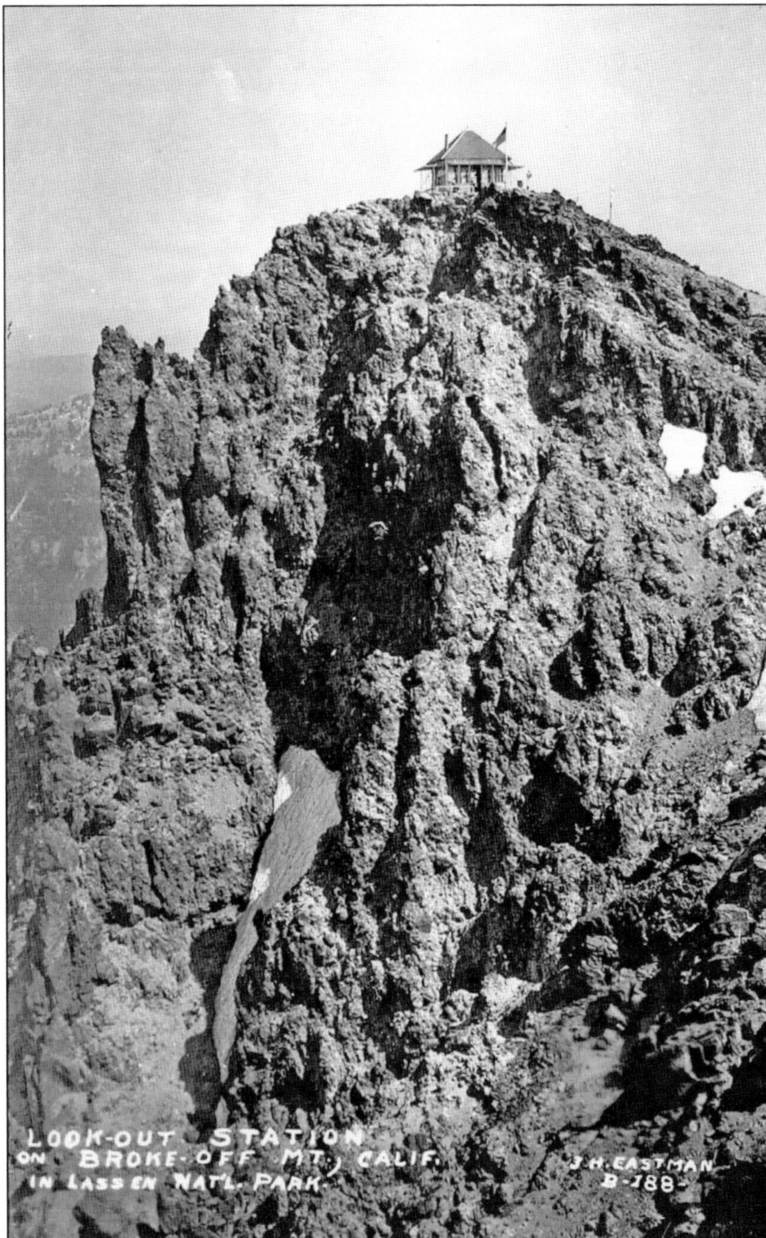

Lassen Volcanic National Park was originally a meeting place for at least four Native American tribes, the Atsugewi, Yana, Yahi, and Maidu. Ishi, the last of the Yahi, who was found in 1911, alone and starving, was taken to Berkeley's Museum of Anthropology to live out the remainder of his life. Because of its elevation and seasonal deer populations, the area was not conducive to year-round living. Jedediah Smith passed through here in 1828, while William Nobles passed through in 1851, and Peter Lassen guided settlers through on what was later called the Lassen Trail. Sections of their trails are visible today. The lookout here is on Broke Off Mountain. It's a three-mile hike to Forest Lake, then 7.4 miles to the summit. On clear days, one can see as far as Nevada to the east or the Coast Range to the west. There are 150 miles of trails, including a 17-mile section of the Pacific Crest Trail.

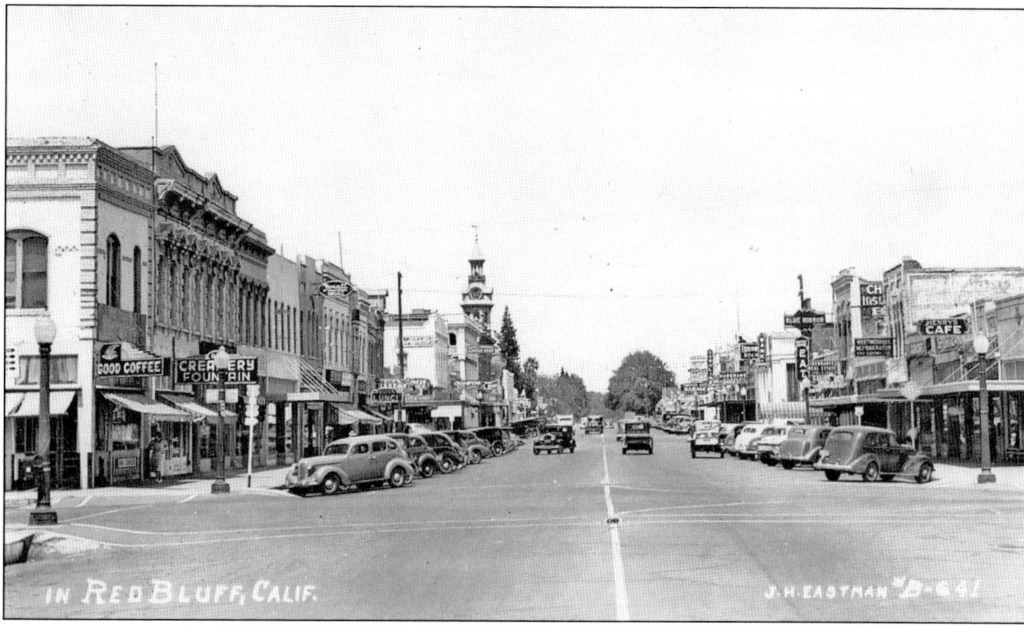

Red Bluff is the county seat of Tehama County, California. It is located along the Sacramento River 30 miles south of Redding. The area was originally home to the Wintu and Yana, but many reportedly died of malaria or smallpox when trappers came through in the 1830s. The first house in Red Bluff was an adobe built by John Myers in 1849. By 1854, the small community was known as Red Bluffs.

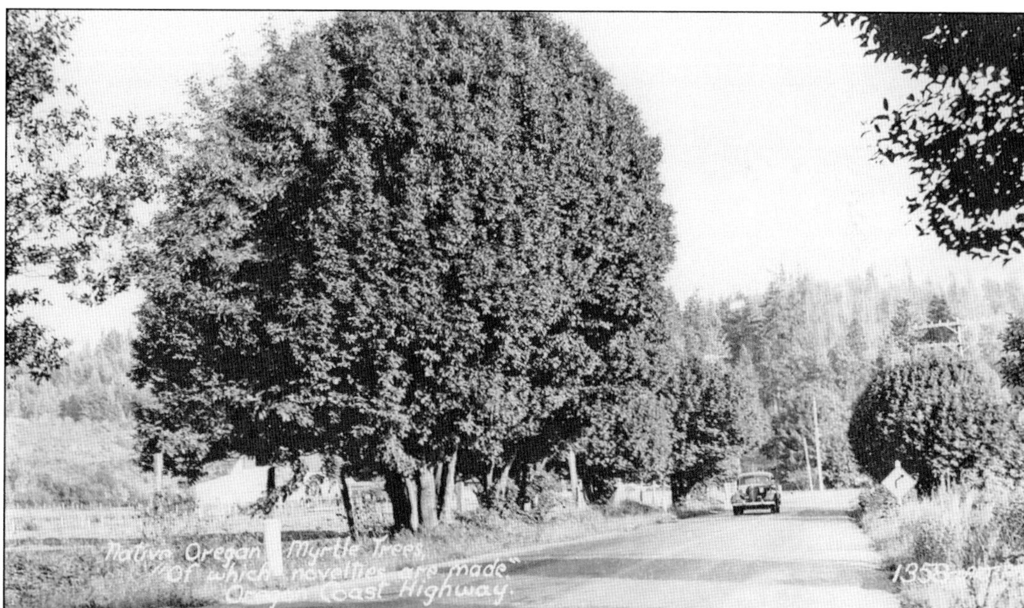

Known in Oregon as Oregon myrtle, this tree in California is known as California laurel. The tree has also been called pepperwood, spicebush, cinnamon bush, pepper nut, headache tree, mountain laurel, and balm of heaven. Its pungent leaves smell like bay leaves, though stronger, and may be mistaken for bay laurel. The dry wood can be blonde like maple to brown like walnut and is sought after by luthiers and woodworkers.

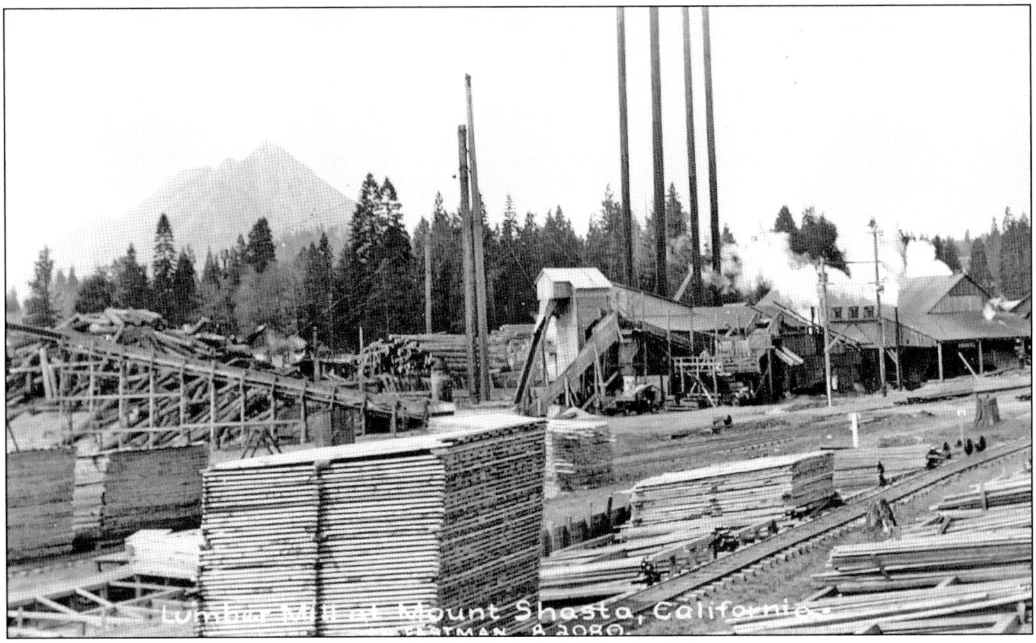

Ross McCloud, an early Siskiyou pioneer, built one of the first lumber mills in the Mount Shasta area. The railroad also triggered an increased demand for lumber. In the 1900s, Italian immigrants added to the pool of labor for timber and millwork; most of them took jobs in the burgeoning lumber industry. With the railroad, the community was given the name Sisson. It was changed to Mount Shasta in 1924.

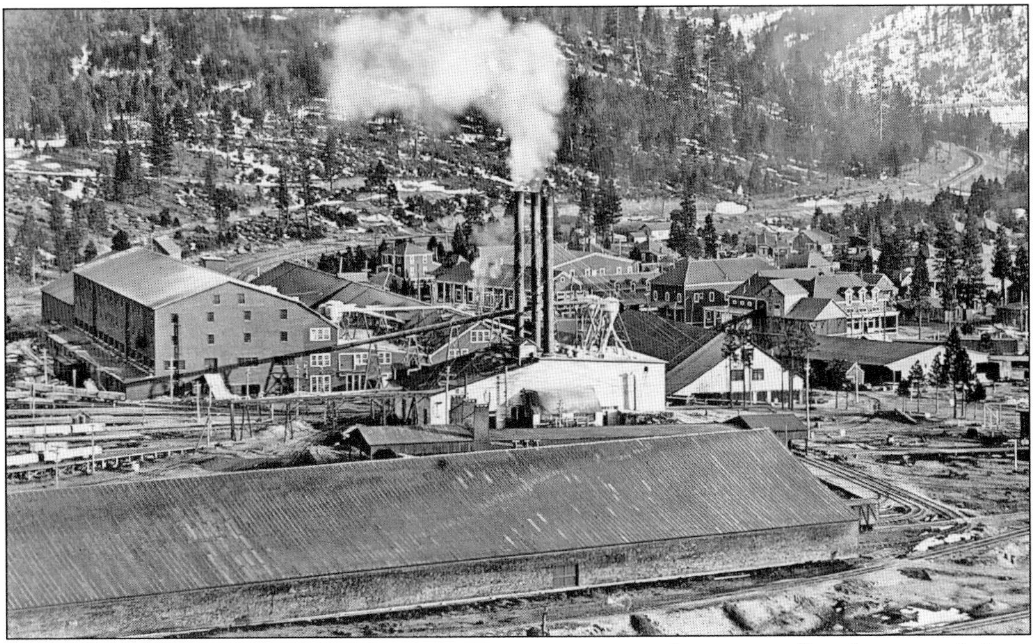

Weed, California, began as lumbering town. Its proximity to the surrounding forests made it an ideal site for a mill. By 1905, there were two mills and a box factory in town. The box factory was built by Abner Weed, the town's founder, in 1902. The factory built fruit boxes as well as doors and window sashes. The boxes were sold as kits and assembled later in the field.

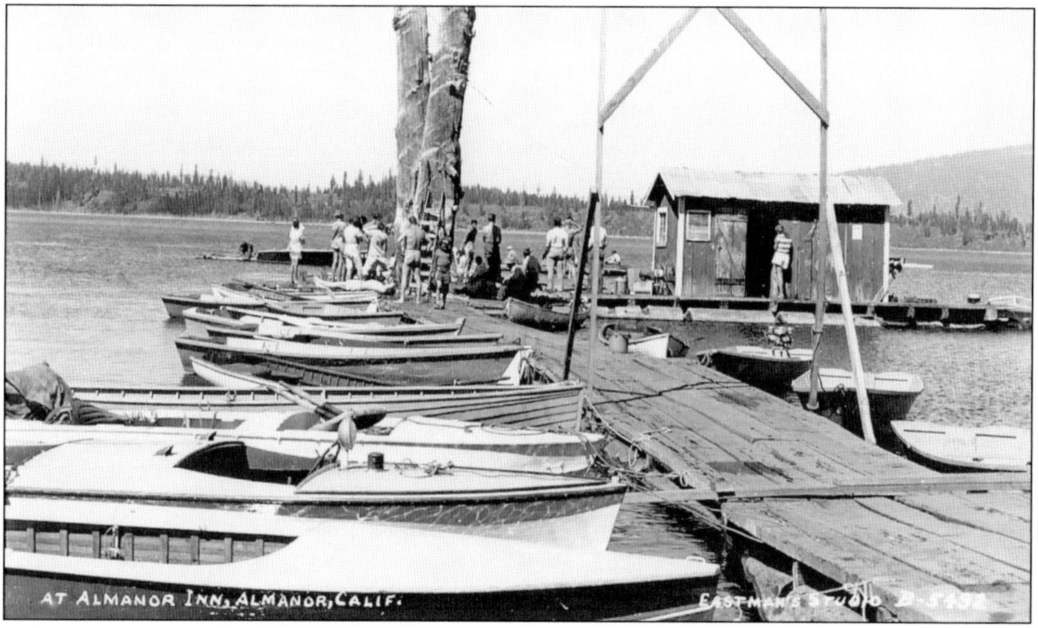

Lake Almanor is a man-made lake in Plumas County, California, created in 1926–1927 by Great Western Power Company. Originally, the land under the lake was called Big Meadows and was a resort area. Old pioneering families like the Bidwells pastured cattle here, and many ranchers still graze cattle across the pastureland. The lake was named for the daughters of Guy Earl, vice president of Great Western Power: *Al*ice, *Ma*rtha, and Elea*nor*.

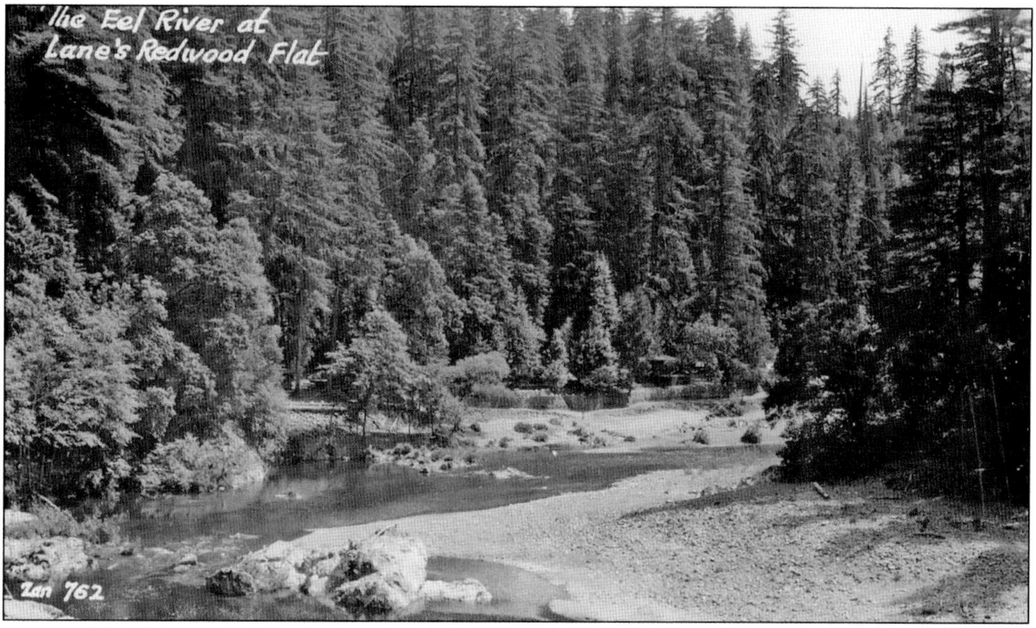

Some of the first inhabitants of the Eel River region were the Sinkyone and Wailaki. They had encampments along the East Branch of the Eel River and in Cooks Valley, California. The first recorded settler in the area was Reuben Reed. He married a Wailaki woman named Nellie, a widow whose first husband accidently drowned in the South Fork of the Eel River. A Canadian immigrant, Henry Devoy, later purchased Reed's property.

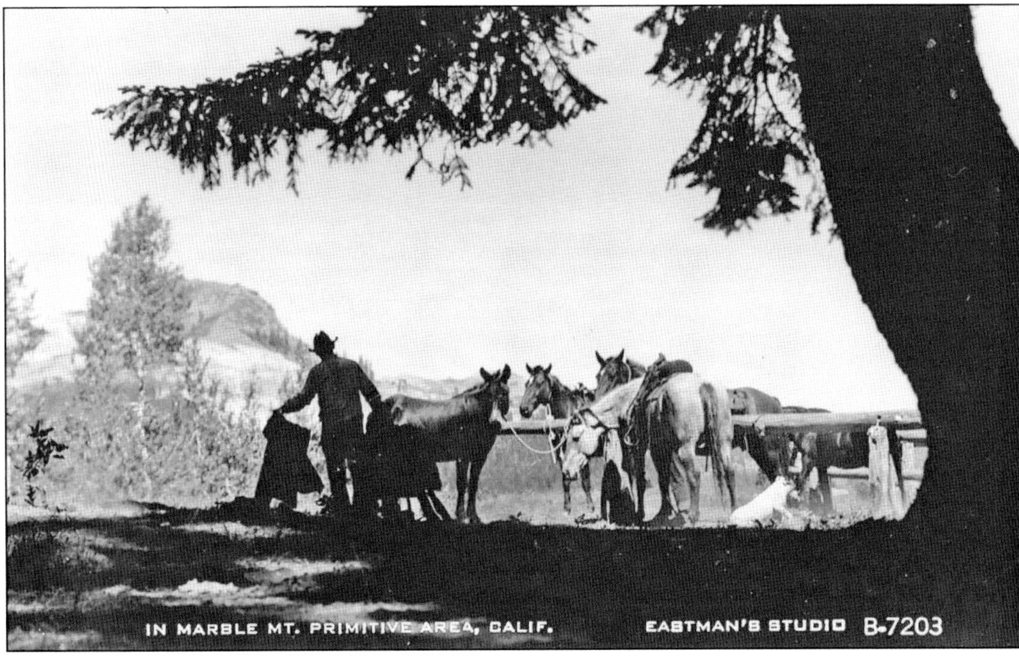

The Marble Mountain Wilderness Area, located in western Siskiyou County, California, encompasses over 240,000 acres. There are 89 lakes, and most of the peaks stand over 6,000 feet. Boulder Peak is the highest point at 8,299 feet. The North Fork of the Salmon has its headwaters in the wilderness area. The region was first labeled a primitive area in 1931. Packers, hunters, and hikers all enjoy the rugged beauty.

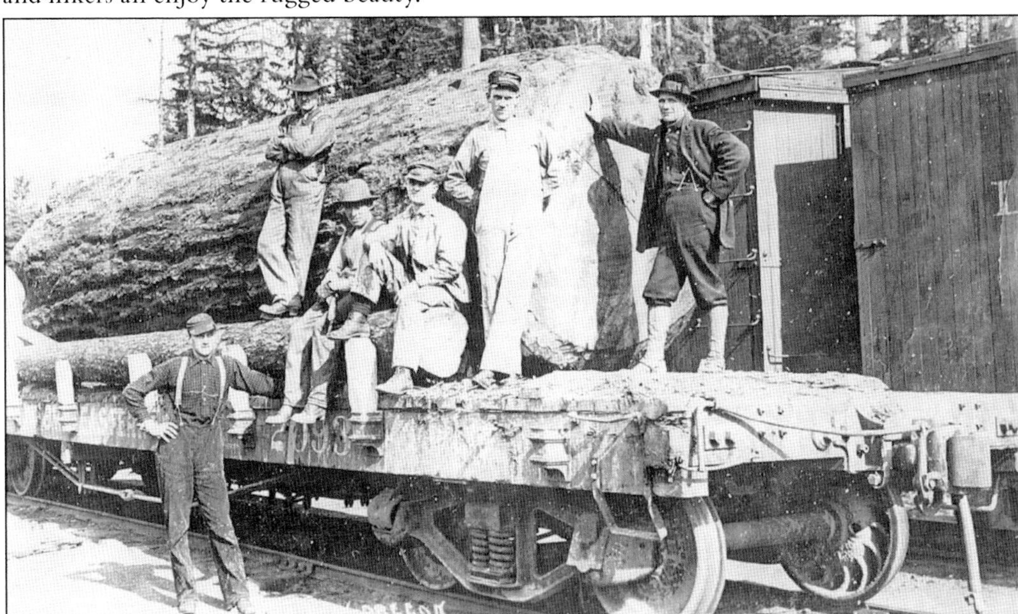

Logging in Oregon and California has undergone dramatic and controversial changes since 1990. For those who have spent generations in the forests or mills in this region, the loss of jobs has meant turning to new occupations and developing new attitudes. Scenes such as this are rarely, if ever, captured in daily life. They are moments only captured on film.

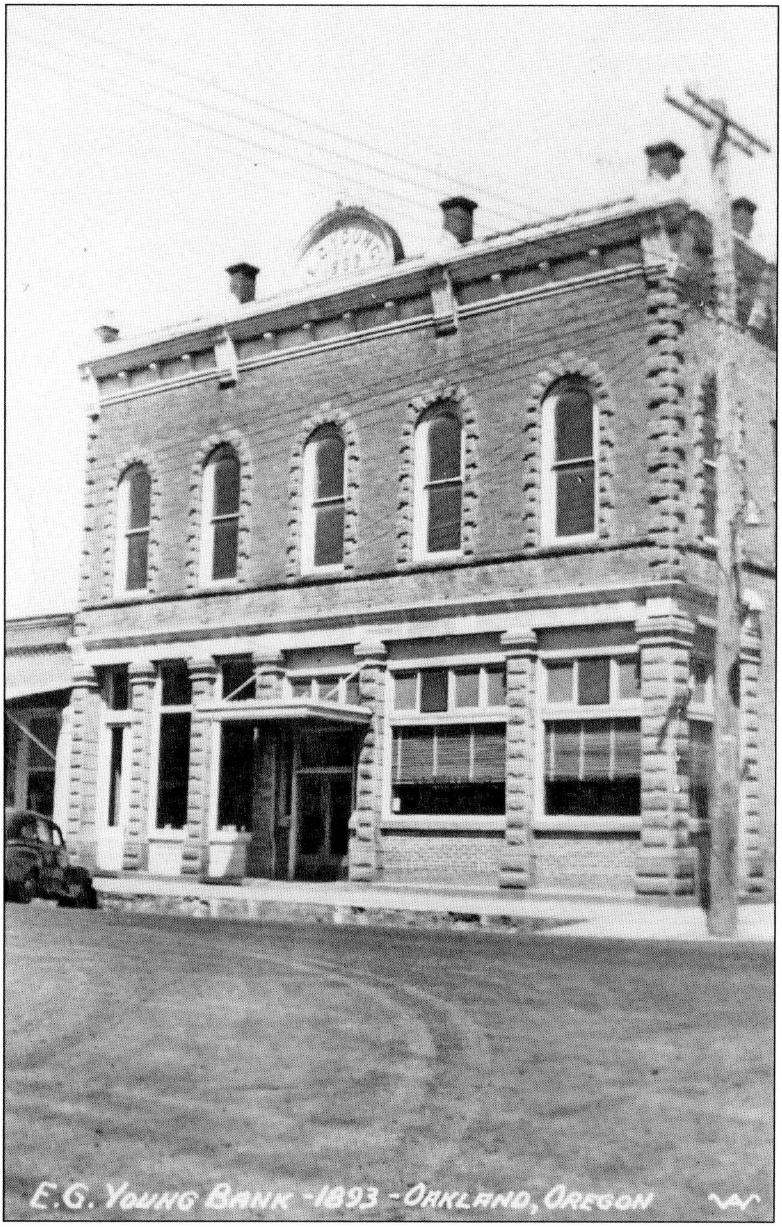

Oakland, Oregon, was the first city to be listed in Oregon's State Historic Register. The city traces its origins to Rev. Joseph Cornwall, who reached the area in 1846, as well as Dr. Dorsey Baker, who established a gristmill in 1851. E.G. Young, another early pioneer, joined Dr. Baker in the operation of the mill. When the Oregon & California Railroad laid out its route and moved into town, Young's bank began providing money to the community. Young and his sons also operated a large turkey packing plant and a store. The brick building seen here was built in 1892 and survived Oakland's fire in 1899. Although Young sold the store in 1909, he continued managing the bank until his death in 1920. Oakland became the turkey shipping capital of the West and the sponsor of the Northwestern Turkey Show, which became the largest in the world. Oakland was also noted for the fact that in the first decades of the 20th century, it boasted more well-to-do people per capita than any town in Oregon.

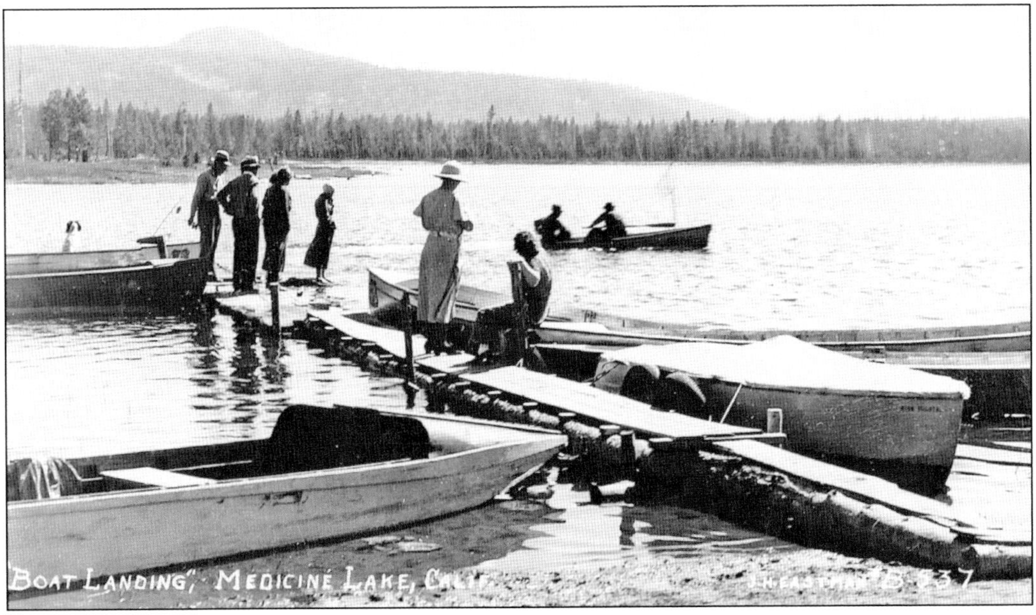

Medicine Lake is located in the northeastern corner of California, 30 miles from Mount Shasta and near the Lava Beds National Monument. It sits within the old caldera of the Medicine Lake Volcano, a shield volcano that is the largest volcano by volume in the Cascade Range. Though active for 500,000 years, its eruptions are not violent like Mount St. Helens but gentle, moving slowly down the sides of the volcano.

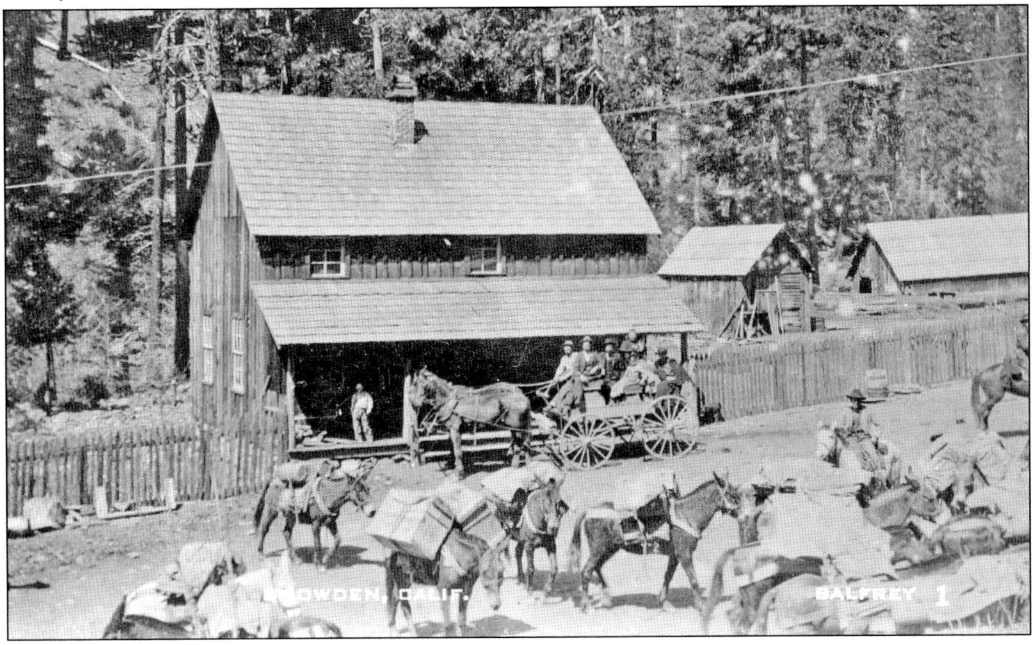

In 1893, John Grant bought property on the North Fork of the Salmon River from James May and built a station, Snowden, for pack trains and freight wagons. Edna Grant operated the station after John's death until she was too ill to carry on. Snowden's post office, established in 1904, was dropped in 1913, then reopened in 1915, when it was moved to Sawyers Bar, California. Snowden is now a private residence.

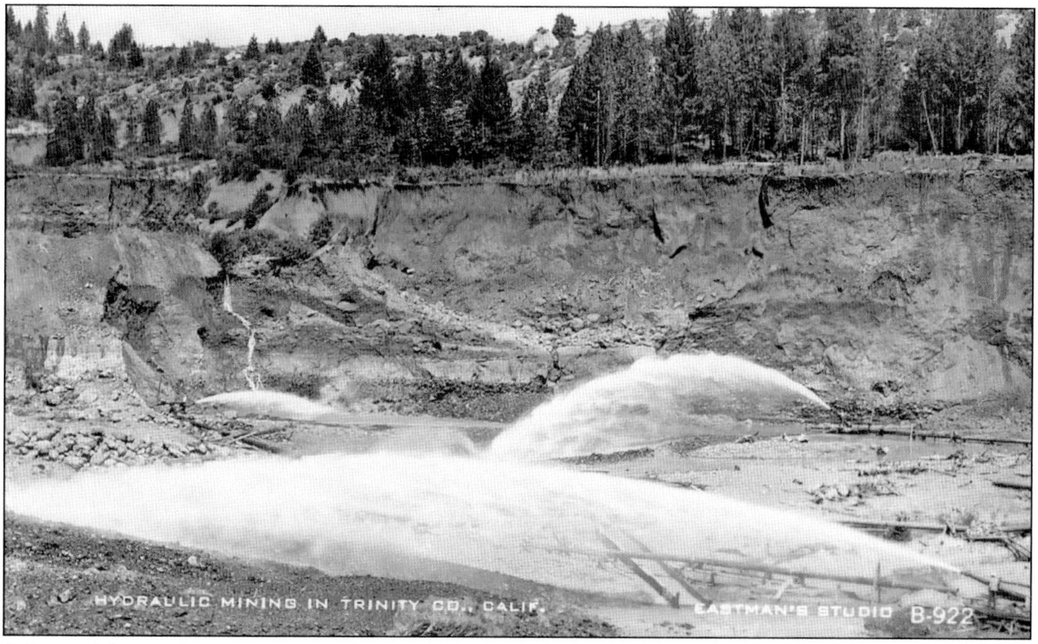

After gold was discovered in the Sierras, it wasn't long before miners headed north to Trinity County, California. Gold was discovered on the Trinity River in 1848, and large-scale hydraulic mining dominated from the early 1860s to well past 1900. Two of the largest hydraulic mines in the world at the time were located in Trinity County, the La Grange Mine and Union Hill Mine.

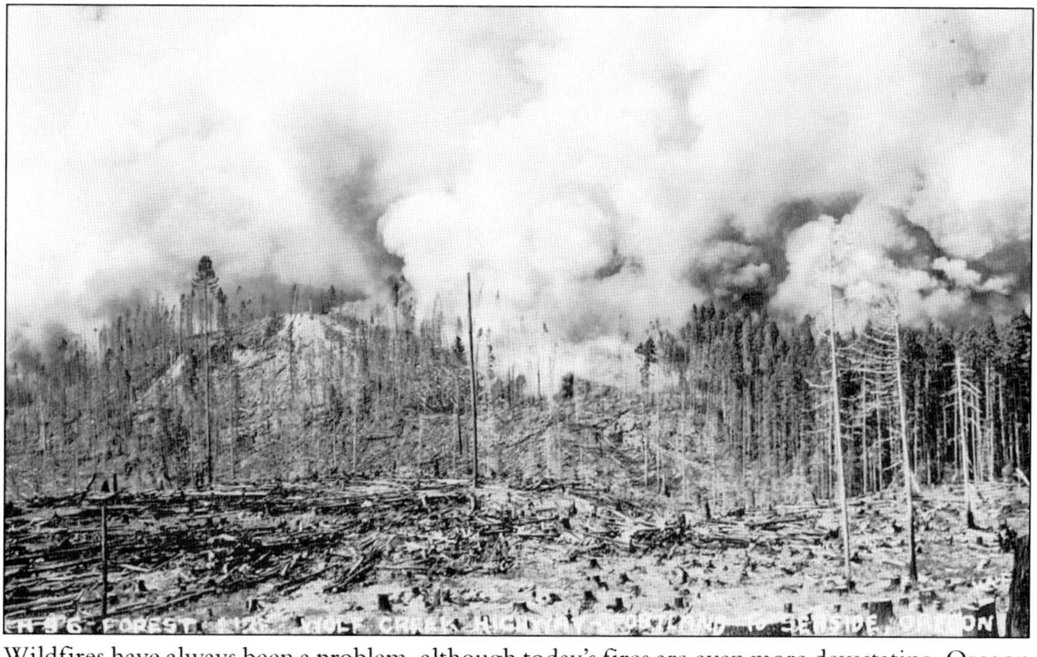

Wildfires have always been a problem, although today's fires are even more devastating. Oregon fires in 1910 burned much of the state's more remote areas, and the 1933 Tillamook Fire burned through the Coast Range. The fire in this photograph occurred along Wolf Creek Highway, also known as the Sunset Highway, named for the US 41st Infantry Division, a Portland National Guard unit that fought in World War II.

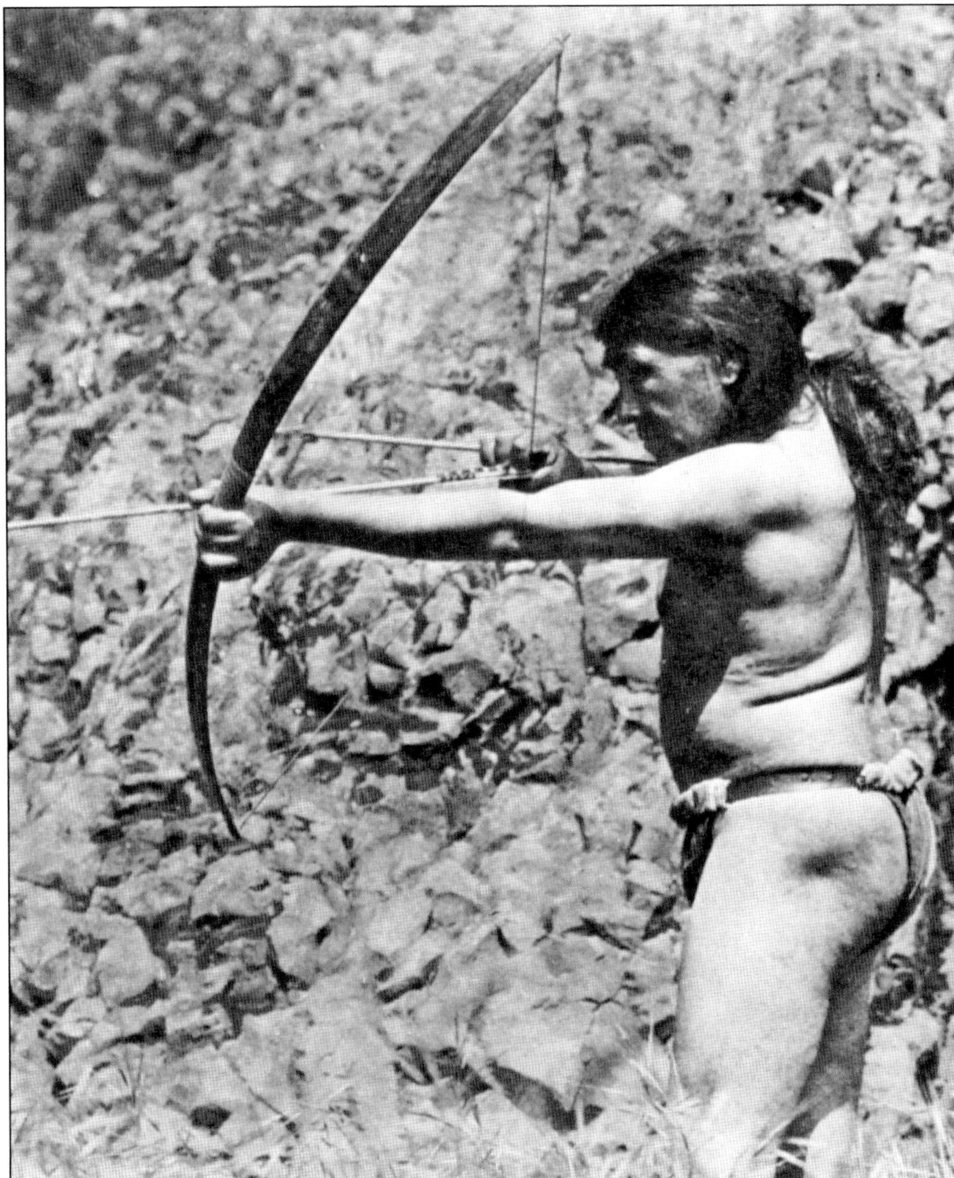

On August 29, 1911, Ishi, the last of the Yahi, was found crouched in the corner of a corral, in Oroville, California, naked, silent, and shivering. The sheriff, not knowing what to do, placed him in a jail cell and for the next few days tried to find someone who could communicate with him. Word of his situation reached the University of California at Berkeley, and Professors T.T. Waterman and Alfred Kroeber headed to Oroville. Waterman, who had studied native languages, was finally able to communicate with the mysterious man. They called him Ishi; in Yahi, *Ishi* meant "man." Ishi never revealed his real name, but for the next five years, he lived at the Museum of Anthropology and taught Kroeber and others about the life of the Yahi and Yani. His people had been massacred, so, alone and starving, Ishi was compelled to seek help, perhaps from the very people who had pursued him. In 1914, he was diagnosed with tuberculosis. He died on March 25, 1916. In 1961, Theodora Kroeber wrote about Ishi in her book, *Ishi, in Two Worlds*.

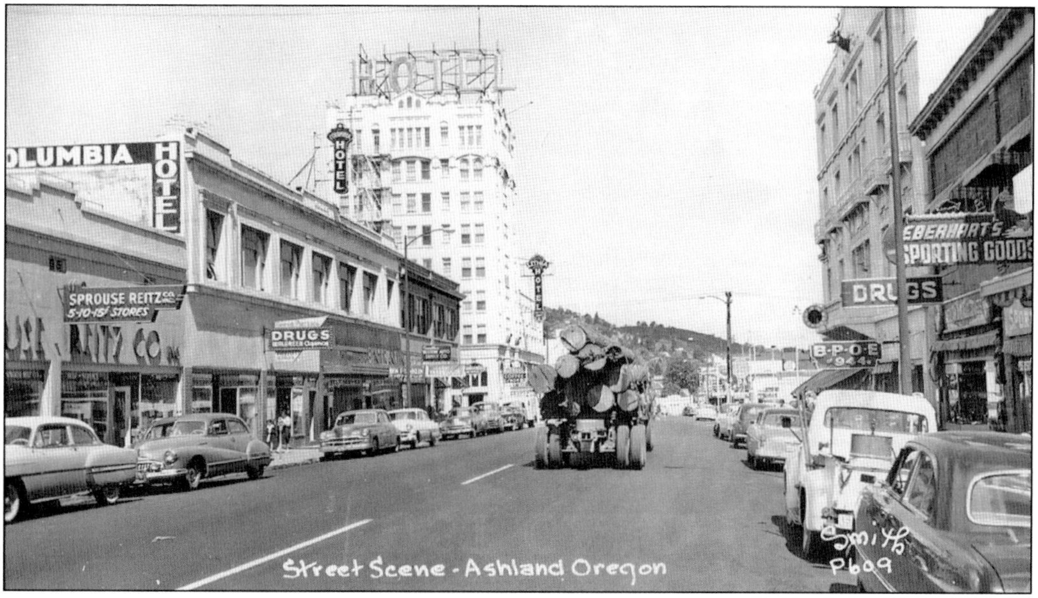

A logging truck moves through downtown Ashland, Oregon, along Old Highway 99 during the 1950s. A city of 20,000 people, Ashland is situated in the Rogue River–Bear Creek Valley at the foot of the Siskiyou Mountains. Much of Ashland's early history is linked to timber. In 1852, Abel Helman, Eber Emery, James Emery, and Robert Hargadine established a lumber mill on Ashland Creek. Today, tourism is Ashland's largest industry.

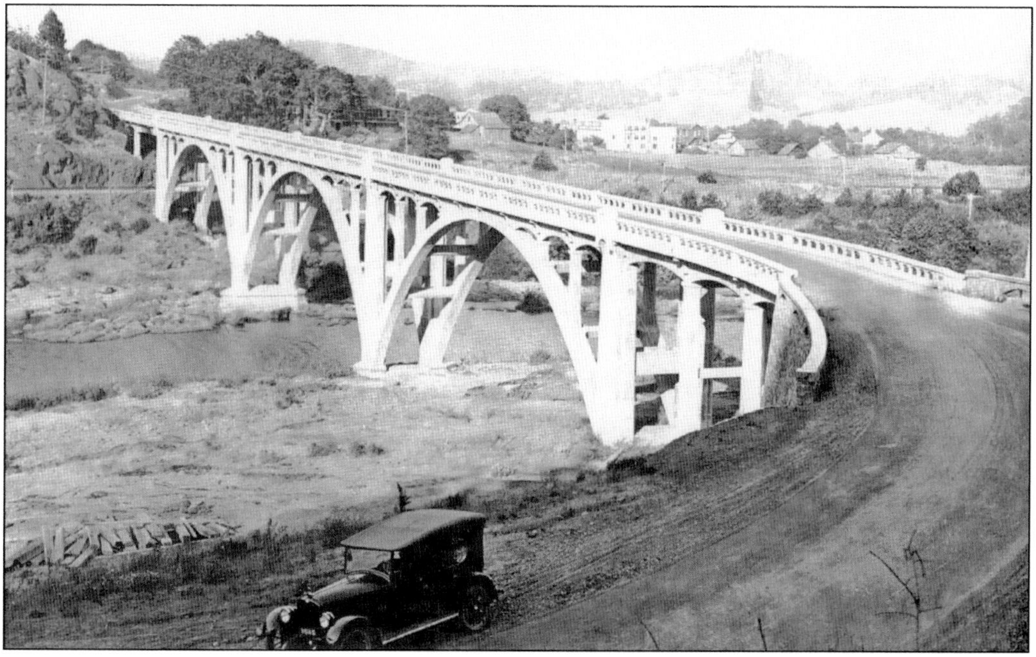

The Myrtle Creek Bridge, built in 1921 by Oregon's "Master Bridge Builder," Conde B. McCullough, was restored and widened in 2007. The bridge crosses the South Umpqua River in Douglas County, Oregon. McCullough headed the Oregon State Highway Department's bridge program, overseeing more than 600 bridge projects. The Myrtle Creek Bridge is characterized by high Gothic arches and Romanesque handrails, which the restoration team kept intact.

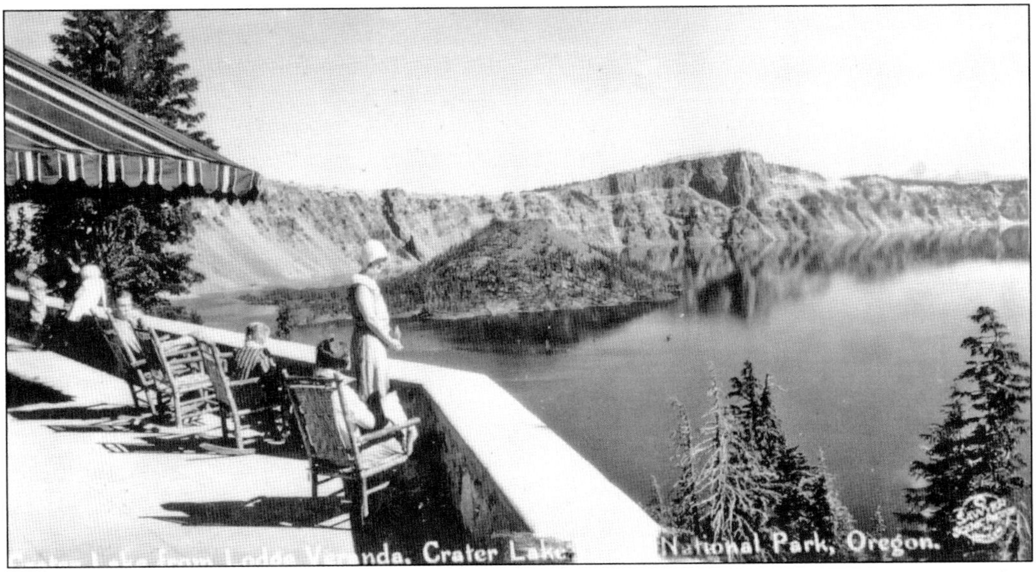

Located on the rim of Crater Lake, the Crater Lake Lodge was built to ensure a view. The lodge had to be designed to carry a heavy snow load for up to eight months a year. In addition, materials had to be trucked in, and workers could only work three months a year. After years of problems, the National Park Service purchased the lodge in 1967. The lodge officially reopened in 1995.

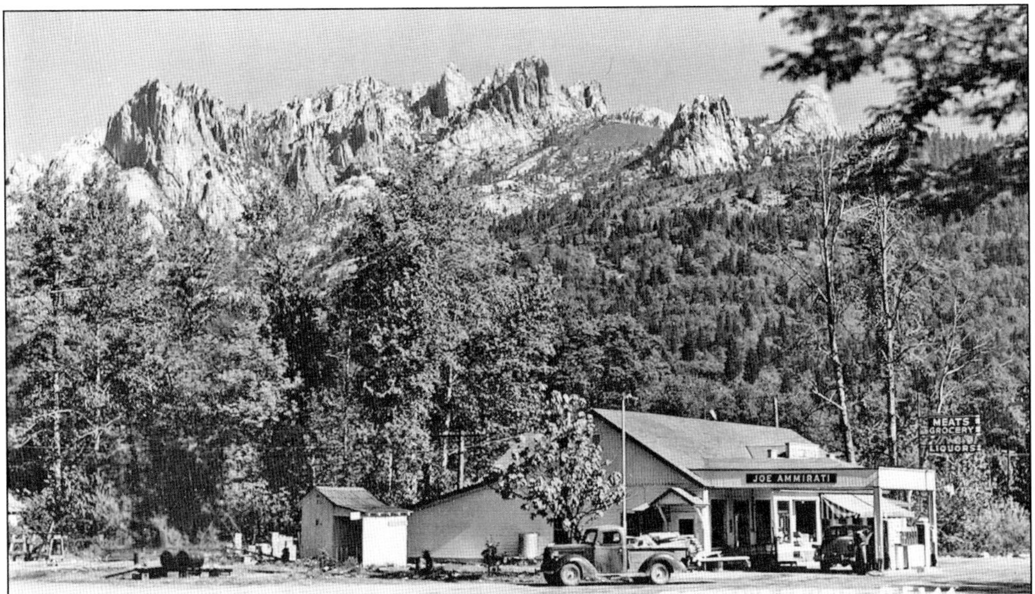

Ammirati's, located in Castella, California, was originally established in 1929. Castella, first called Castle Rock, sits at the foot of the awe-inspiring Castle Crags. A number of resorts were built in the area late in the 19th century, including Bailey's Station at Lower Soda Springs and Castle Rock Springs Hotel, both renowned for their mineral baths. The original Ammirati's Grocery Store and Boarding House were replaced by Ammirati's Market.

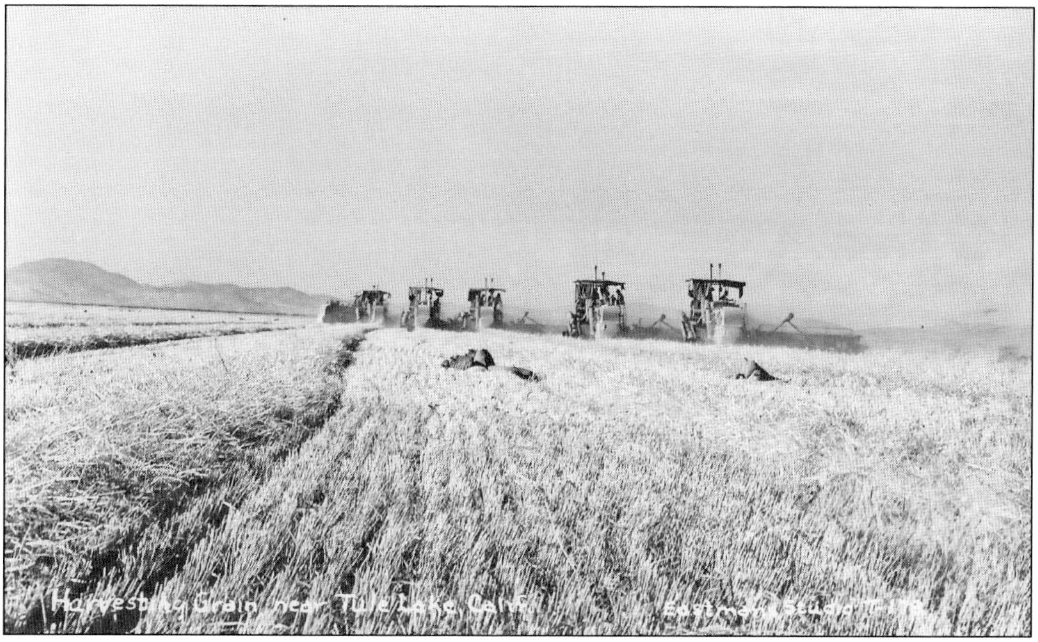

The 16,400-acre Klamath Basin, which connects northern California and southern Oregon, is larger than nine states. It's an important region for waterfowl and wildlife as well as for agriculture. Many came to the Klamath Basin to homestead, including veterans after both world wars. Some did not stay, but others established productive farms. The region has become the center of continued controversy over access to water in the first decade of the 21st century.

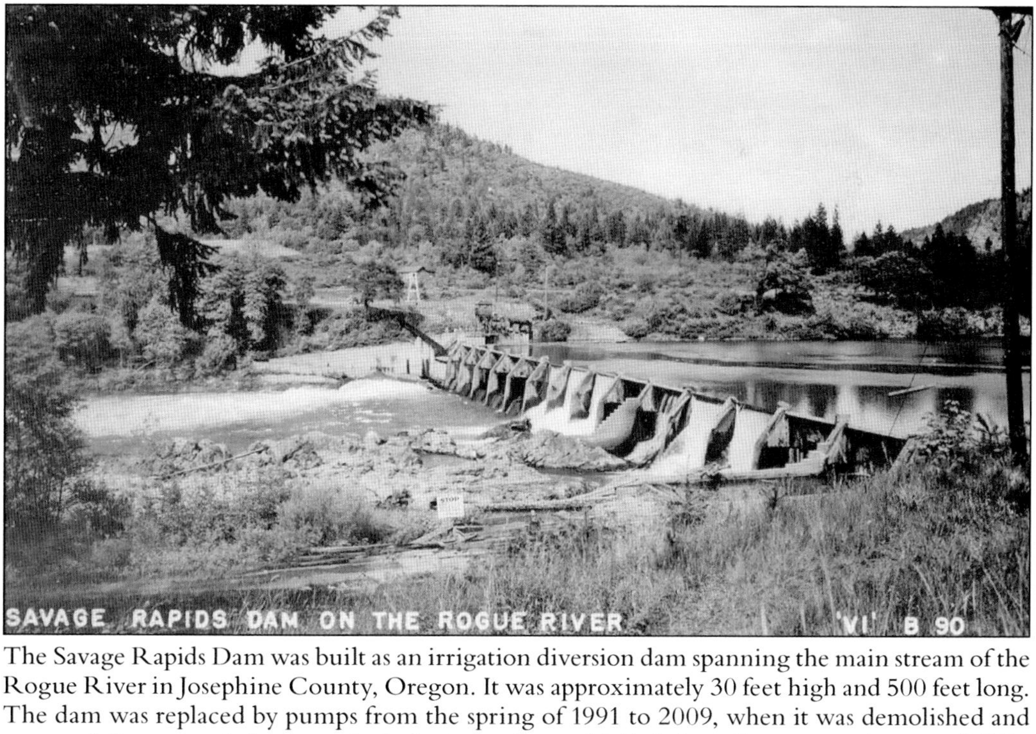

The Savage Rapids Dam was built as an irrigation diversion dam spanning the main stream of the Rogue River in Josephine County, Oregon. It was approximately 30 feet high and 500 feet long. The dam was replaced by pumps from the spring of 1991 to 2009, when it was demolished and removed. It was used almost entirely for irrigation, with little benefit to recreation or wildlife.

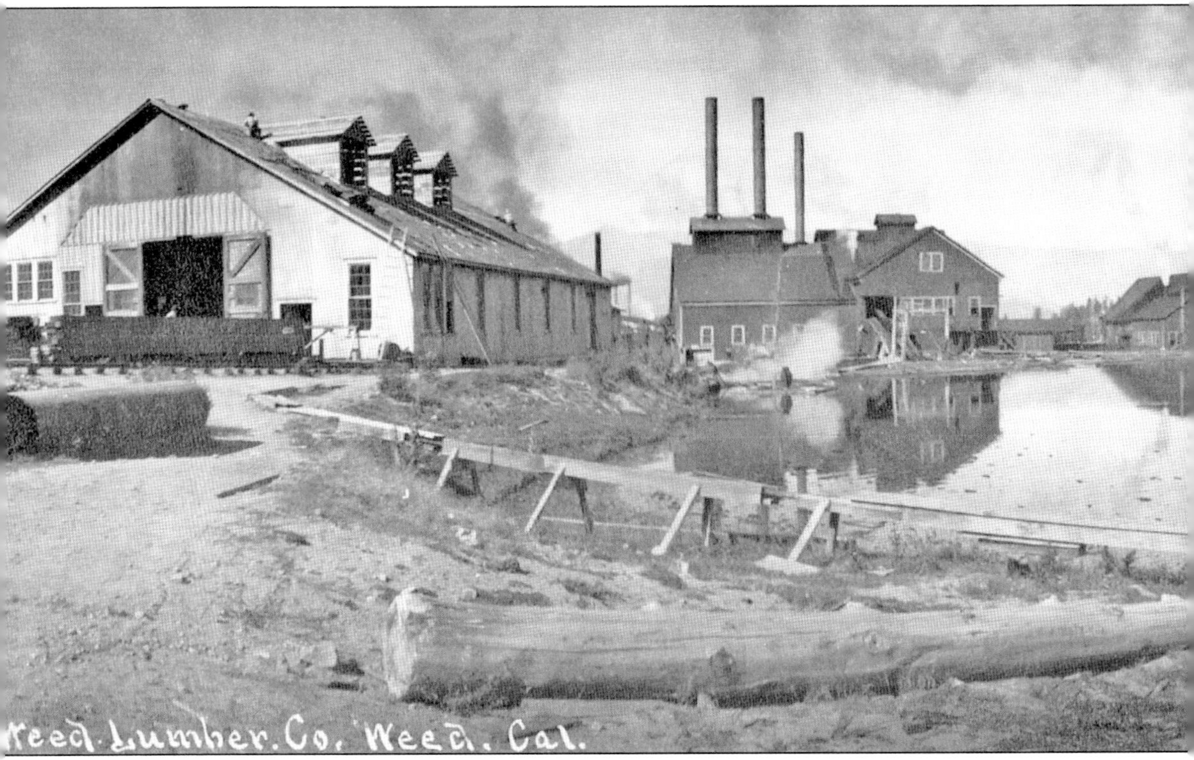

Abner Weed arrived in California from Maine and soon after purchased a mill (known as Mill No. 1) and 280 acres of land west of Mount Shasta and north of Black Butte. In 1901, he established the Weed Lumber Company. With the lumber company came the birth of the town of Weed. In 1902, he purchased a second mill (known as Mill No. 2) and moved it to sit alongside his first mill. In its first years, Weed Lumber Company produced 60,000 feet of lumber a day. In 1904, the company was turned into a corporation, with R.A. Long and the Long-Bell Lumber

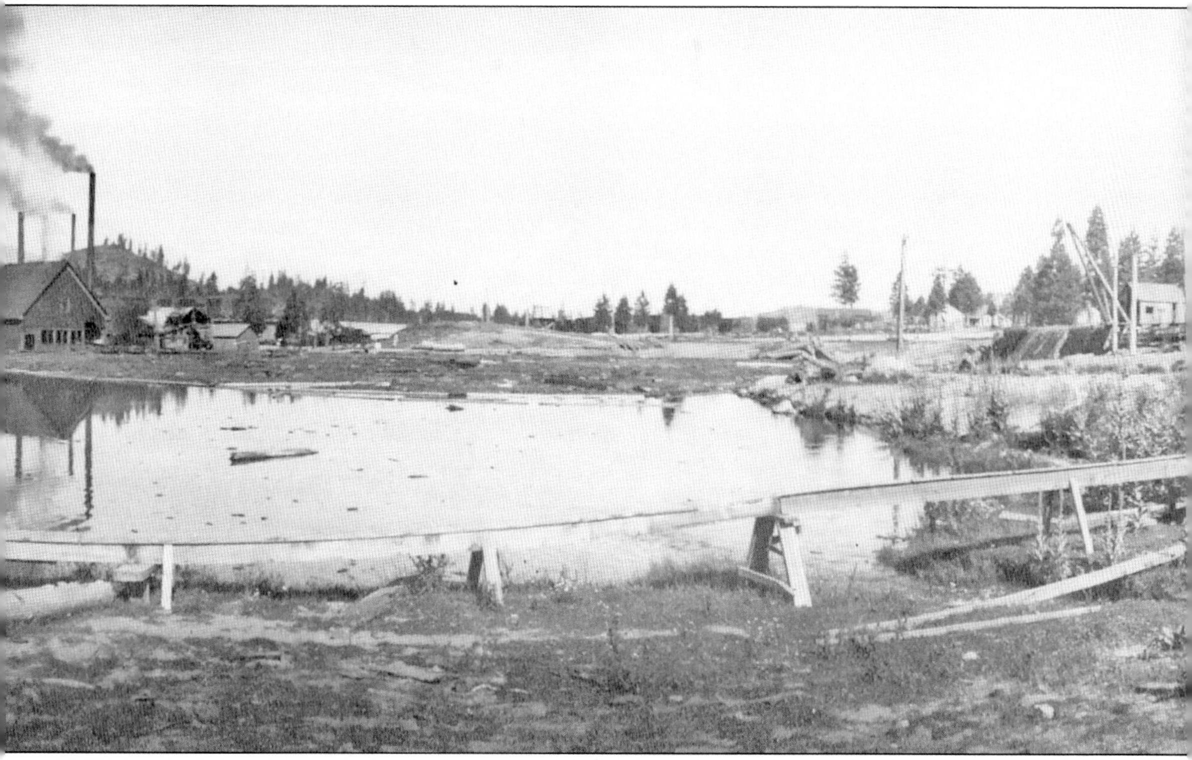

Company as its major shareholder. In 1905, Long-Bell Lumber bought out Abner Weed's share of the company for approximately $2 million. Long-Bell built a new mill and, by 1918, was milling over 250,000 board feet a day. After Weed's original two mills burned down in 1919, Long-Bell built a new firehouse and hired seven firemen. The company not only provided jobs, it also provided housing for its workers, and Weed remained a company town until the 1950s.

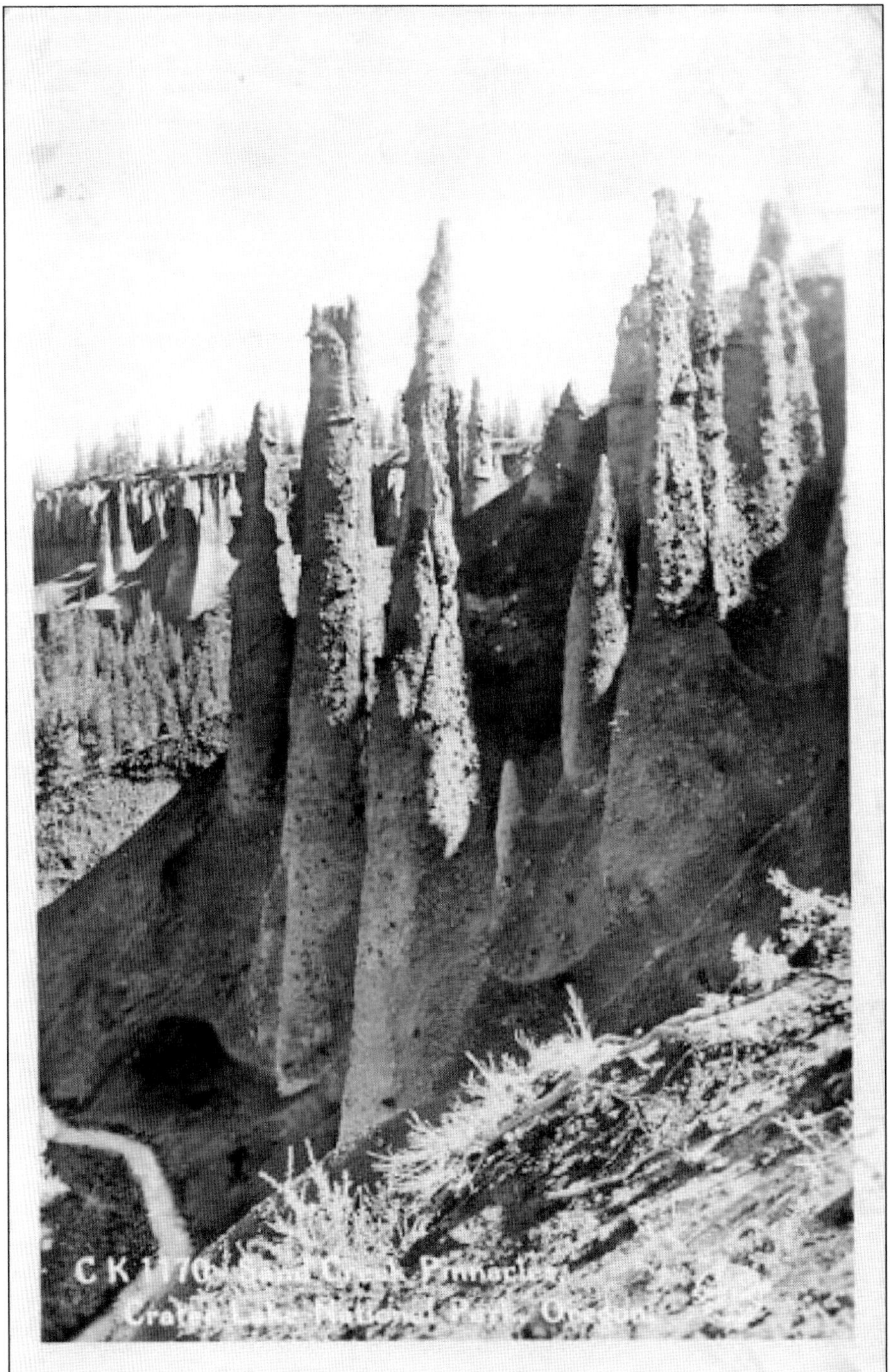

These towering needle-like formations of rock, called fossil fumaroles, stand up along the Sand Creek Canyon floor in the eastern part of Crater Lake National Park. The pinnacles were formed some time before Mount Mazama's collapse 7,700 years ago, probably as a result of stream erosion and wind abrasion. As hot volcanic pumice escaped and cooled, steam and gases were released through vents that hardened into tubes, creating the spires seen here.

Three

Fall

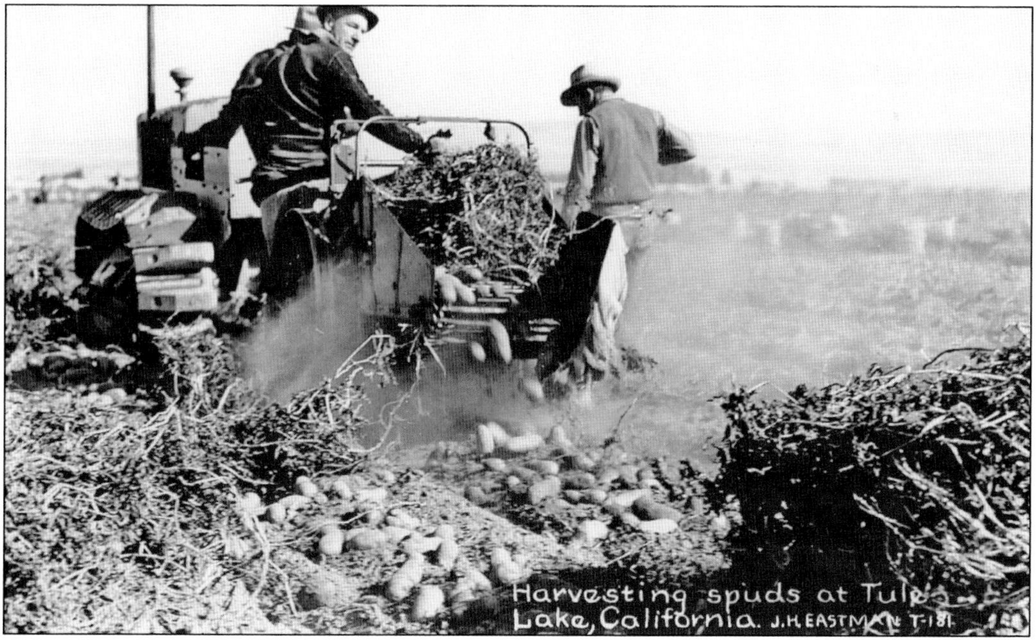

Every leaf speaks bliss to me, fluttering from the autumn tree.

—Emily Bronte

Potatoes have been grown in the Klamath Basin for several generations. Joe Obed Short is thought to be the first person to grow potatoes commercially in the 1890s. C.A. Henderson helped organize an association of growers in 1923; as a result, the first crop of potatoes was shipped by rail in 1924. By 1944, potatoes were being grown on 27,000 acres and, in 2007, on more than 36,500 acres.

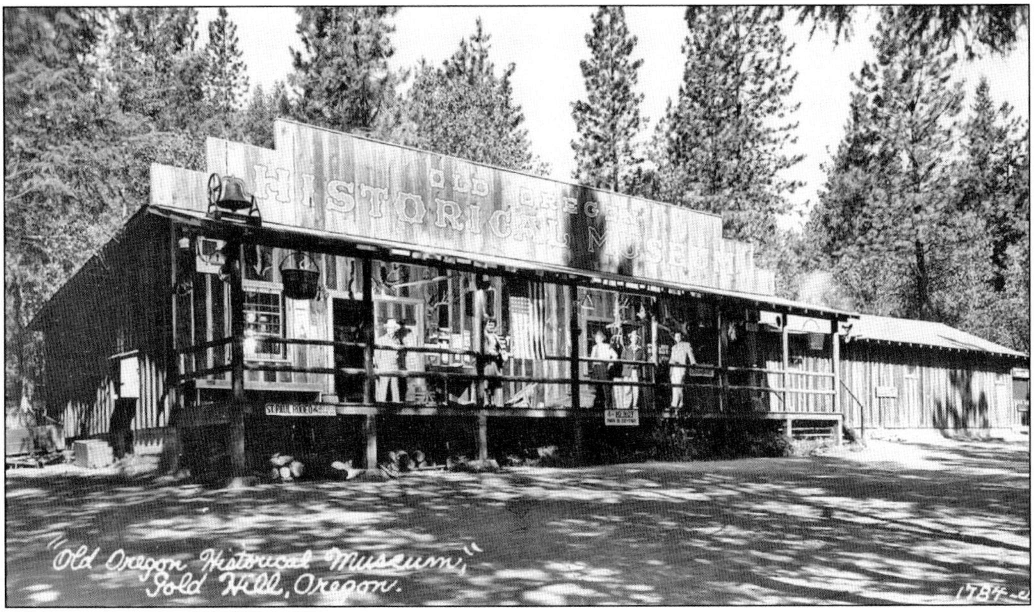

According to one old-timer, the Old Historical Museum in Gold Hill, Oregon, was "part of a group of roadside attractions, including the Oregon Vortex, Trees of Mystery, the Prehistoric Gardens (with replicas of prehistoric animals), a petting zoo, and whatever else could be thrown in to draw a crowd." Today the Gold Hill Historical Society's museum is located in the Beeman-Martin House, built in 1901 in downtown Gold Hill.

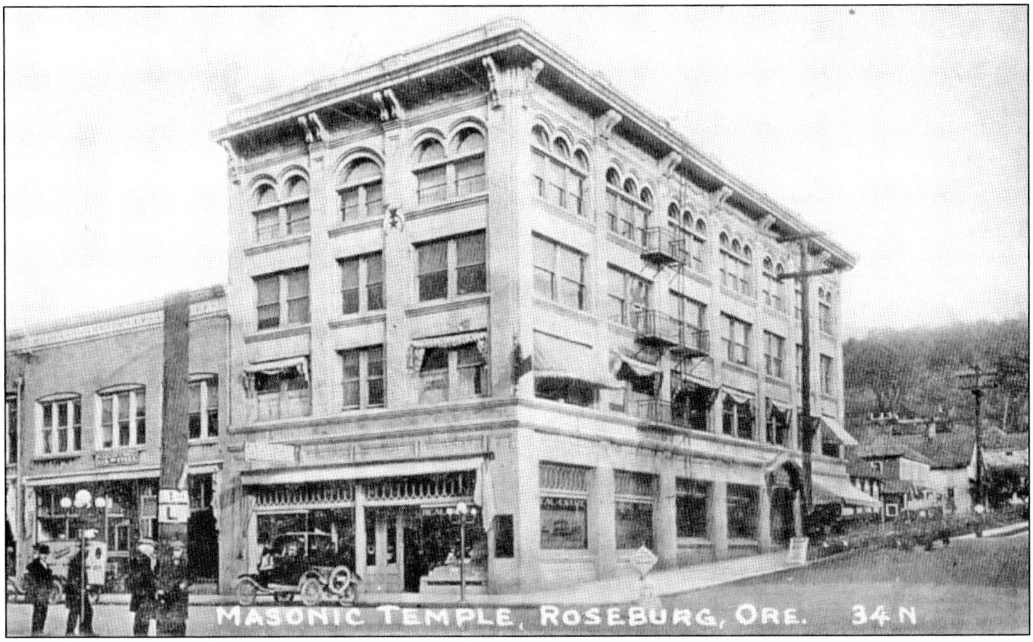

Chartered in 1857, after the Brethren of Winchester changed their location to Roseburg, Oregon, Masonic Laurel Lodge No. 13 celebrated its 150th anniversary in 2008. There have been many staunch members of the lodge, including relatives of some of Roseburg's earliest pioneers. The list of members includes names such as Rose, Flint, Mosher, Floed, Watson, Booth, Rice, Parrot, Calkins, Dillard, Sutherlin, Eddy, Lane, Chadwick, Stephens and Fullerton.

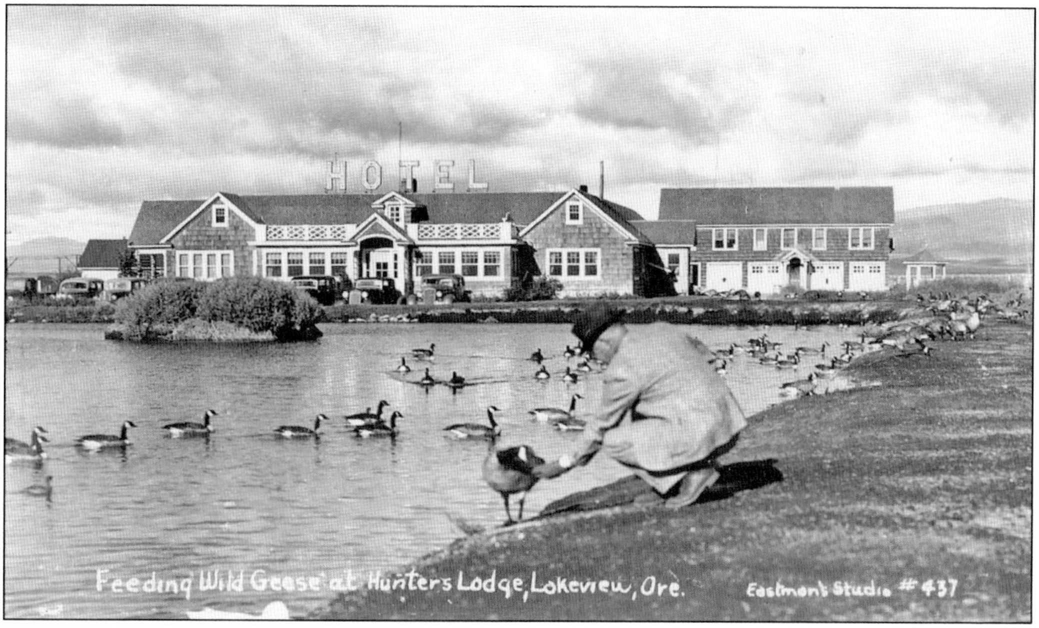

A guest is feeding geese at Hunters' Hotel in Lakeview, Oregon, around the 1940s. Lake County, located in south-central Oregon, was established in 1874 and formed by taking the southern part of Wasco County and the eastern part of Jackson County. It was named for the many lakes found in the region. Lakeview, which was named for its "lake view" by pioneer John A. Moon, is the county seat and overlooks Goose Lake.

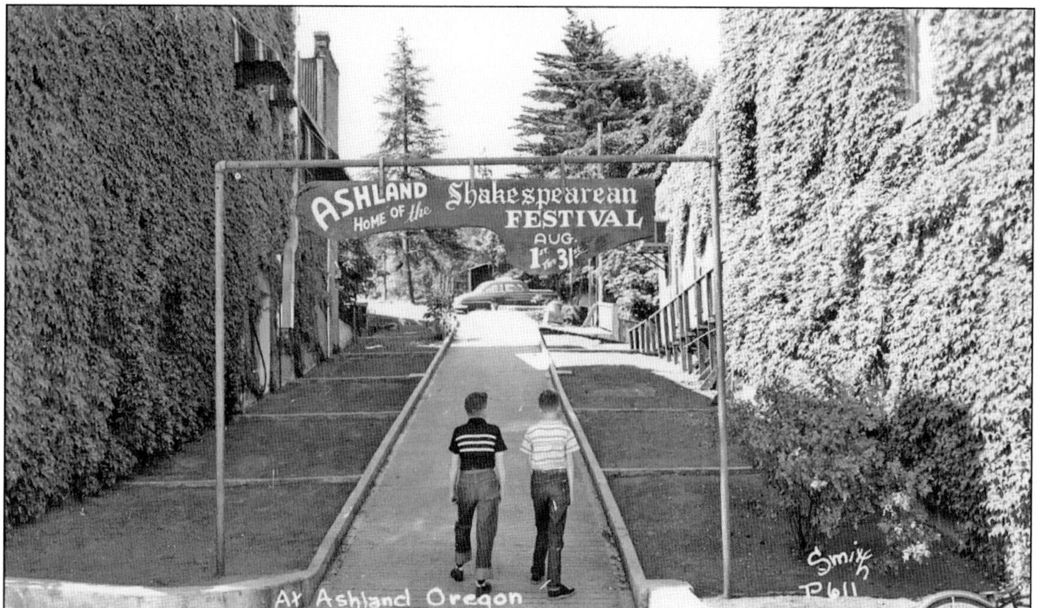

The Chautauqua movement of the late 1800s inspired Oregon's Shakespearean Festival. Angus Bowmer, a young teacher at Ashland's normal school in the 1930s (now Southern Oregon University), designed a festival for the community: two plays to be performed within the Chautauqua's original walls, which still stand today. Oregon's Shakespearean Festival was born on July 2, 1935, with a production of *Twelfth Night*.

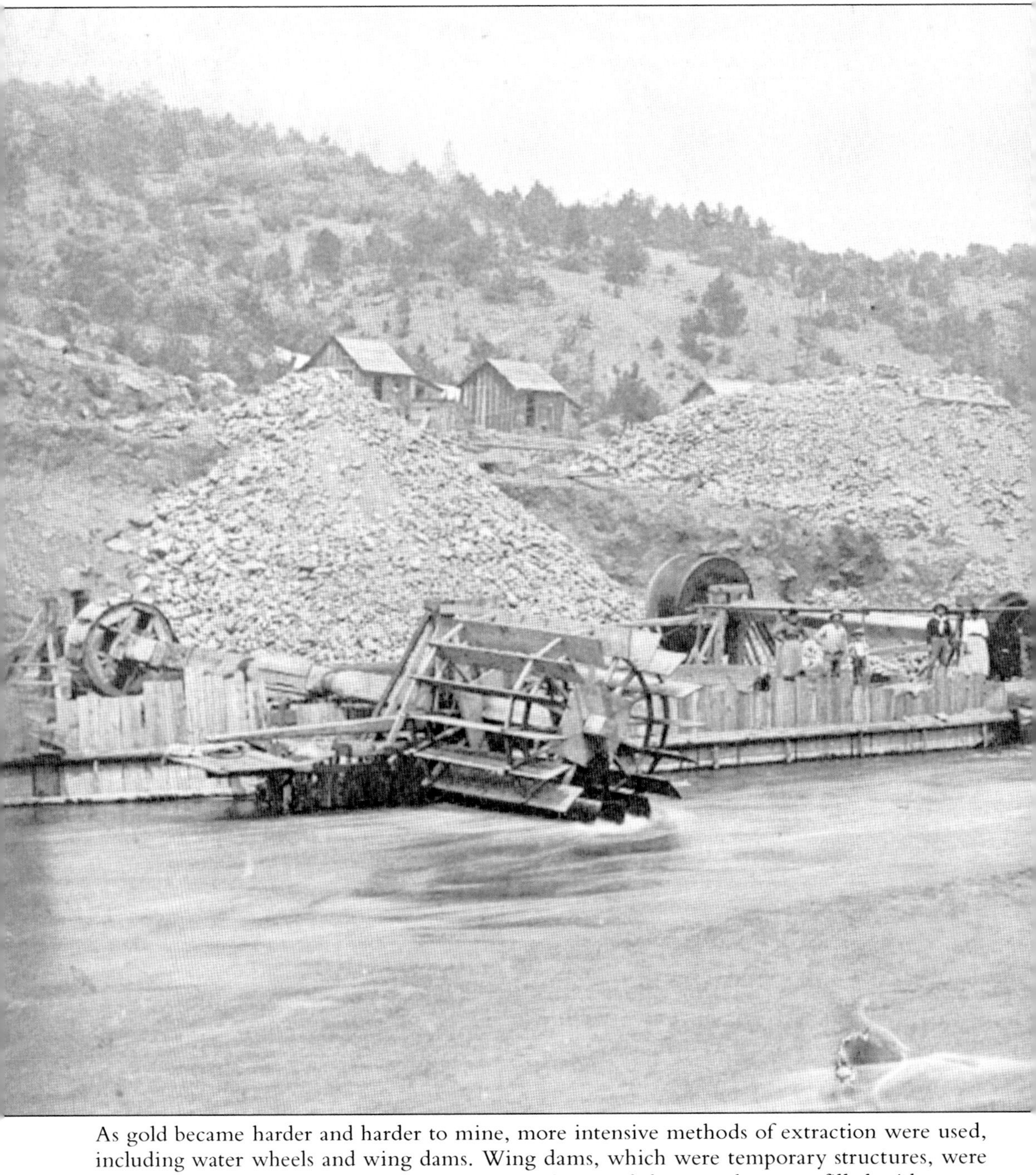

As gold became harder and harder to mine, more intensive methods of extraction were used, including water wheels and wing dams. Wing dams, which were temporary structures, were placed at two ends of a river bar. Walls were built up and the space between filled with coarse material and gravel. Pumps were used, driven by wheels placed alongside the dam parallel to the

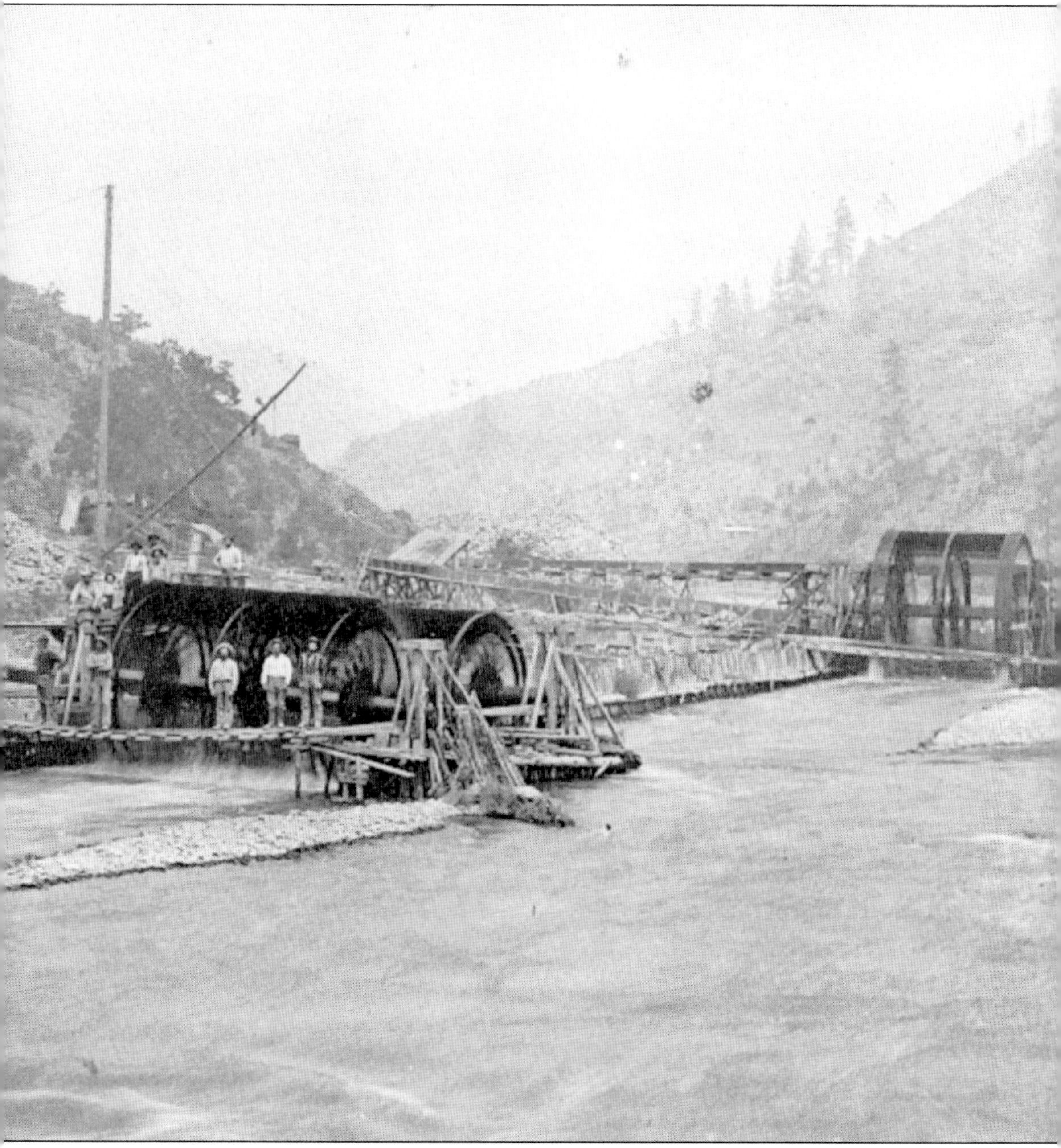

stream. This allowed miners to pump the water out and work the shallower enclosed streambed. Once one side of the river was mined, the wing dams were moved to the next bar. These wing dams were used throughout California's rivers, including the Klamath and Trinity. (Courtesy of the Fort Jones Museum.)

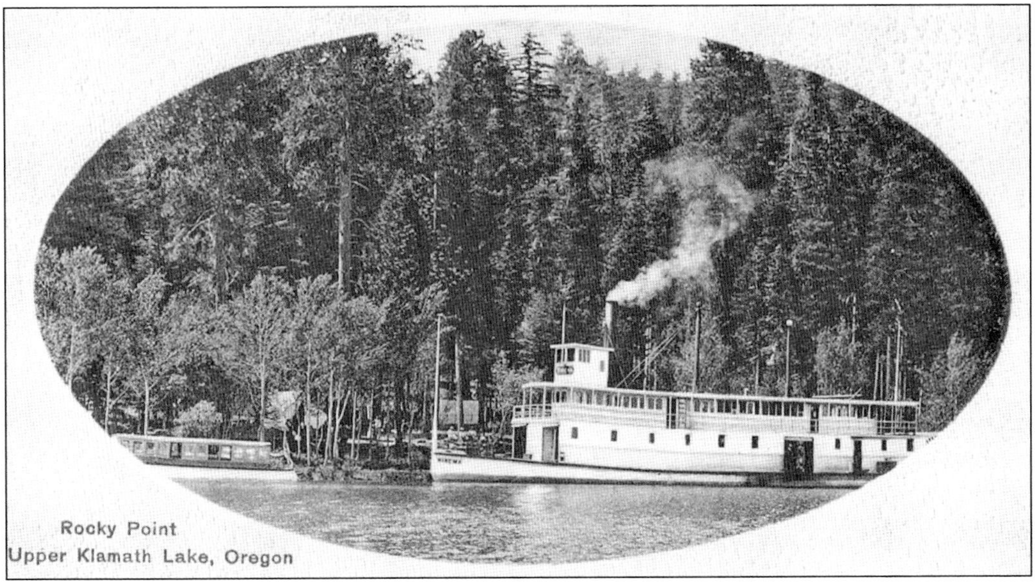

Originally, four vacation or resort lodges were built along Upper Klamath Lake. They included Eagle Ridge, Odessa, Harriman Springs (built by E.H. Harriman), and Point Comfort. Point Comfort was built in 1912. Steamboats traversed Upper Klamath Lake and Goose Lake, not only for tourists but also for locals. Rocky Point Resort sits on the northwest shore of Upper Klamath Lake and features cabins, a lodge, a restaurant, and more.

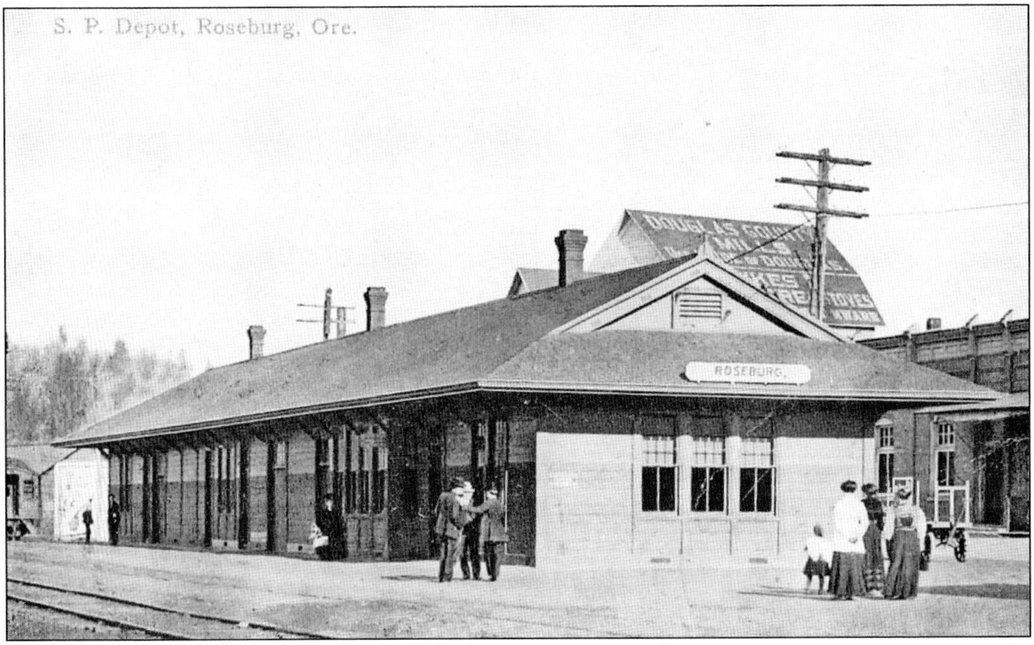

Before the city of Roseburg, Oregon, existed, there was a small settlement known as Deer Creek, but Aaron Rose, who arrived in Oregon in 1851, donated land and money for a courthouse. He also owned the first inn and operated a local tavern. Today the building that was once Roseburg's Southern Pacific train depot is a popular pub and brewery that retains much of its original architecture and artifacts.

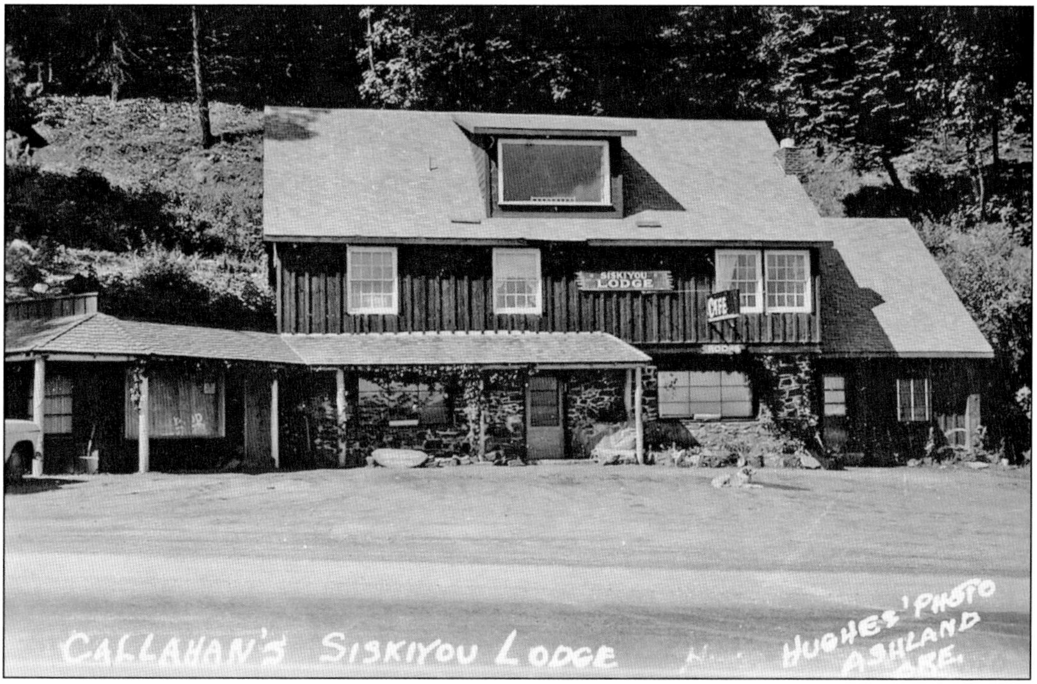

Callahan's Lodge is a landmark for those crossing the Siskiyou Mountains into Oregon. Oregon native Don Callahan dreamed of opening a lodge in the Siskiyous. In 1944 he purchased land on Highway 99, and later began carving out a site from the hillside. In 1947, he opened Callahan's Siskiyou Lodge. Today, Callahan's is a large and elaborate lodge, but it still caters to travelers and locals alike.

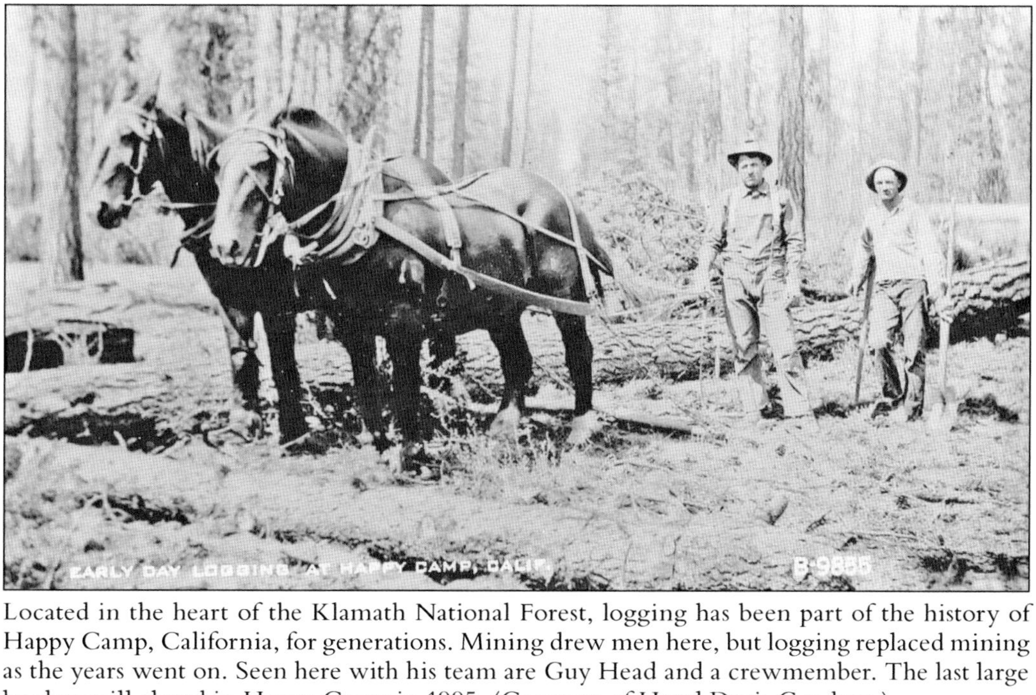

Located in the heart of the Klamath National Forest, logging has been part of the history of Happy Camp, California, for generations. Mining drew men here, but logging replaced mining as the years went on. Seen here with his team are Guy Head and a crewmember. The last large lumber mill closed in Happy Camp in 1995. (Courtesy of Hazel Davis Gendron.)

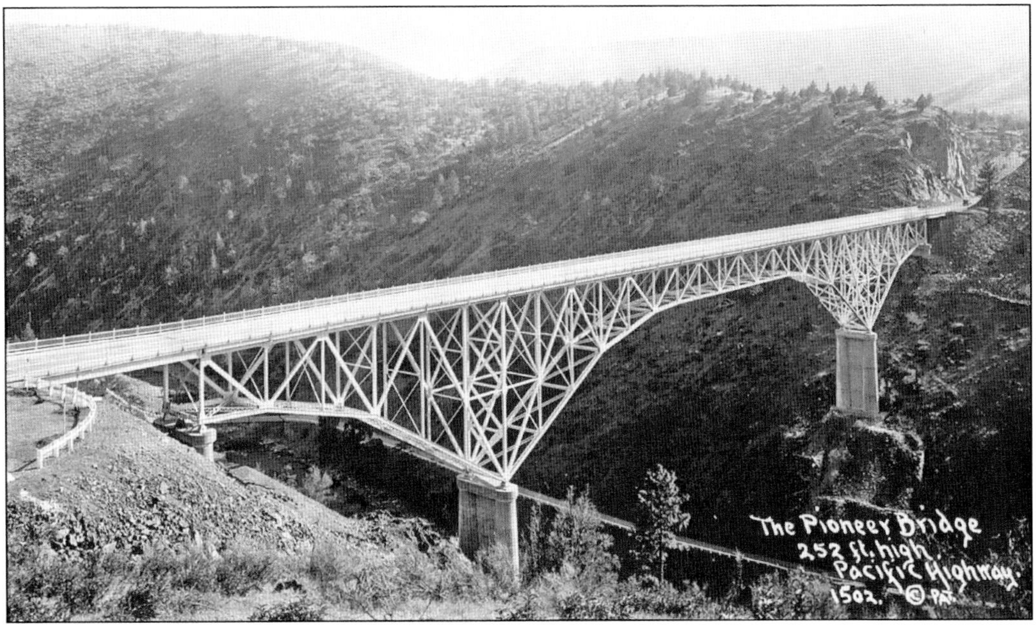

Built in 1931, the Pioneer Bridge spans the Shasta River along Old Highway 99, also known as Highway 263. Located 3.6 miles from Hawkinsville and six miles from Yreka, California, the dramatic structure stands 2,234 feet above the ground. In 2011, the bridge was temporarily closed in order to repaint it. F.D. Thomas Construction of Central Point, Oregon, oversaw the $1.98-million project.

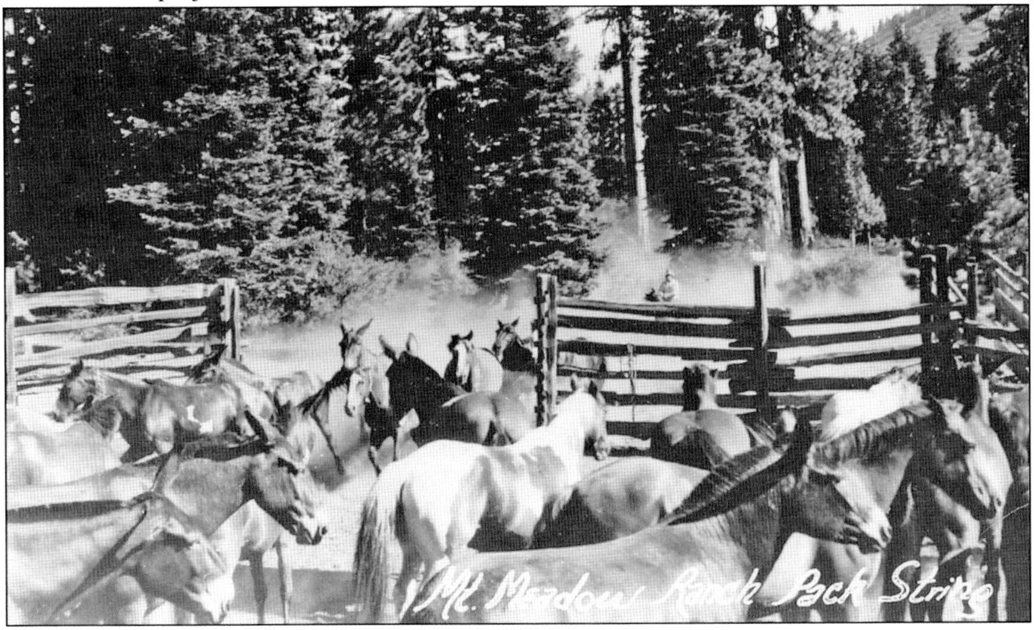

Mountain Meadow Resort, located on Big Flat up Coffee Creek in Trinity County, California, was originally the site of the Abrams' Cabin, built during the Gold Rush and used as a trading post. In 1932, Nathan and Ethel Steele established a packing station there to serve local miners. Eventually, the station became a resort. They sold the ranch in 1976. The horses here were part of Steele's pack string. The station is still a private resort.

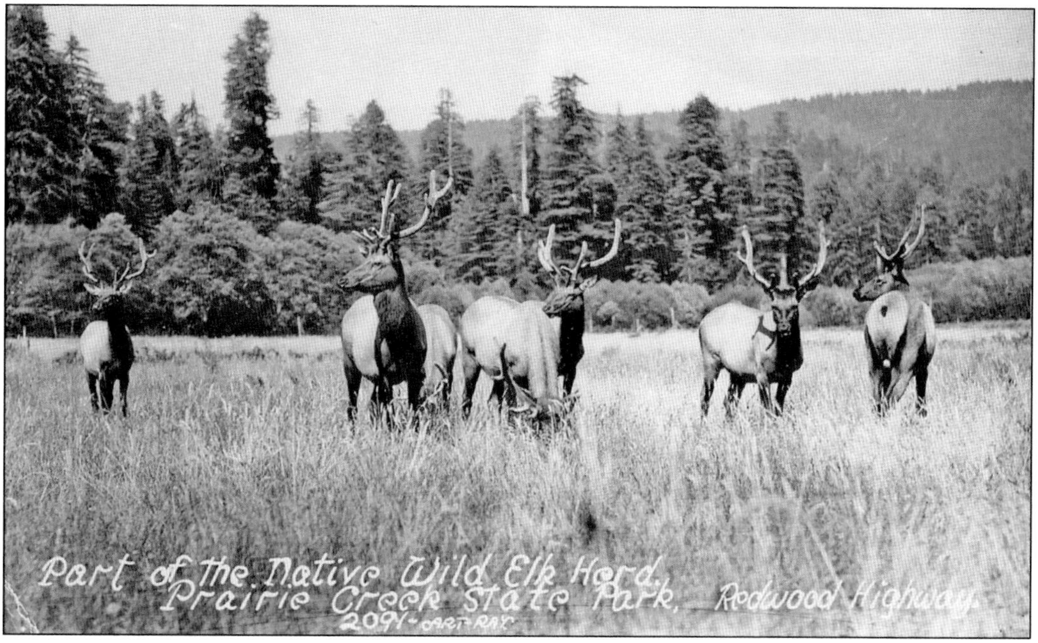

Native wild elk are found at Prairie Creek State Park in California. Set aside in the early 1920s by the people of California and the contributions of the Save-the-Redwoods League, Prairie Creek State Park is a sanctuary of old-growth coast redwoods. The elk are a conservation success story. Once near extinction, they now number in the thousands. Prairie Creek is 25 miles south of Crescent City, California.

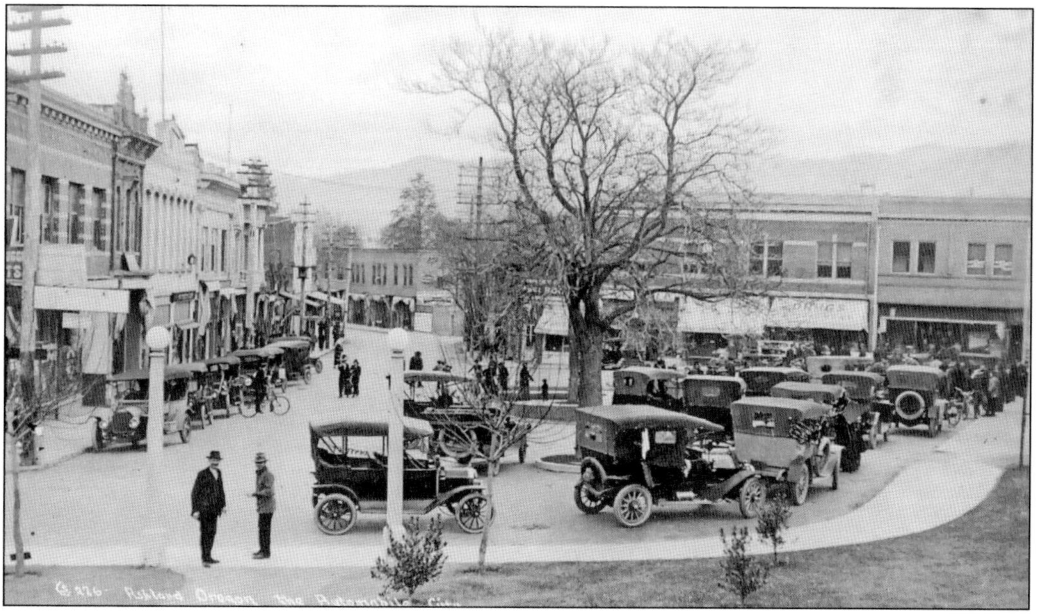

Ashland, Oregon, was home to southern Oregon's Chautauqua festival, which brought the arts to rural areas. It was held for two decades in a special beehive-shaped building. Later, this evolved into the renowned Oregon Shakespearean Festival. With the university as well as the city's historic plaza, Ashland secured its place as one of the region's more interesting and commercial cultural centers. People flock to the city.

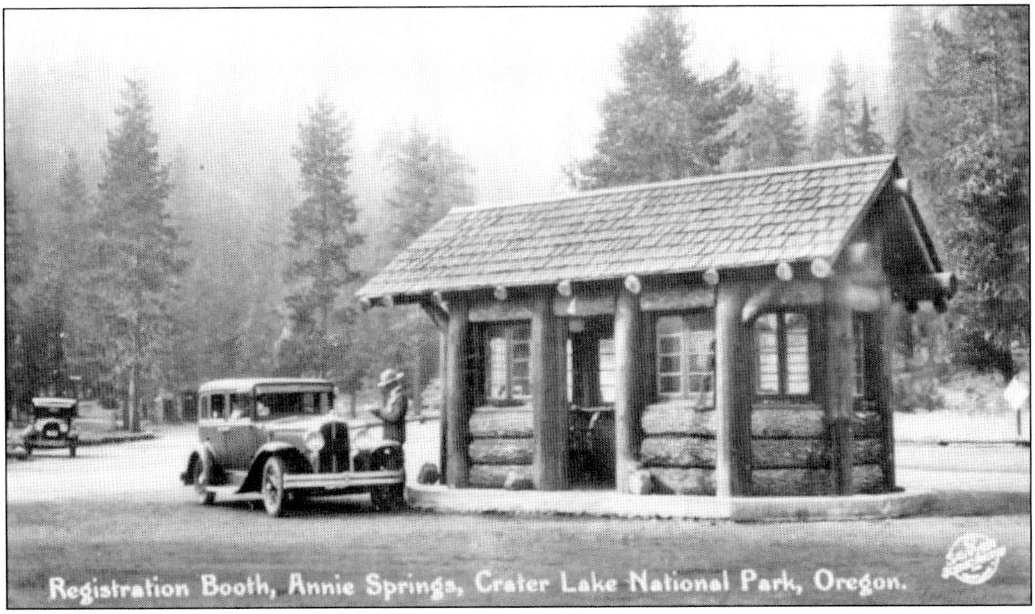

Annie Springs, seen here around 1930, is one entrance into Crater Lake National Park in Oregon. As a national park, Crater Lake is not very large. The only long trail inside the park is a portion of the Pacific Crest Trail. After entering the park, the highway leads south to the Annie Springs Registration Booth and Entrance Station. This is the entrance used when traveling from the west. (Courtesy of the Betty Jane Young Collection.)

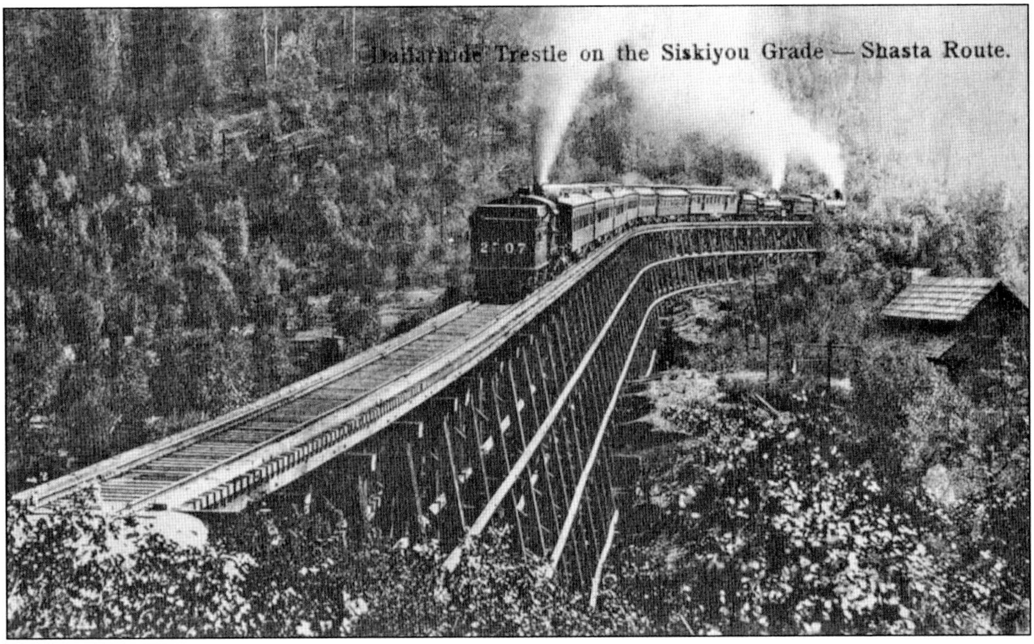

In 1869, the Dollarhide family moved to Jackson County, Oregon, and purchased the right-of-way for a section of the Applegate Trail that ran from the Siskiyous down to the town of Hornbrook, California. They also purchased a sawmill; the lumber they produced was used by Southern Pacific Railway (formerly Oregon & California Railway) to build the Dollarhide Trestle across a canyon in the Siskiyous.

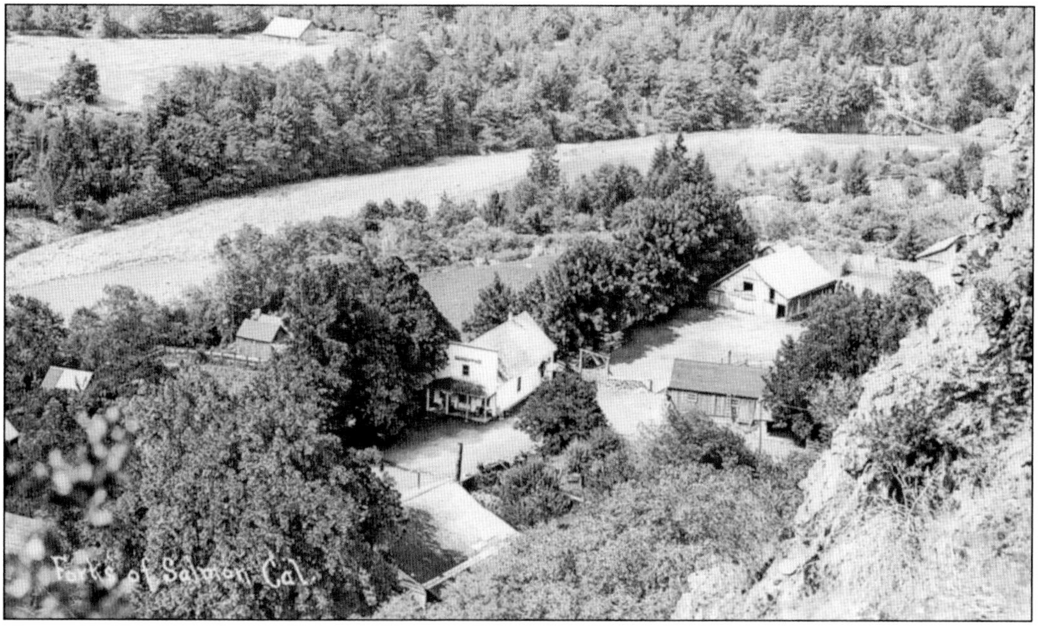

Forks of Salmon, California, located at the junction of the North and South Forks, was mined extensively. The town was part of Klamath County in 1874, then absorbed into Siskiyou County. An important supply center, it had a sawmill, two-story hotel, bars, and a store. The post office was built in 1858. The hotel included a butcher shop, bar, kitchen, dining room, eight rooms, and an extra room with 10 beds.

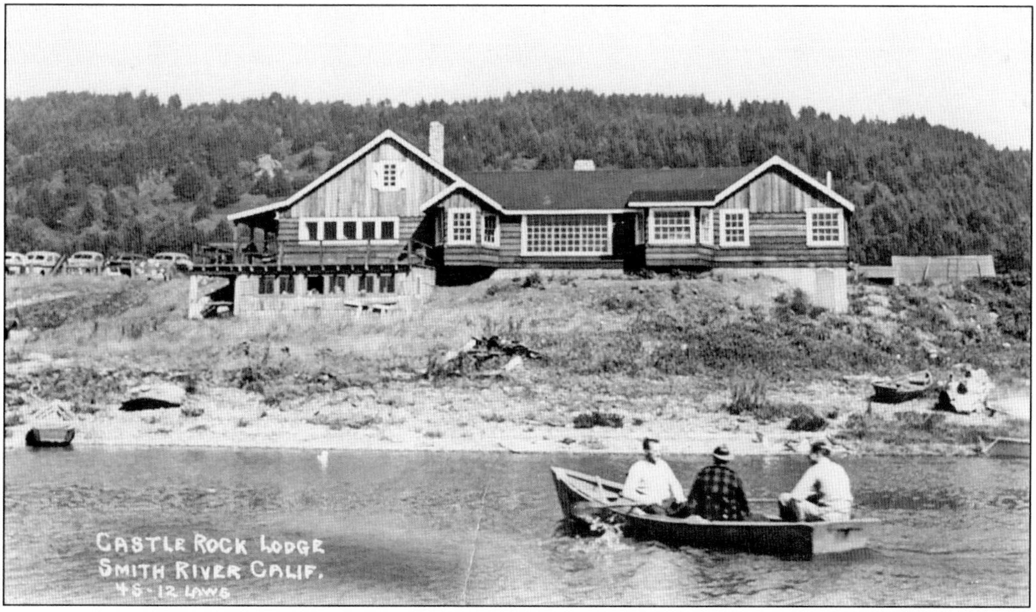

The Castle Rock Lodge at Smith River is located near Castle Rock Refuge, which stands a half-mile offshore from Crescent City, California. This coastal rock is approximately 14 acres and rises steeply to 335 feet above sea level. The refuge provides sanctuary for Canada geese and nesting seabirds and is the second largest nesting seabird colony south of Alaska (after the Farallon Islands).

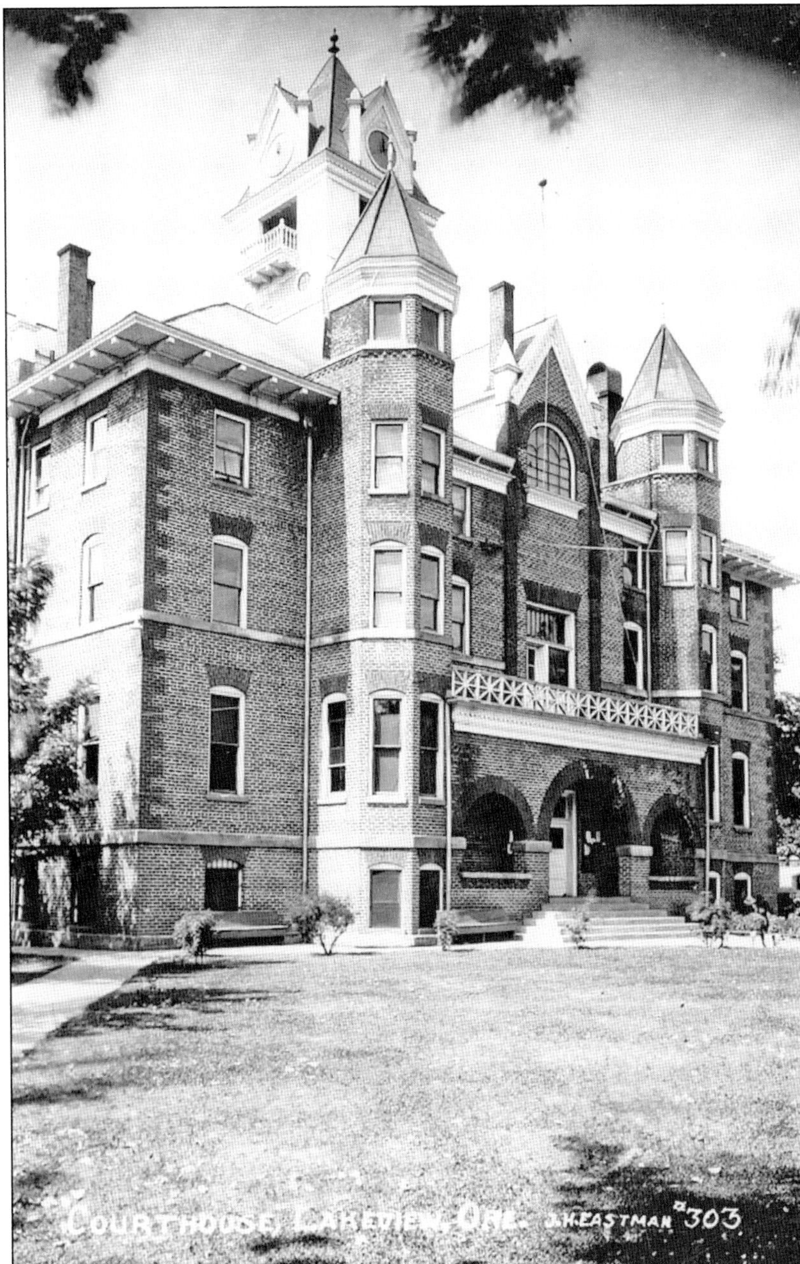

The town of Lakeview, Oregon, dubs itself the "Tallest Town in Oregon" because of its elevation. It was first known as Bullard's Ranch or Bullard's Creek. Situated in the Goose Lake Valley at the foot of the Warner Mountains, the region boasted five lumber mills. The courthouse was completed in 1909, a sketch of it appearing in the *Lake County Examiner* on June 25, 1908, which noted that Charles W. Casky of Seattle was the carpenter and W.A. Wingate of Lakeview the overseer of brickwork. The design was apparently based on a Nebraska courthouse from 1876 or 1886. With a bell tower with chimes imported from Baltimore, the residents felt the building projected their good future. Unfortunately, the region suffered terribly with the loss of lumber mills and jobs. The courthouse was replaced by a single-story concrete building in 1954.

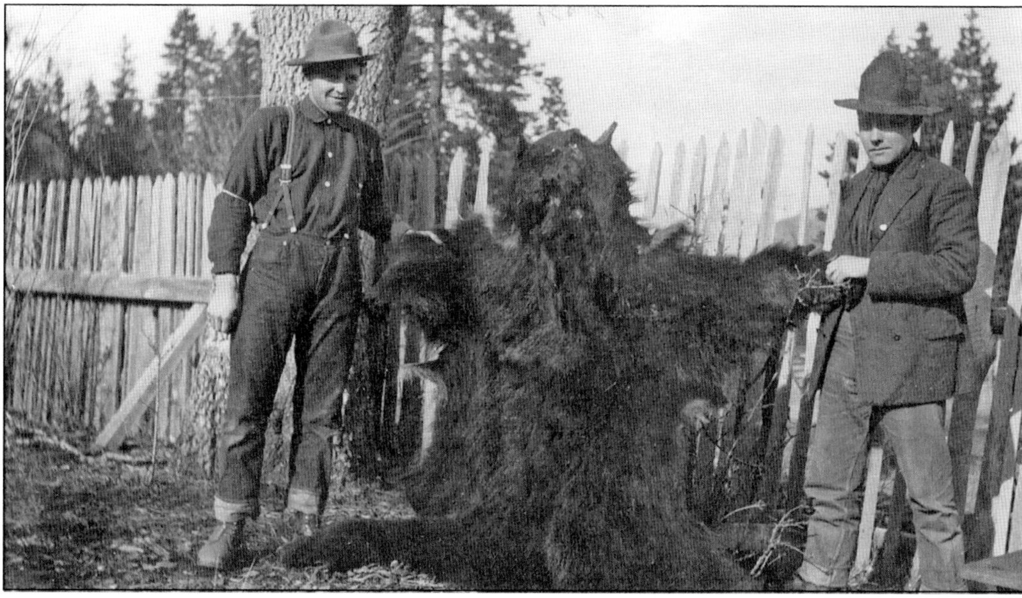

Hunting bear was common in the early years of settlement in northern California and southern Oregon for protection, sport, and furs. Until 1948, there were no restrictions on when or how many bear could be killed. This bear was killed near Miner's Creek. From left to right are Ray Vanderpool and Ralph Look standing in the yard at the Vanderpool and Lloyd Ranch. Today, bear hunting is seasonal and requires a tag and license.

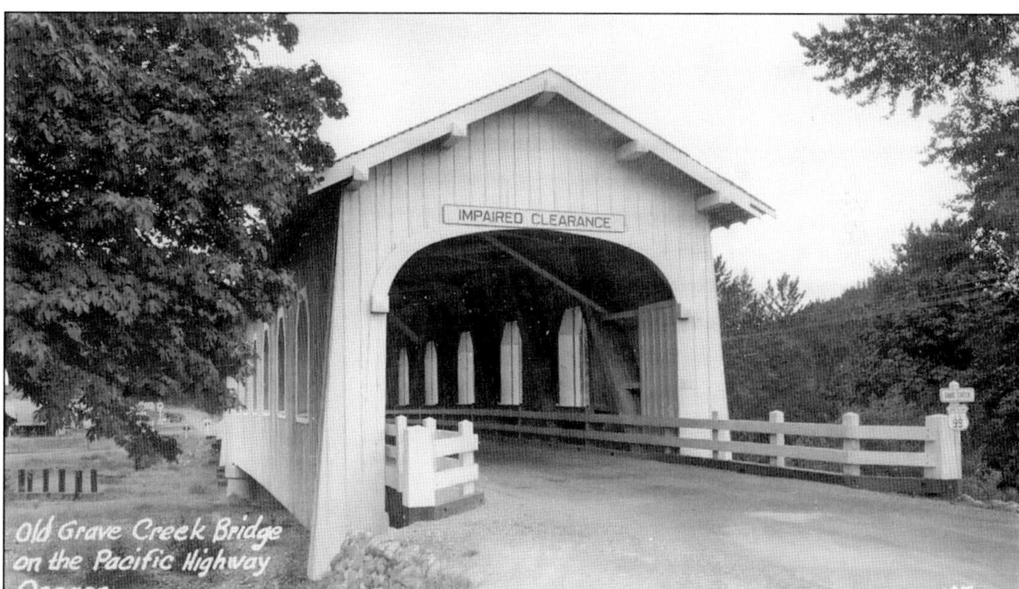

Grave Creek Covered Bridge is 14 miles north of Grants Pass, Oregon. It is the only covered bridge visible from Interstate 5. In 1846, the first immigrant train to travel the Applegate Trail to Willamette Valley camped on the north side of the creek, then called Woodpile Creek. Martha Crowley, 16 years old, died of typhoid and was buried 150 feet from the creek, giving it its name.

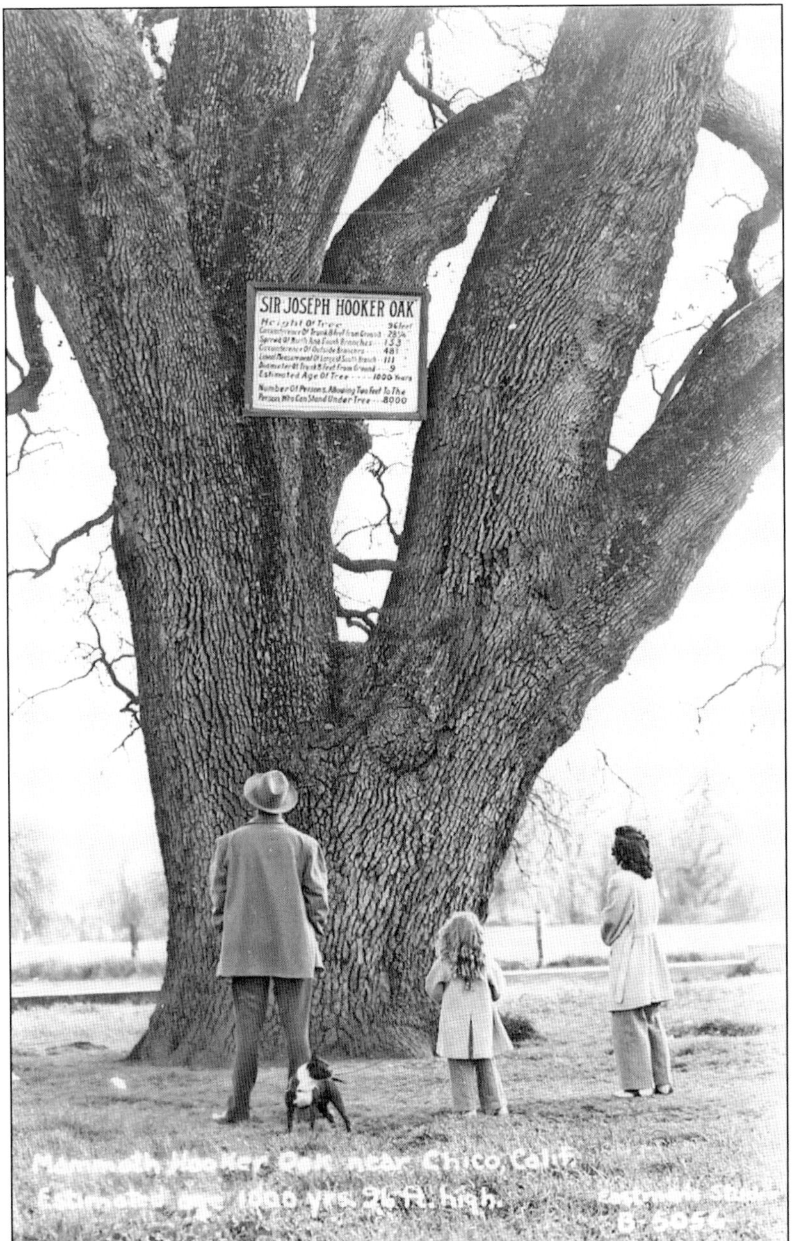

Hooker Oak, located in Chico, California, was declared "the largest of its species in the known world" by English botanist Sir Joseph Dalton Hooker in 1877. In 1887, Annie Bidwell, wife of Gen. John Bidwell, named it in honor of the botanist. In 1921, the oak reportedly stood 110 feet tall, and it was estimated that 7,885 people could stand under its massive reach. The tree appeared in the 1938 film *The Adventures of Robin Hood*, starring Errol Flynn. When the tree fell on May 1, 1977, it measured 29 feet in circumference, and the largest branch measured 111 feet. But what was thought to be one tree was actually two, and rather than a thousand years old, each was more likely only 325 years old. After the tree fell, city leaders were not sure what to do with the wood. In the end, it was milled and given to local artisans. Today, the city's gavel and the park benches inside the city council's chamber have all been made out of Hooker Oak.

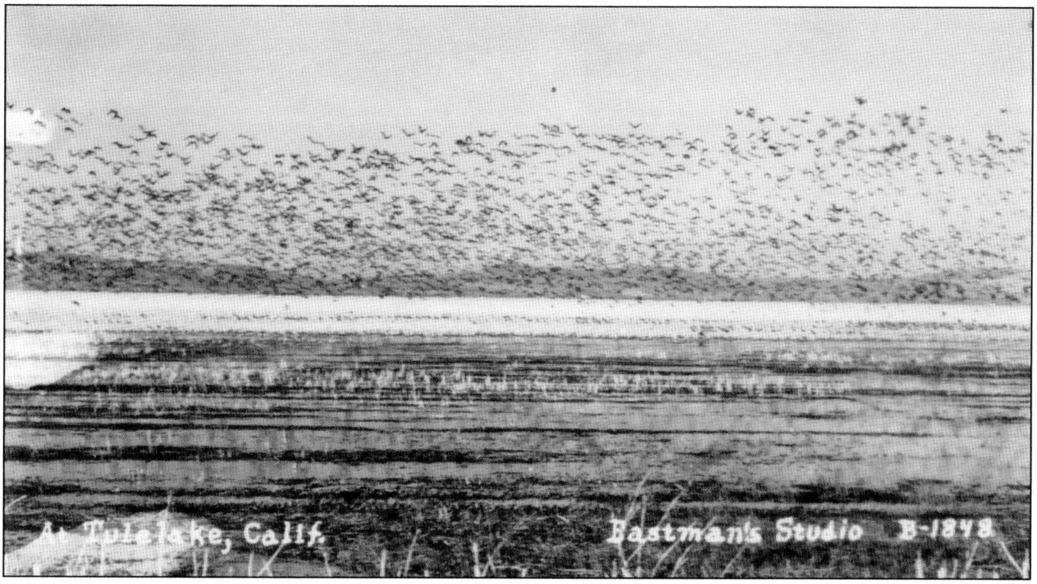

The Klamath Basin straddles the border of California and Oregon. The area provides critical habitat for wintering and nesting birds and other wildlife. Bald eagles, white pelicans, and osprey are among the birds seen throughout the year. The Klamath Wildlife Area is located four miles south of Klamath Falls on Highway 97. Habitat areas here vary and include developed agricultural land and seasonal and permanent wetlands. Of the approximate 2,400 acres, 1,200 acres are either seasonal or permanent wetlands. Agricultural producers in the region have become involved in providing additional habitat and have added to the area where birds are found. Recent evidence suggests that landowners in the flyway zones in the western United States have provided at least 75 percent of habitat. The best viewing times for spotting birds in the Klamath area include October to December for waterfowl, winter months for raptors, and spring for migrating or nesting birds.

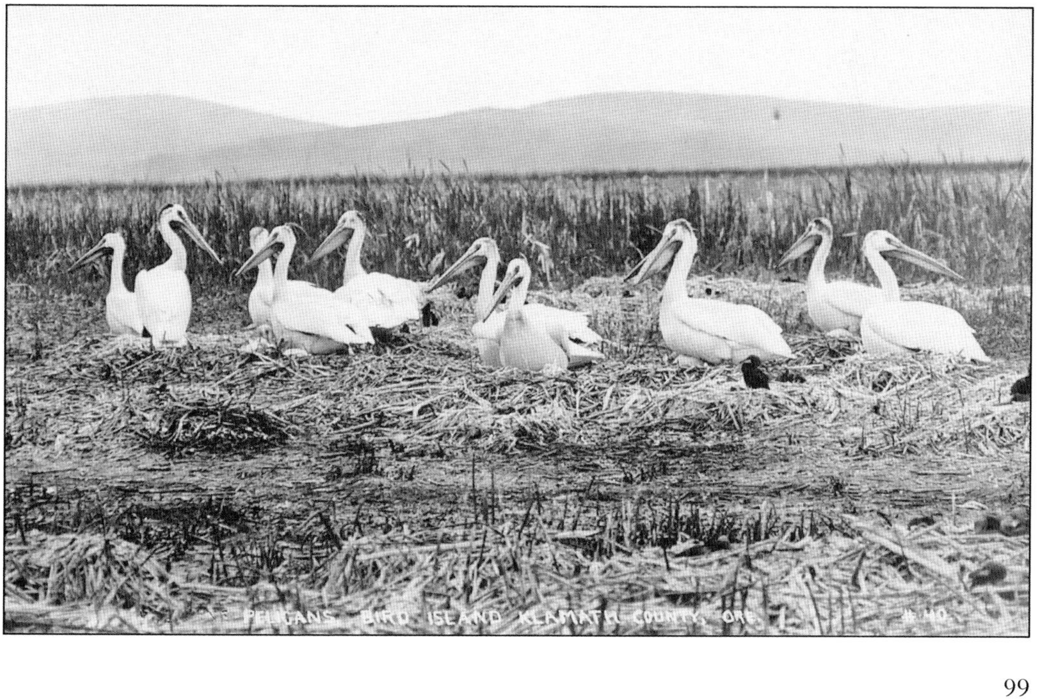

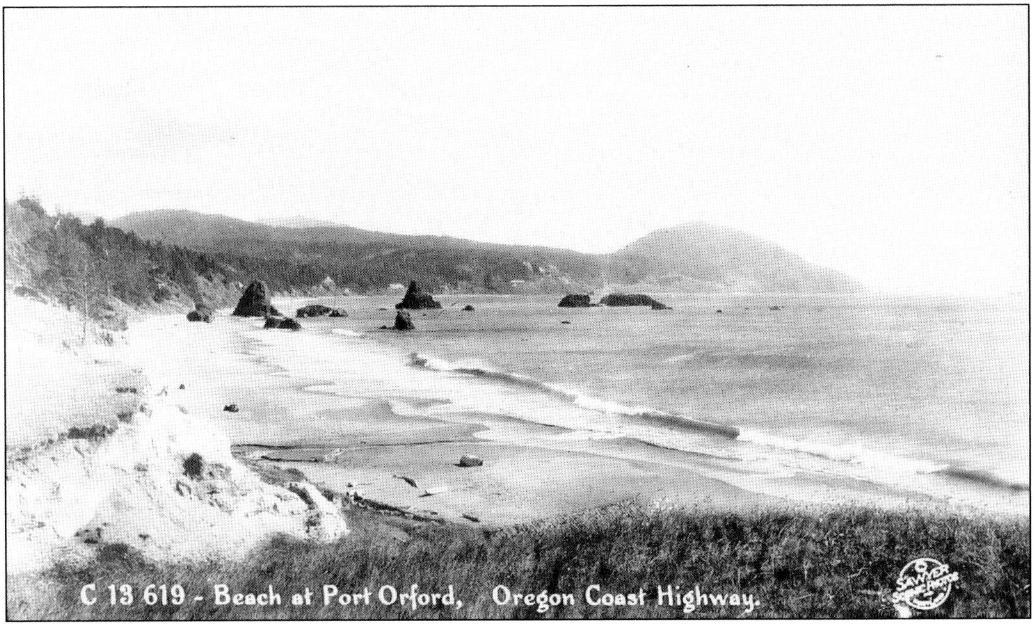

Port Orford is located in Curry County, Oregon, on the southern Oregon coast. The area was originally the home of the Tututni tribe, members of the Athabaskan language family group. Port Orford was officially founded in 1856 and became a receiving port for mercantile and fishing. Within a few years, it was also an important shipping port for local cedar. Eventually it suffered a decline in both fishing and timber sales.

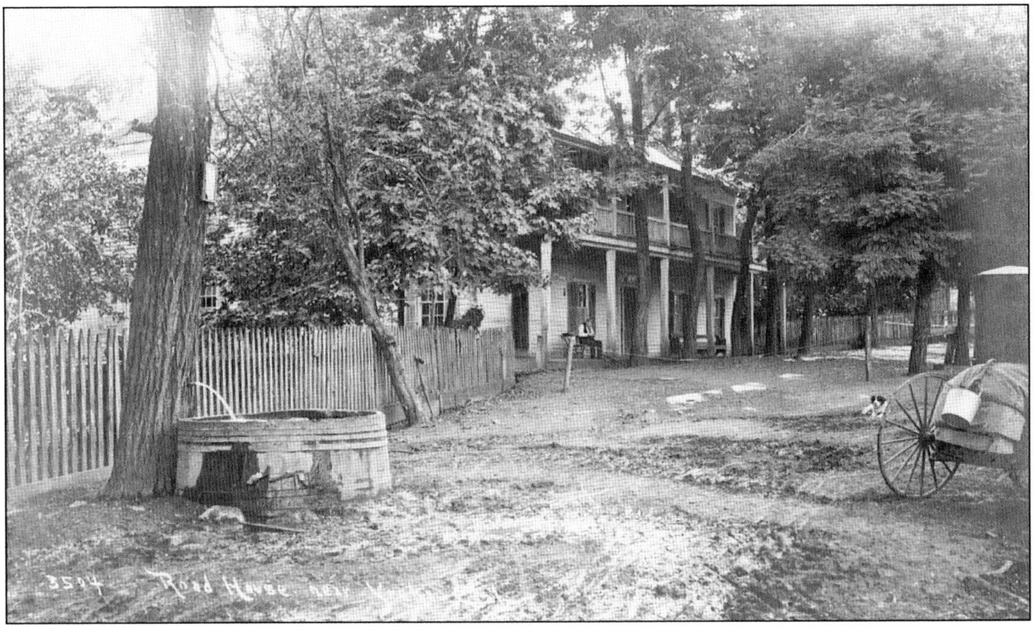

The Forest House, seen here around 1900, sits at the base of Forest Mountain on what was once a toll road between Yreka and Scott Valley, California. The road was "freed up" in 1864, when tolls were abolished. A popular stage stop, the Forest House was known for its hospitality, complete with ballroom where dances were held "until six in the morning." The Forest House had hundreds of fruit trees and was well known for its apple brandy.

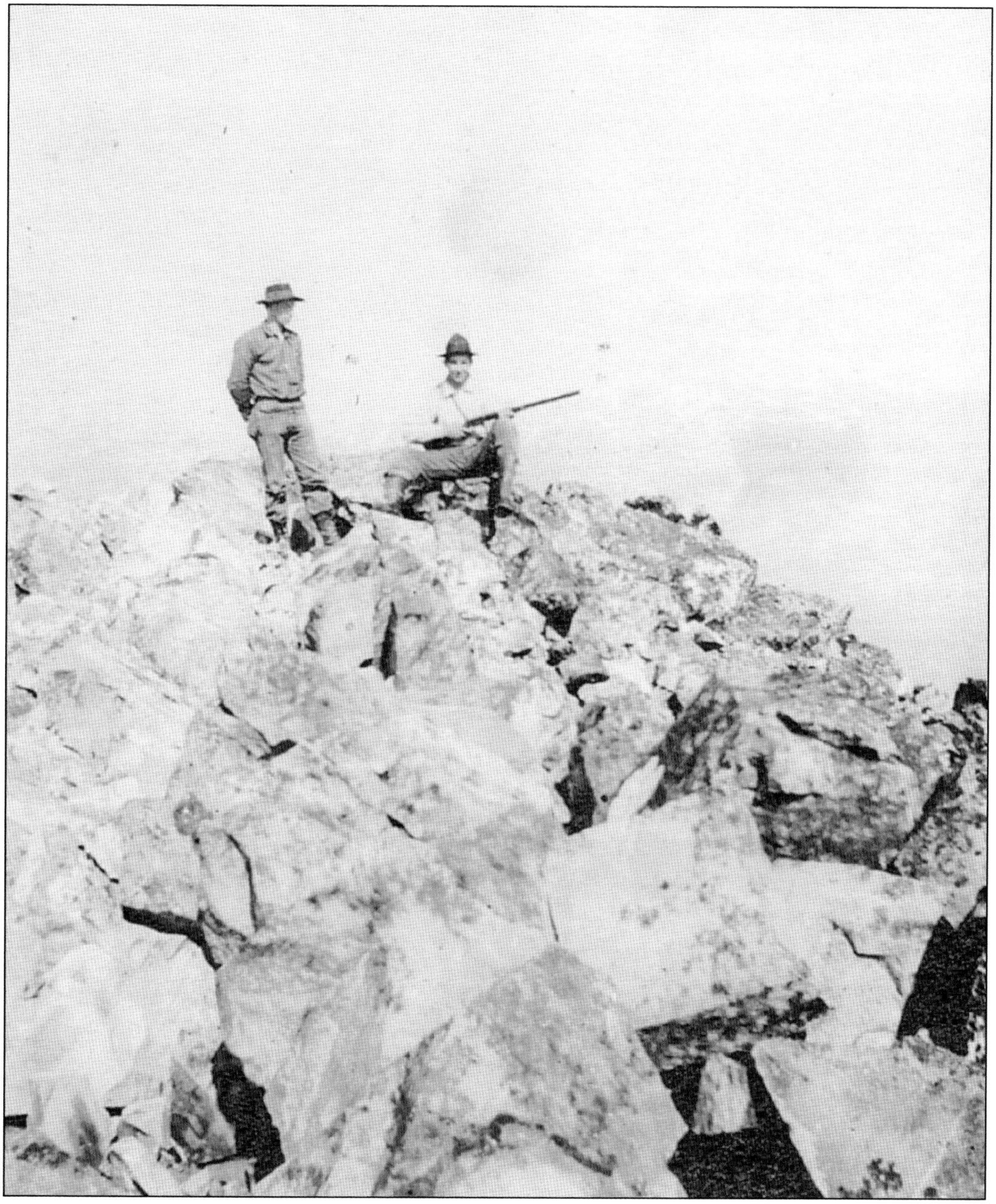

The Trinity Alps Wilderness Area covers 517,000 acres, making it the second largest in California. In 1932, it was designated the Salmon–Trinity Alps Primitive Area. The backbone of the Trinity Alps is the Salmon and Scott Mountains. The ridge tops are often hot and dry. Popular destinations include Canyon Creek Lakes, Emerald and Sapphire Lakes, and Granite Lake. The historic Carrville Inn was located along the Oregon-to-California Stage Road. James E. Carr was one of those responsible for building the road over Scott Mountain. When his wife fell in love with the Curry and Noyes Ranch, he purchased it. It became one of the more popular stage stops on the road from Trinity over to Scott Valley. The inn went through a renovation in the 1980s. Today, under new ownership, it remains a popular tourist bed-and-breakfast destination. This photograph dates to 1909.

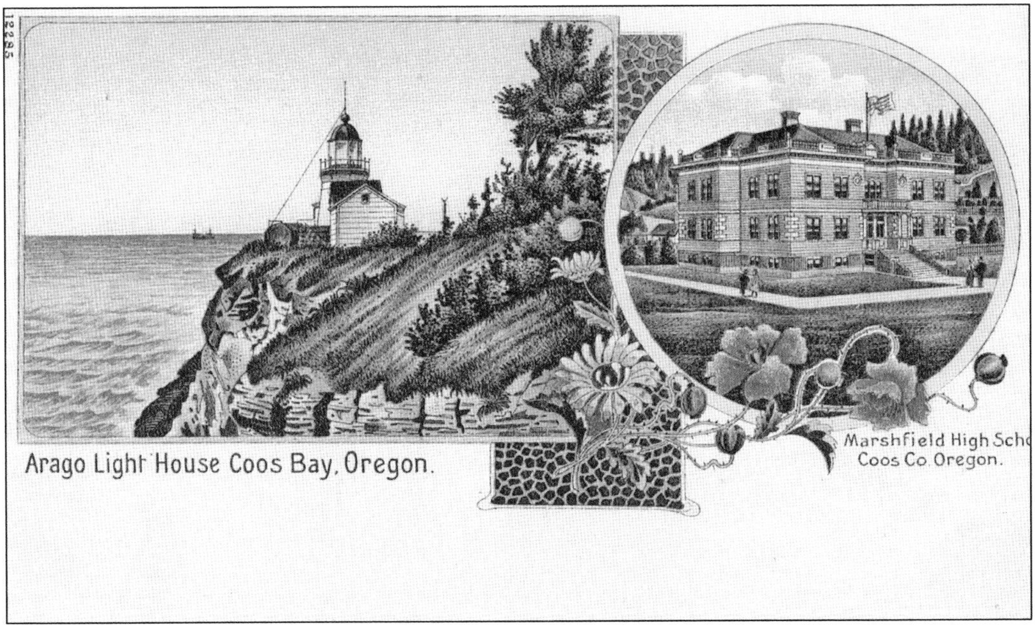

Survivors of a shipwreck settled Coos Bay, Oregon, in 1852. Originally, the town was called Marshfield, but in 1940, it was changed to Coos Bay. Because of the port's growing importance, there was a need for a lighthouse; in 1864, funds were raised to build a harbor light, and in 1866, Cape Arago was established. A second lighthouse was built in 1909, and a third was built in 1934.

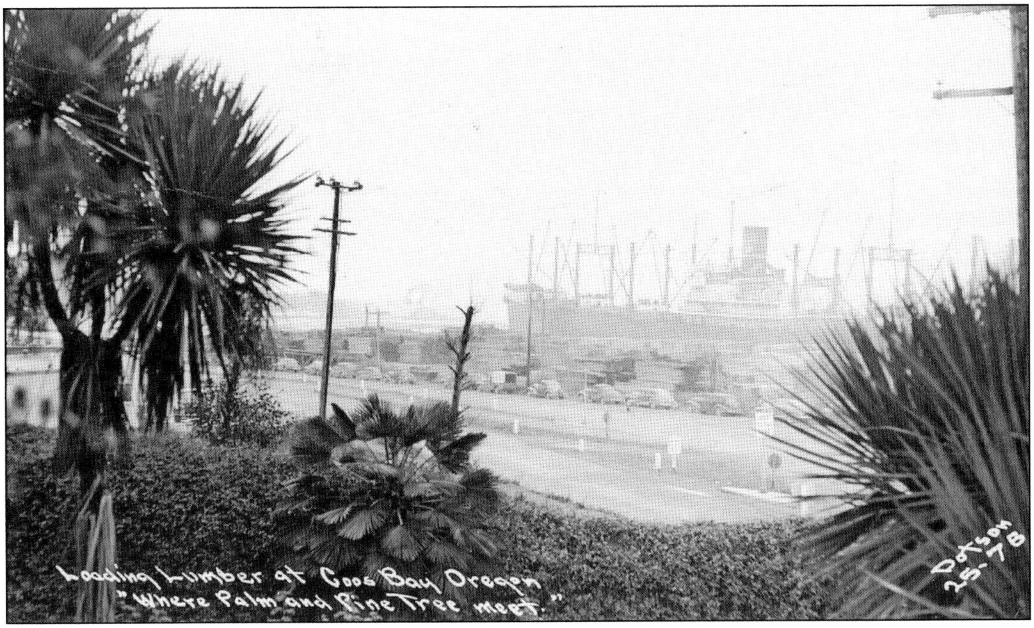

Beginning in the mid-1800s, Coos Bay became an important shipping point on the Pacific coastline; it is still Oregon's largest coastal estuary and shipping port. As a midway point between the ports of San Francisco and Portland, local products, including lumber, coal, salmon, and other agricultural products, could be shipped either north or south. In 1908, the C.A. Smith Lumber mill was the largest mill on the Pacific coast.

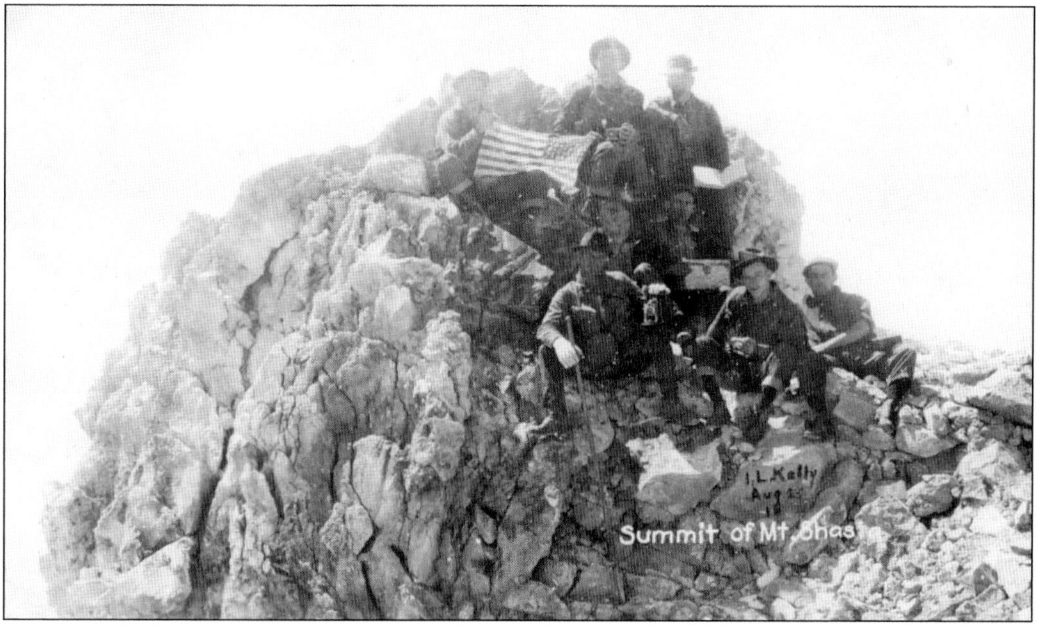

The completion of a stagecoach road between Yreka and Upper Soda Springs, California, in the late 1850s led to the building of Sisson's Hotel as a stop for travelers and the more adventurous tourists hoping to climb Mount Shasta. Here a group of men, names not known, sit atop the summit of Mount Shasta. Note the flag and camera. Also, there is a name on the rock: "I.L. Kelly, Aug. 25, '16."

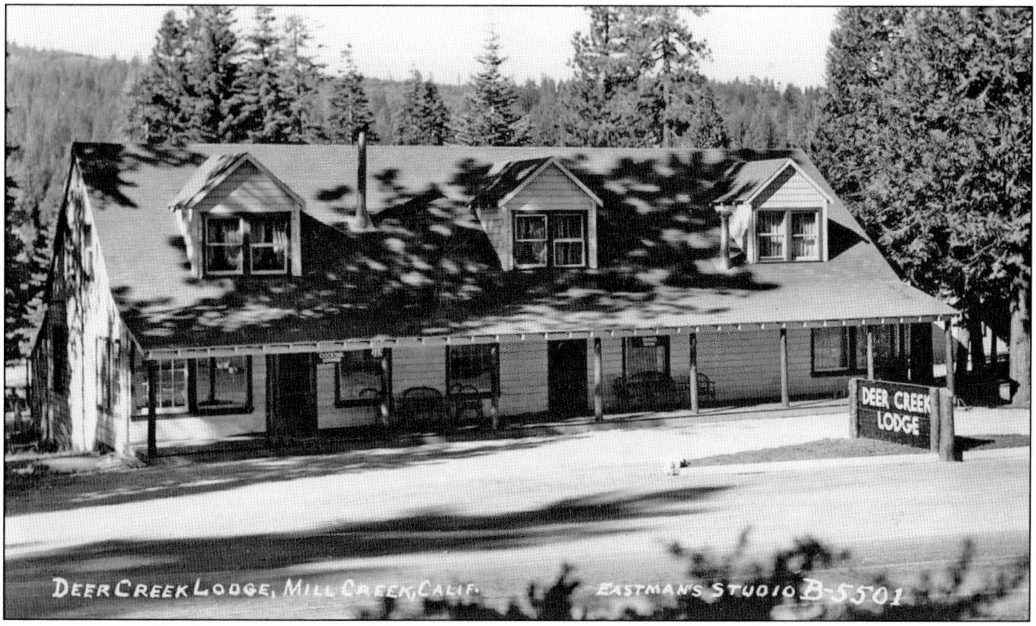

Deer Creek Lodge is located in Mill Creek, California, not far from Lassen National Park and Chester, California. This was the land of the Yahi and Yana people and likely the site where four Yahi people were accosted by whites. Several years later, accompanied by Professors Alfred Kroeber and T.T. Waterman, Ishi, last of the Yahi, revisited his homeland. Ishi's doctor, Saxton Pope, wrote, "When Ishi passed away, the Yahi passed away."

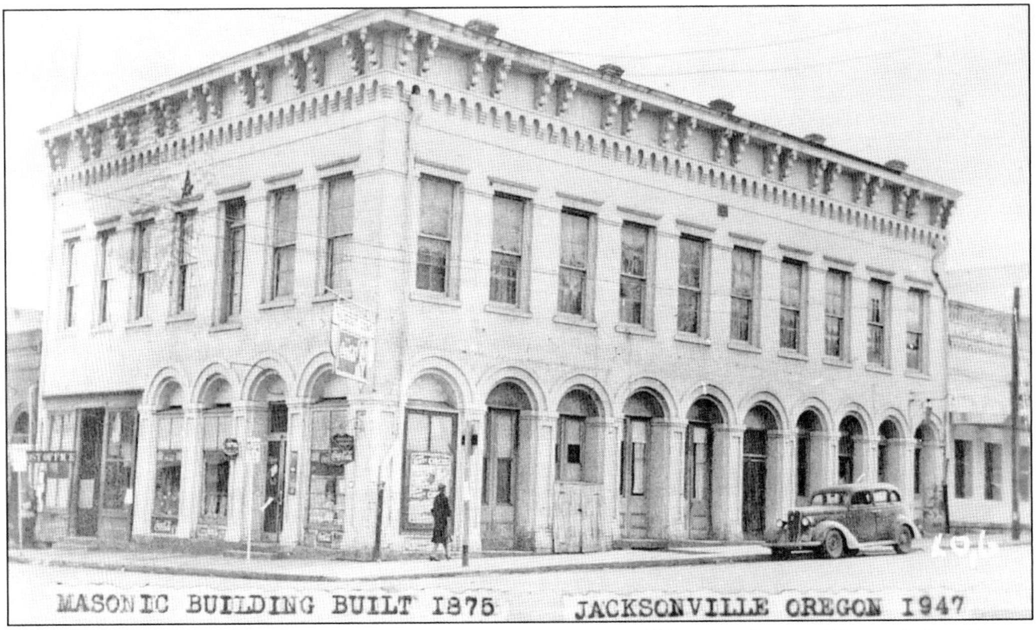

The Masonic fraternity in Oregon Territory sent out a call in the first edition of the *Oregon Spectator* of Oregon City: "The members of the Masonic Fraternity in Oregon Territory are respectfully requested to meet at the City Hotel, in Oregon City, on the 21st to adopt some measure to obtain a Charter for a Lodge. February 5, 1846." Jacksonville's lodge, built in 1875, was known as Warren Lodge No. 6.

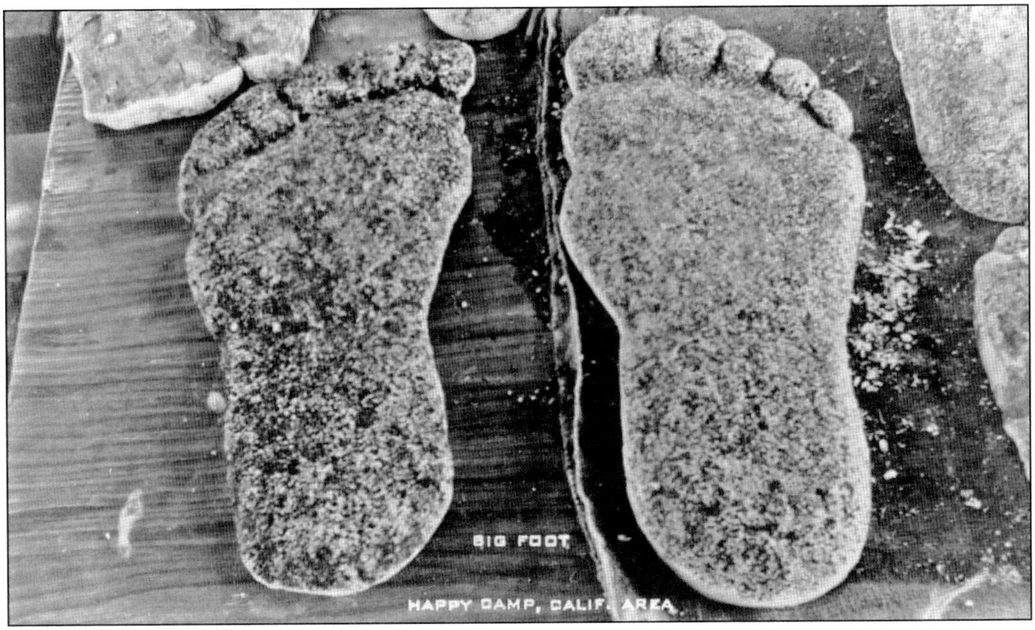

Bigfoot, or Sasquatch, is the name given to a human-like creature that some believe lives in the Pacific Northwest. Many sightings have been reported in Oregon and California; one report indicates at least 350 sightings in northern California alone. Two communities that celebrate Bigfoot are Hoopa and Happy Camp, California. *The Hoopa Project* was written about Bigfoot sightings. The Hupa tribal lands stretched from the Trinity River to the Klamath River.

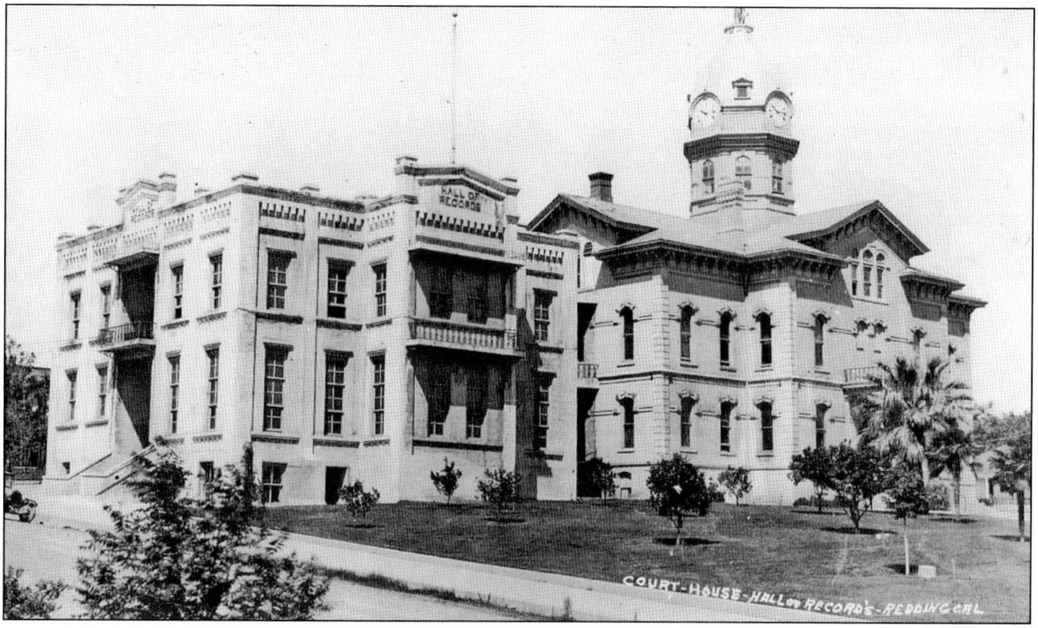

This two-story, 75-by-92-foot, cruciform brick building was Redding, California's, third county courthouse. Begun in 1888 and completed a year later, the large building stood at the crossroads of Yuba, Butte, Court, and West Streets. On the dome was raised a statue, the *State of Justice*. After the building was torn down in 1963, the statue stood for many years in front of the new courthouse. It is no longer there.

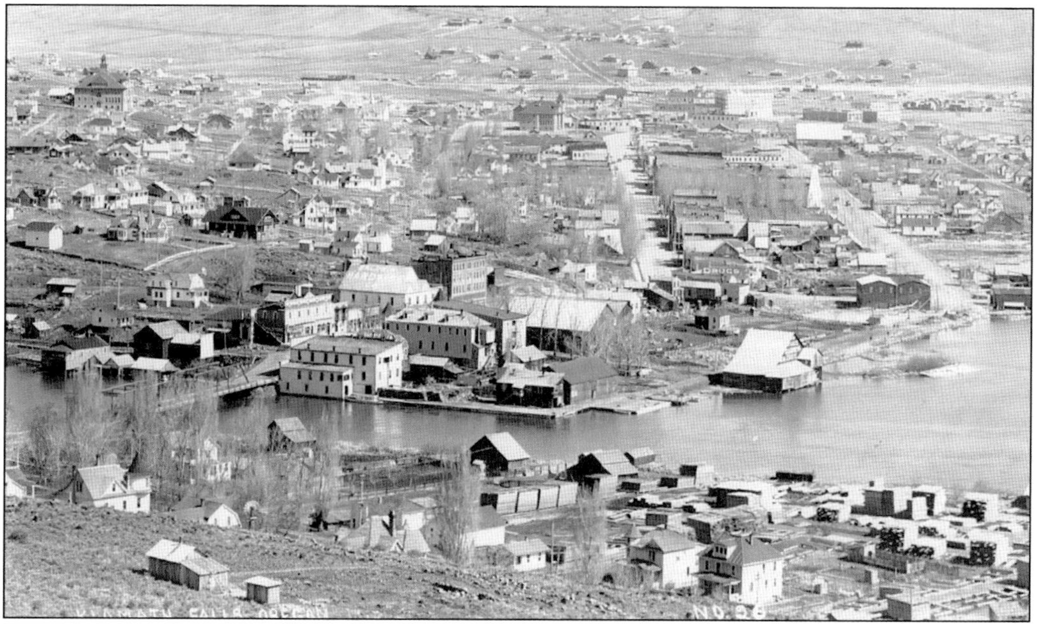

Located in the south central portion of Oregon, Klamath Falls was first called Linkville. A booming logging town, in 1893 the name was changed. The arrival of the Southern Pacific Railroad in 1909 brought further prosperity. That ended with the Great Depression. The city is only 60 miles south of Crater Lake and sits on the southern edge of Upper Klamath Lake. The area is home to the largest concentration of bald eagles in the Northwest.

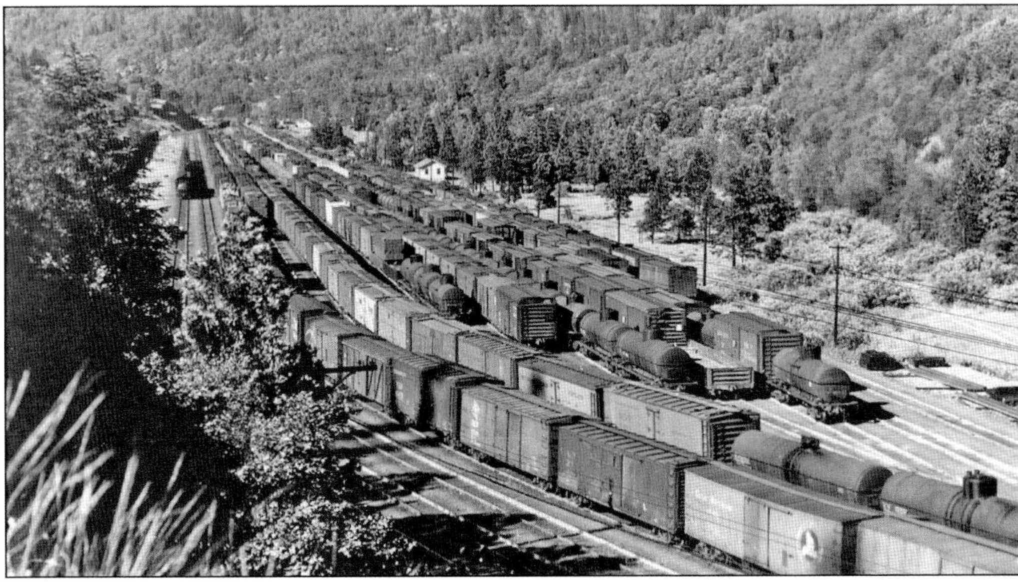

Dunsmuir, California, was a railroad town. A roundhouse, a station, and rail yards were built to accommodate the trains moving up and down the Sacramento River Canyon. The town was incorporated in 1909 and began to boom. In fact, Dunsmuir was the most prosperous town in Siskiyou County in the early 1950s because of the prosperous railroad industry. After diesel trains were introduced, however, the boom was over.

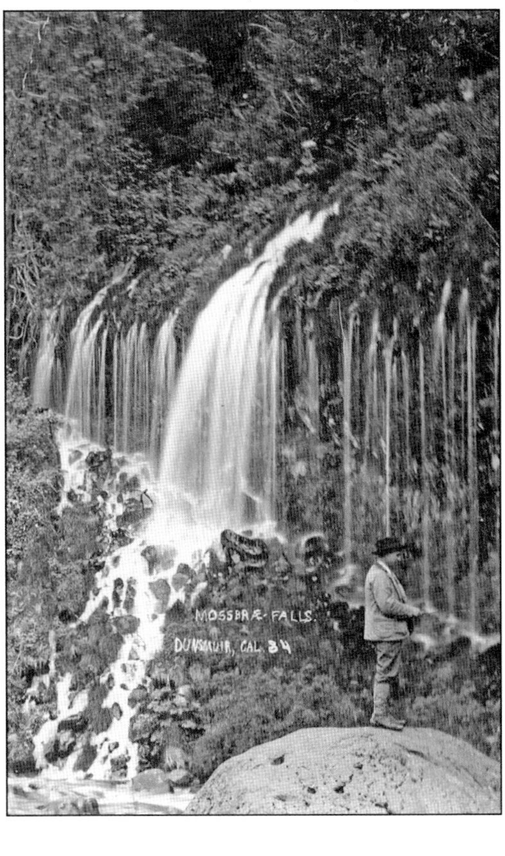

Mossbrae Falls is an unusually beautiful waterfall. Located near Dunsmuir, California, the 50-foot-high falls are fed by springs above the Sacramento River. The effect is a series of waterfalls, although the upper range of the falls cannot be seen through the heavy growth. Unfortunately, viewing access is challenging, since the falls are located on the Union Pacific Railroad tracks and an alternative route has yet to be designed. Visitors have noted that the hike is discouraging, as they must walk down the tracks. One visitor wrote, "trains DO run on those tracks, and in the wrong spot you pretty much will have to scurry down a gravel slope." This postcard is dated 1918 and doesn't reveal how close to the tracks the falls might be or what kind of hike visitors had to make to get to the site. In 2011, the falls were closed for at least part of the season.

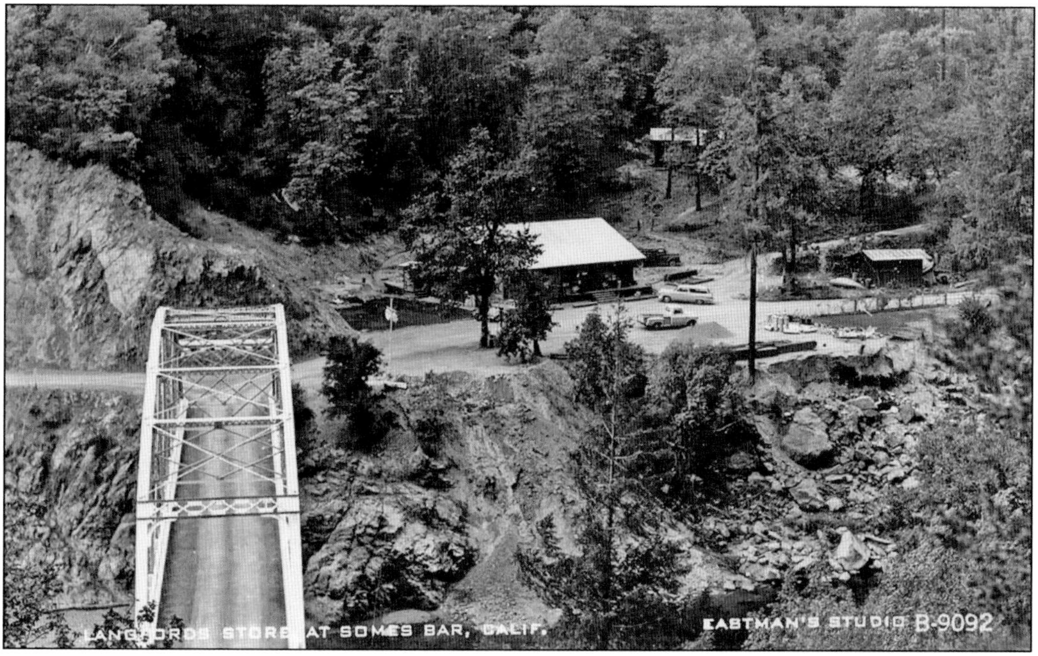

Somes Bar, California, was named for George Somes, a miner who settled in this area along the Salmon River, 12 miles northwest of Forks of Salmon. The post office at Somes Bar was established in 1850, and although the unincorporated town is now in Siskiyou County, it was first located in Klamath County until that county was dissolved.

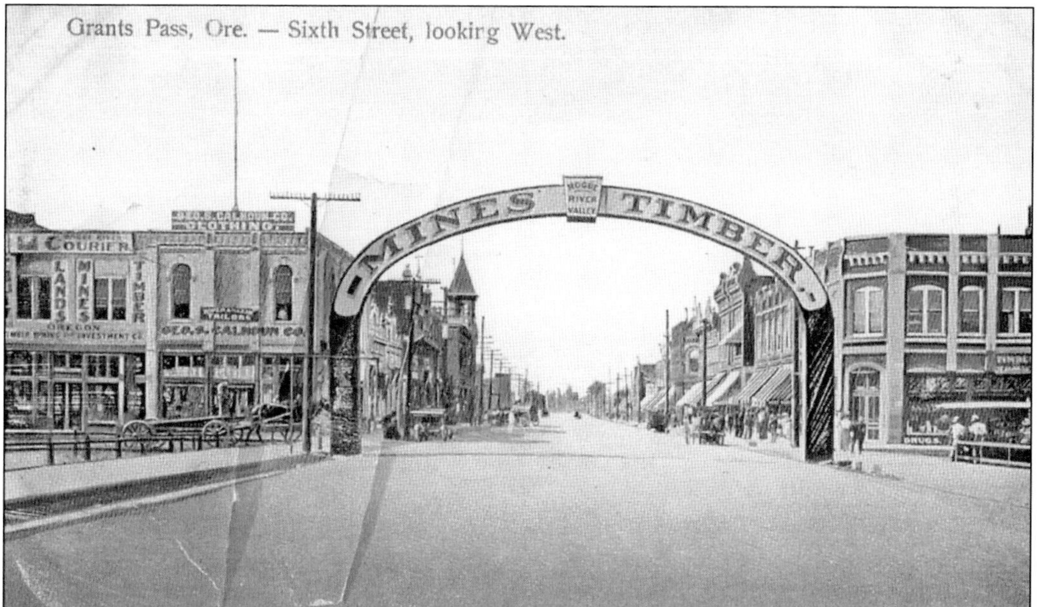

Like many towns, Grants Pass, Oregon, owes its existence to the railroad as well as to the industries of mining and timber. This c. 1910 view of Grants Pass shows a sign reading "Mines—Rogue River Valley—Timber" stretching across the road. This city is known for its array of signs; on another postcard, a sign reads: "It's the Climate." Note the office of the *Rogue River Courier* to the left.

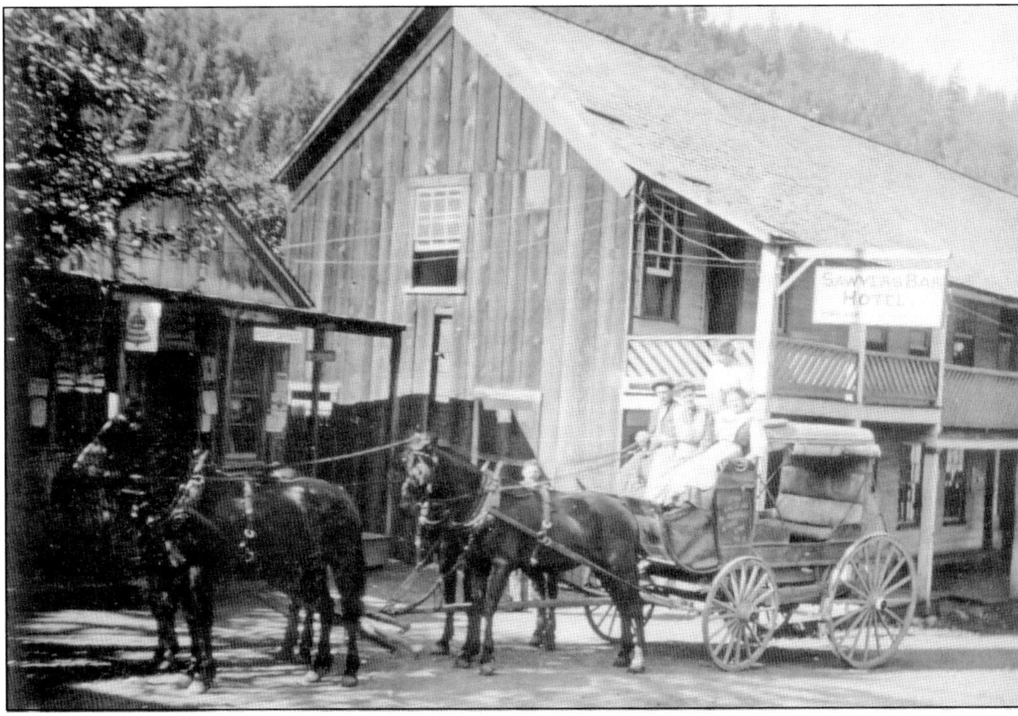

The earliest stagecoaches were through-brace types, supported by heavy leather straps and built to withstand rough roads. Mud wagons were also used, though they weren't as comfortable. In 1883, L. Swan of Yreka, California, built half a dozen new stages. Drivers, called *jehus*, were heroes, especially since stages were subject to occasional holdups. Black Bart was one of the bandits who held up stages from northern California to southern Oregon.

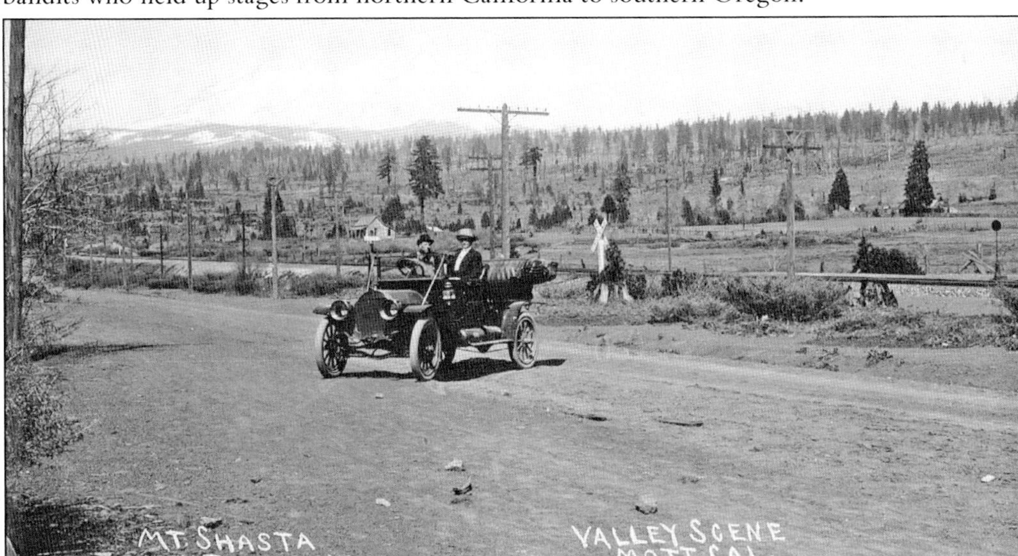

Mott, California, was a fast-growing town named for M.H. Mott, Southern Pacific's road master. Established in 1887, its life was not long. When the mills closed down and a fire swept through most of the town, not much was left. The post office was moved to Shasta Springs in 1910. Today, nothing remains of Mott.

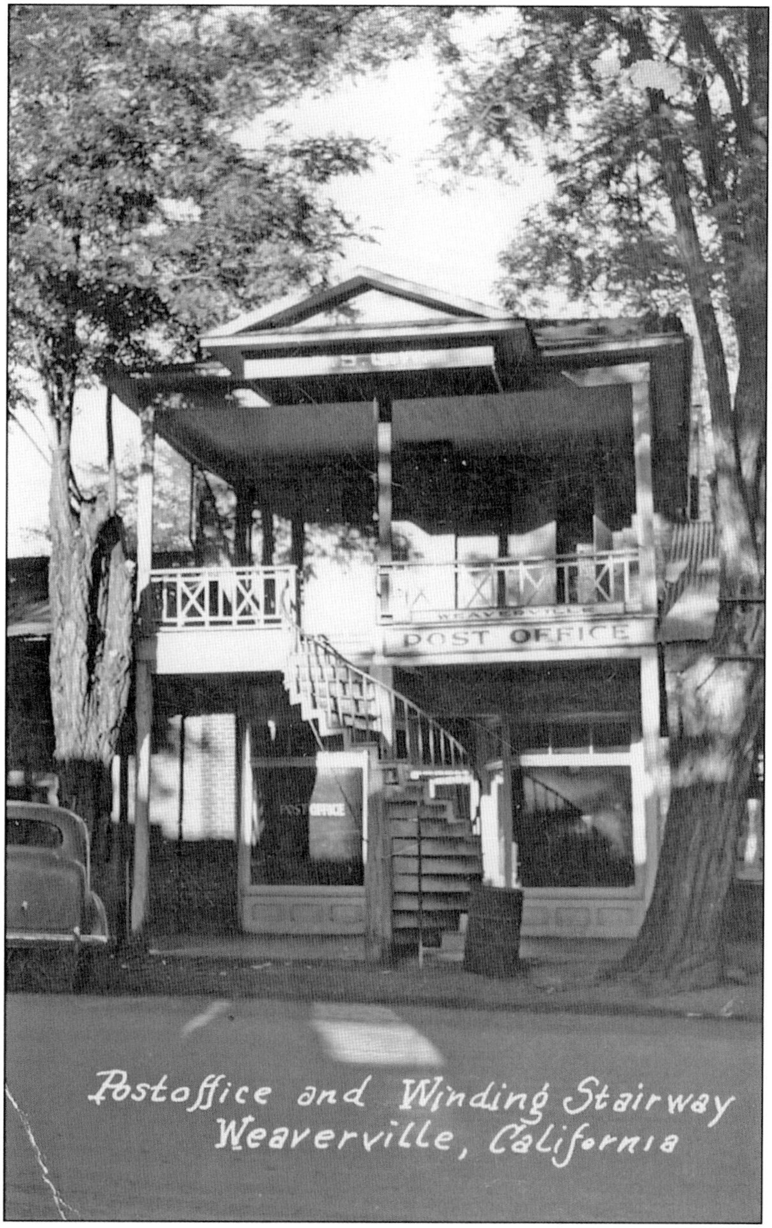

Weaverville, California, is listed in the National Register of Historic Places; it is also the county seat of Trinity County. In 2006, Weaverville became a Preserve America Community. Trinity County was originally the homeland of the Wintu tribe. Though probably visited by fur traders like Jedediah Smith in the 1820s and 1830s, the area's first documented visit was by Maj. Pierson P. Reading, who named the Trinity River in 1845 on the assumption that the river emptied into the Pacific Ocean at Trinidad Bay. Four years later, two miners headed to the ocean found that the Trinity flows into the Klamath River. The rush for gold in the Trinity River region began in late 1849 or early 1850. Weaverville and Trinity Center became boomtowns. Miners came from all over; there were even about 2,000 Chinese in Weaverville at this time, although Chinese mining their own claims had to pay a $4-per-month head tax while white miners paid nothing. There were more people living in the Trinity area in the 1850s than there are now.

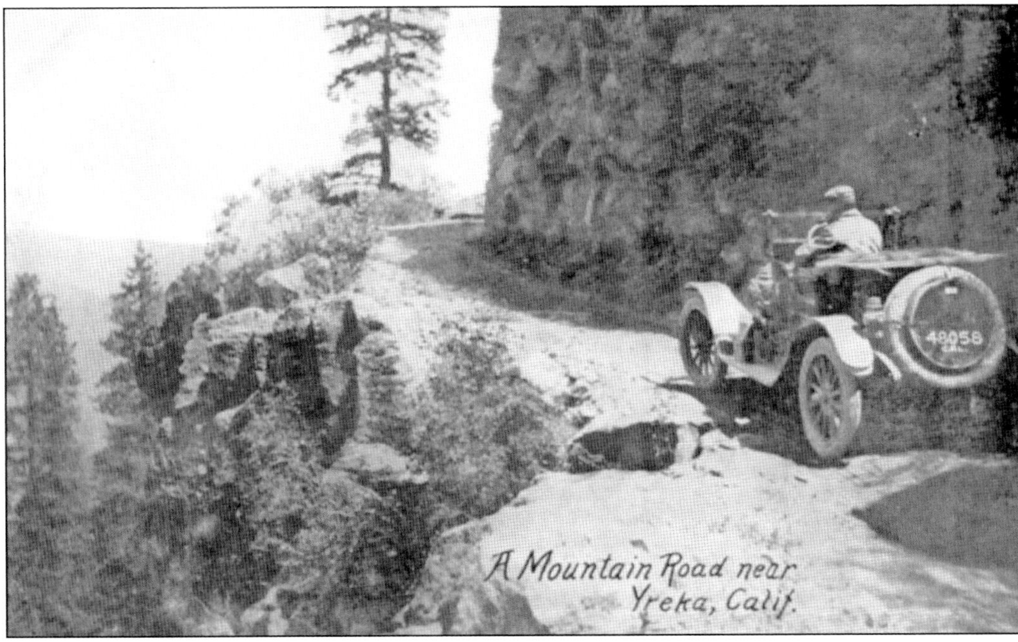

The road from Yreka, California, into Scott Valley is over Forest Mountain, with a summit of 4,097 feet. In the early days, it was a toll road, but in 1864, the toll was eliminated. Still, it was a rugged, winding road. Not until the 1960s were the harshest turns eliminated. The road pictured here gives credence to the State of Jefferson assertion that its roads were "unpassable, not even jack-assable!"

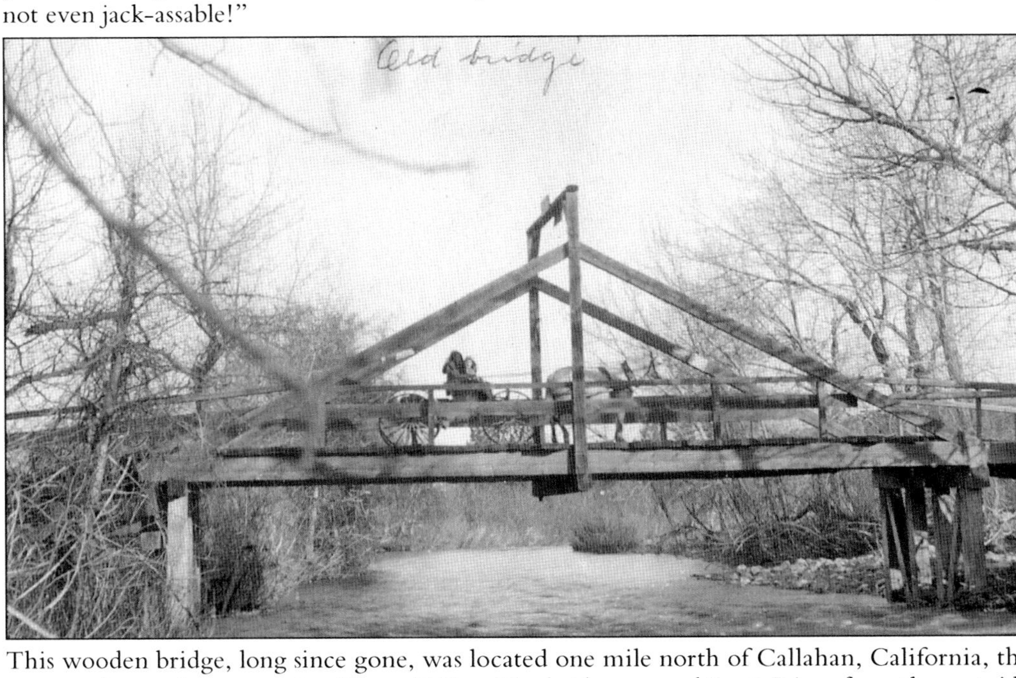

This wooden bridge, long since gone, was located one mile north of Callahan, California, the town at the southernmost tip of Scott Valley. The bridge crossed Scott River from the east side to what is now called Highway 3. Scott River is a 60-mile-long tributary of the Klamath River, and Scott Valley, discovered by Stephen Hall Meek and other Hudson Bay Company trappers, is primarily a ranching community.

Four

WINTER

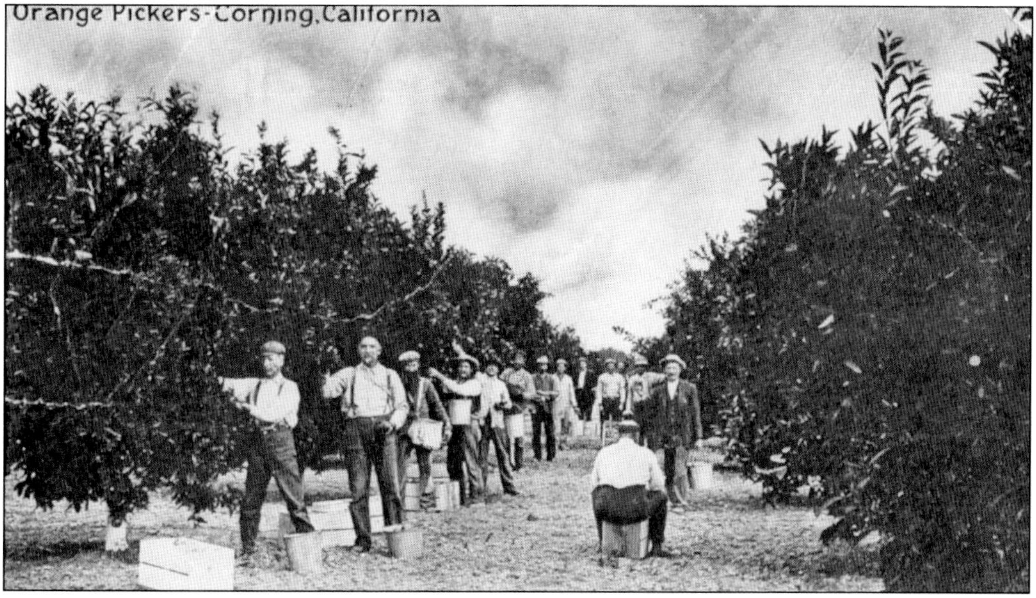

Oh! The snow, the beautiful snow, filling the sky and the earth below.

—J.W. Watson

Corning, California, was named in honor of John Corning, who worked for the Central Pacific Railroad. The first railroad arrived in Corning in 1882. From the beginning, it was an agricultural area. The first olives were planted in the 1890s, and they were used in oil production. In 1923, Corning was dubbed "The Olive Town." Oranges also became a product of Corning farmers.

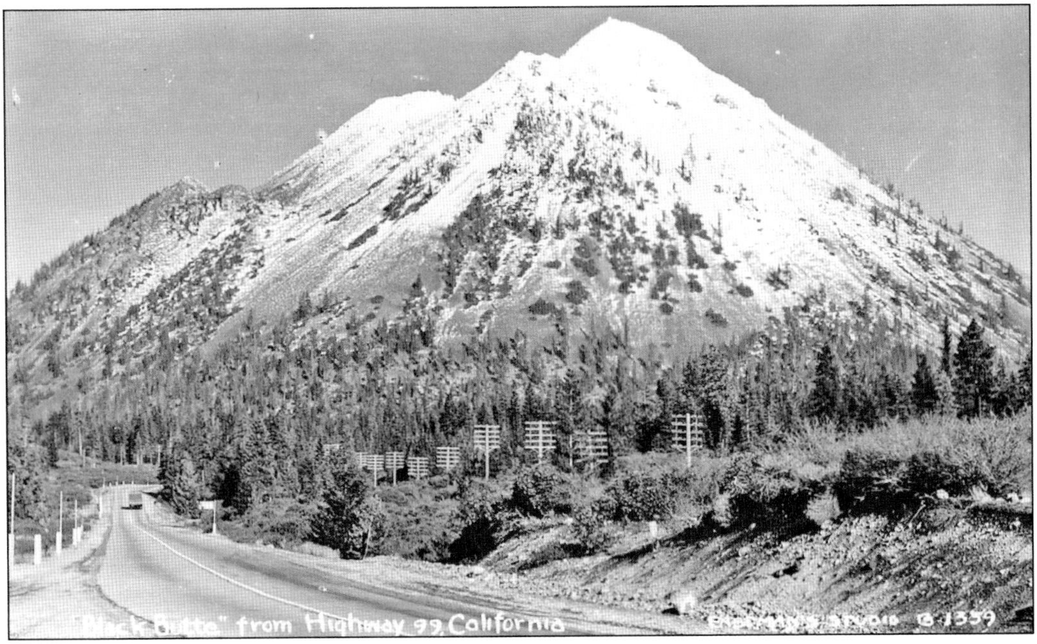

Black Butte stands almost in the shadow of Mount Shasta along Interstate 5 near Weed, California. A plug volcano, it rises 6,325 feet. Often it only receives a dusting of winter snow, the rough sides of the mountain still appearing almost dry. The term *butte* comes from the French word for "ridge."

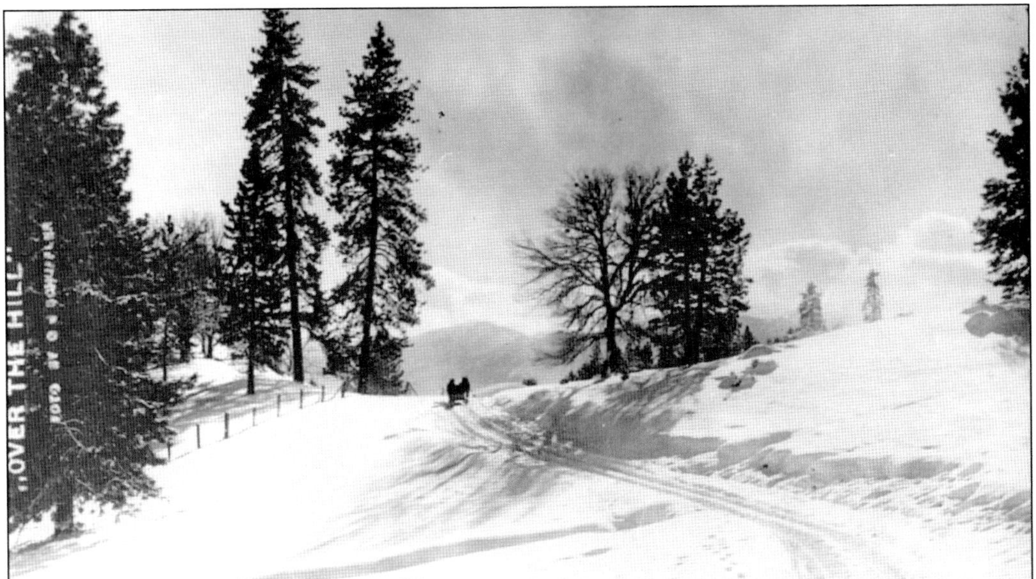

Titled *Over the Hill*, this postcard depicts the road going from Greenview to Fort Jones, California. A distance of roughly four or five miles today, it wound its way more gently in earlier days. Greenview was first known as Hayes Corner. The Hayes Hotel, built on "the hill," was a popular dance hall. The Green family established a home here, and it is from "Green's view" that the name of the town is derived.

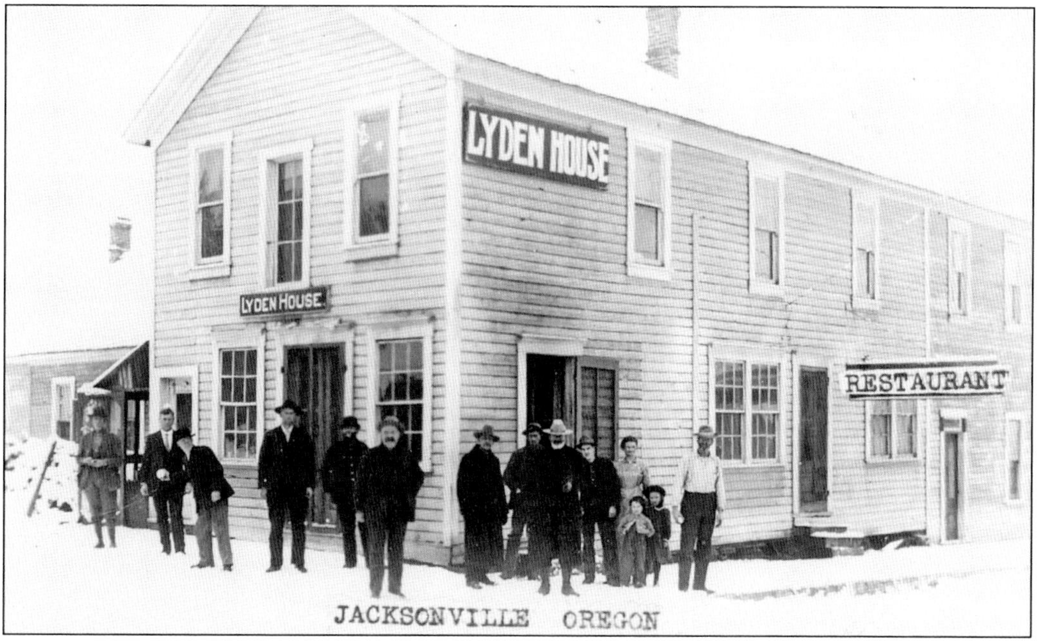

The Lyden House in historic Jacksonville, Oregon, once housed the business of J.C. Whipp, a tombstone cutter. Although Jacksonville prospered in the 1850s and a new courthouse was built in 1884, the Oregon & California Railroad passed it by. As a result, Jacksonville's economy flagged for many years. During the 1930s, many residents returned to some forms of mining. With its designation as a historic district, the town has been revived.

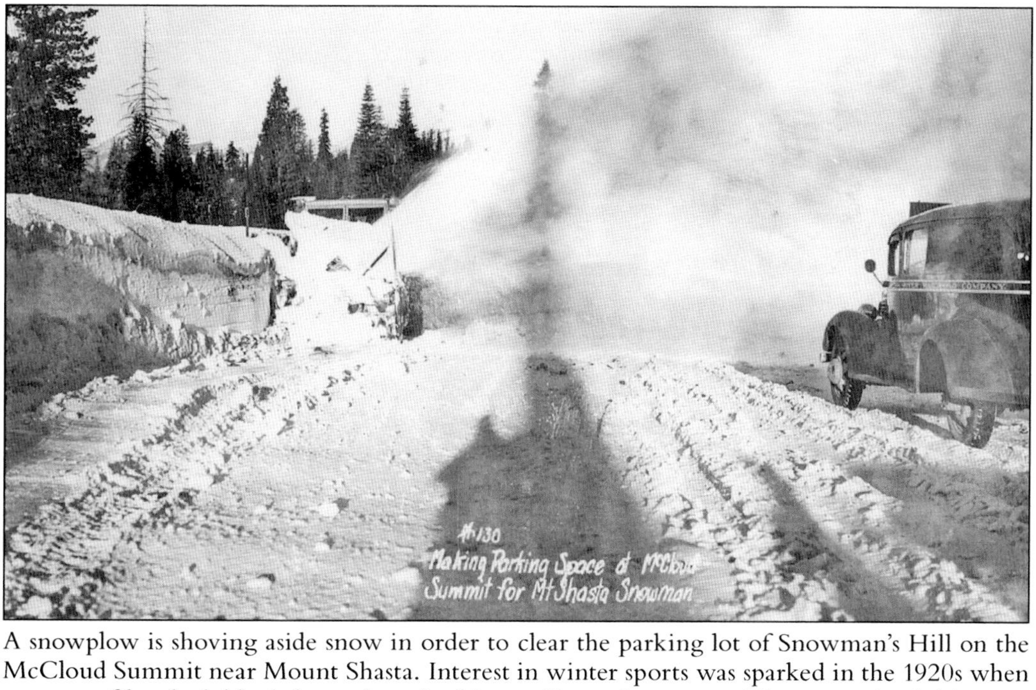

A snowplow is shoving aside snow in order to clear the parking lot of Snowman's Hill on the McCloud Summit near Mount Shasta. Interest in winter sports was sparked in the 1920s when a group of locals dubbed themselves the Mount Shasta Snowmen. They organized ski meets under the direction of John M. Schuler.

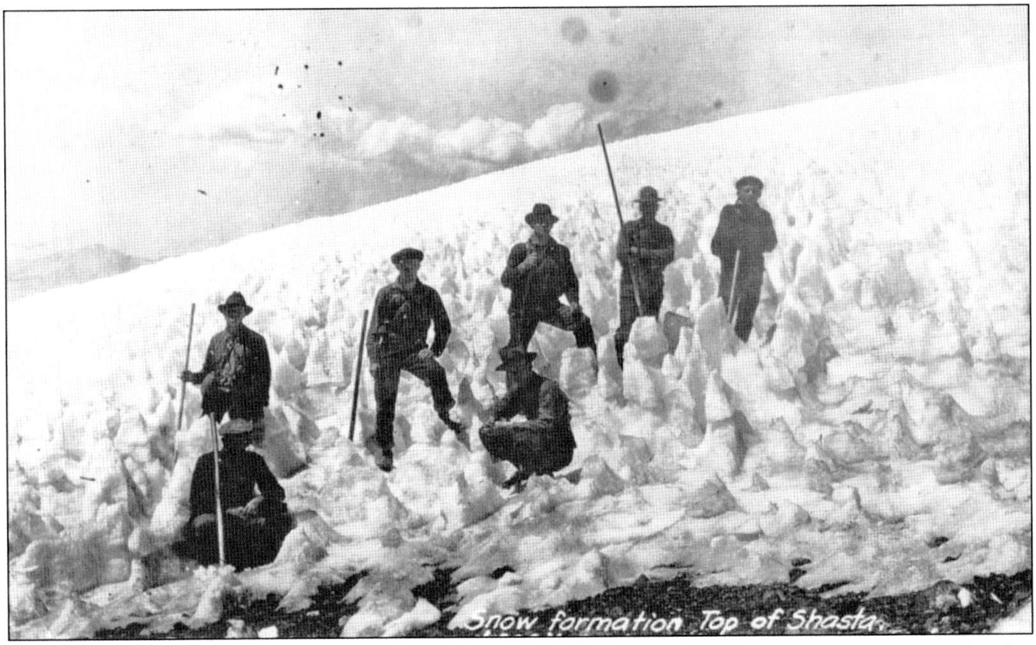

The snow formation on top of Mount Shasta, captured in this photo postcard, is an unusual sight. Identified as *nieves penitentes*, these tall thin blades of ice or hardened snow appear as pinnacles. Some can be as tall as a person, and they lean in the general direction of the sun. Nieves penitentes are only found at high altitudes, such as on Mount Shasta.

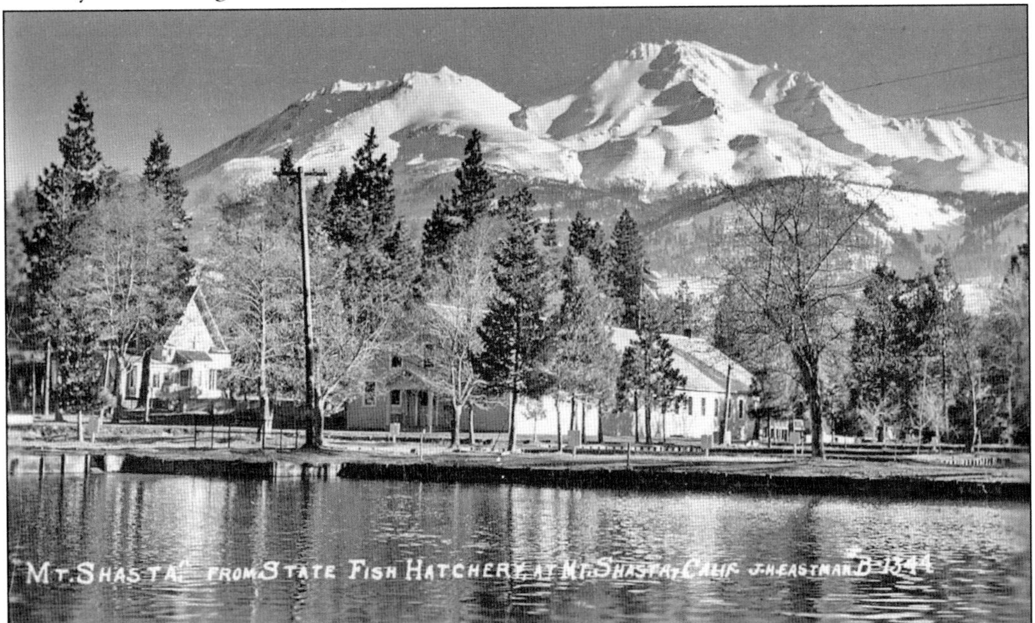

This is a view of Mount Shasta from the Mount Shasta Fish Hatchery, the oldest working fish hatchery in California. It was established in 1888 by the California Fish and Game Commission on land donated by Justin Sisson on Big Springs Creek. At first it propagated only salmon, but later it also propagated trout for stocking streams and lakes. Viewing is open to the public on Tuesdays.

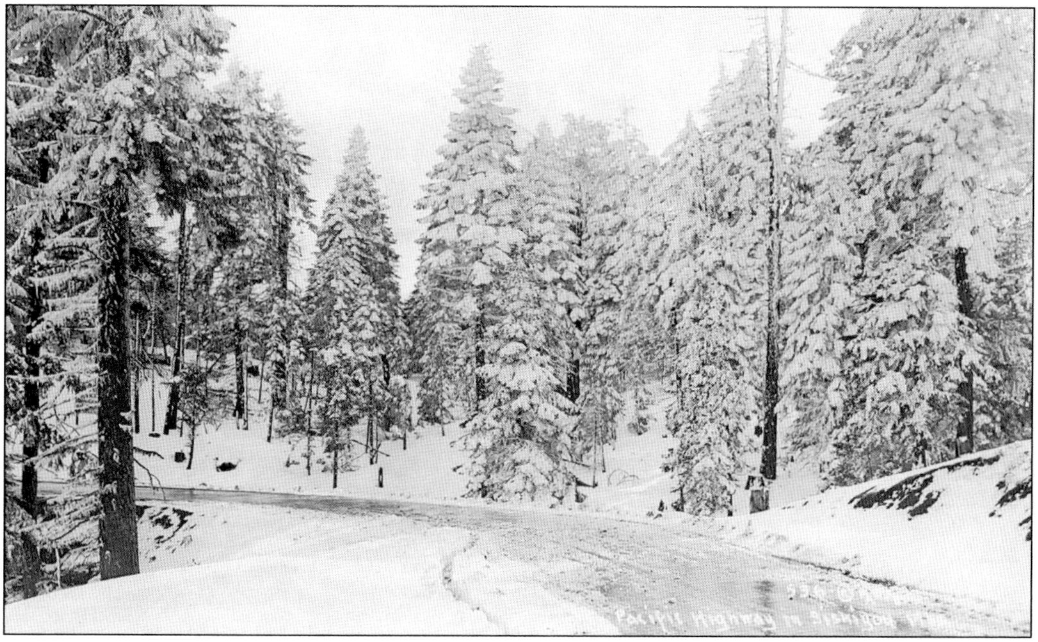

The Pacific Highway over the Siskiyou Mountains into California was frequently covered with snow in winter; however, even today, the old highway is often more passable than Interstate 5. The old highway wends its way more gently over the summit and lacks as many cars and trucks. It begins at the south end of Ashland, Oregon, and emerges at the Hilt, California, exit.

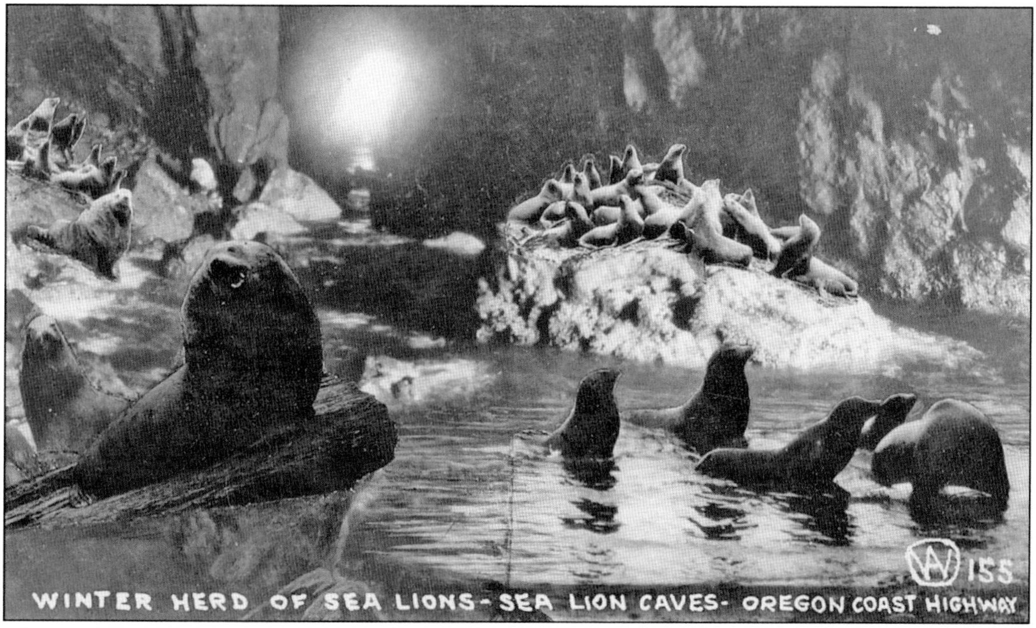

The Oregon Sea Lion Caves feature the largest sea cave in the world, as high as a 12-story building inside and as long as a football field. Scientists estimate it was formed 25 million years ago. The roar of Steller sea lions, seen here, coupled with the sound of the ocean rushing in and out of the cave, is, according to many, unforgettable.

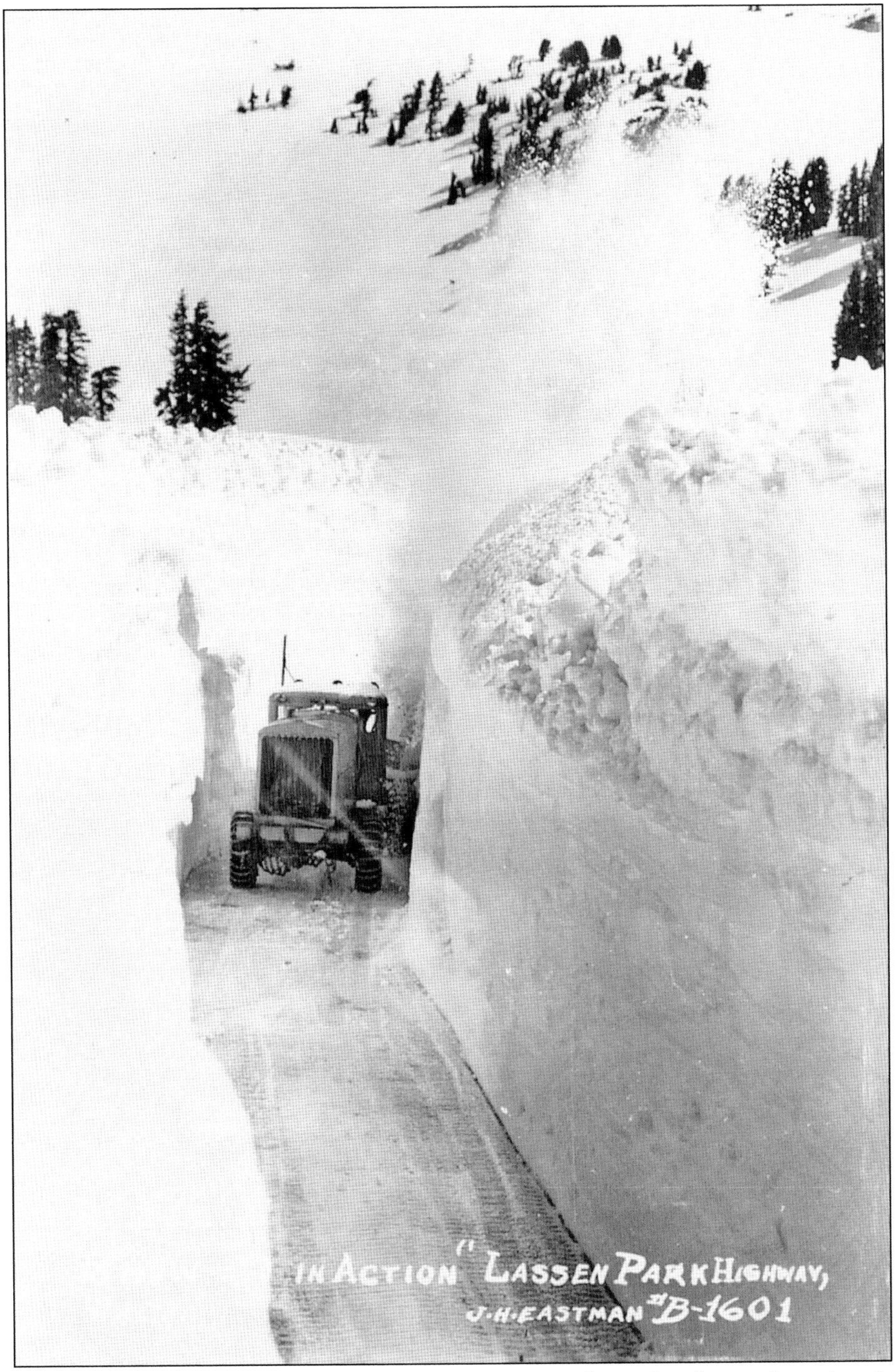

Winter in Lassen Volcanic National Park often comes as early as October and persists through June or July. The main park road is often closed by mid-November, even though the park is open all year. Throughout the winter, the main park road is plowed to the Southwest Parking Area, where there are several sledding hills. It is also plowed on the north side of the park down to the Loomis Museum.

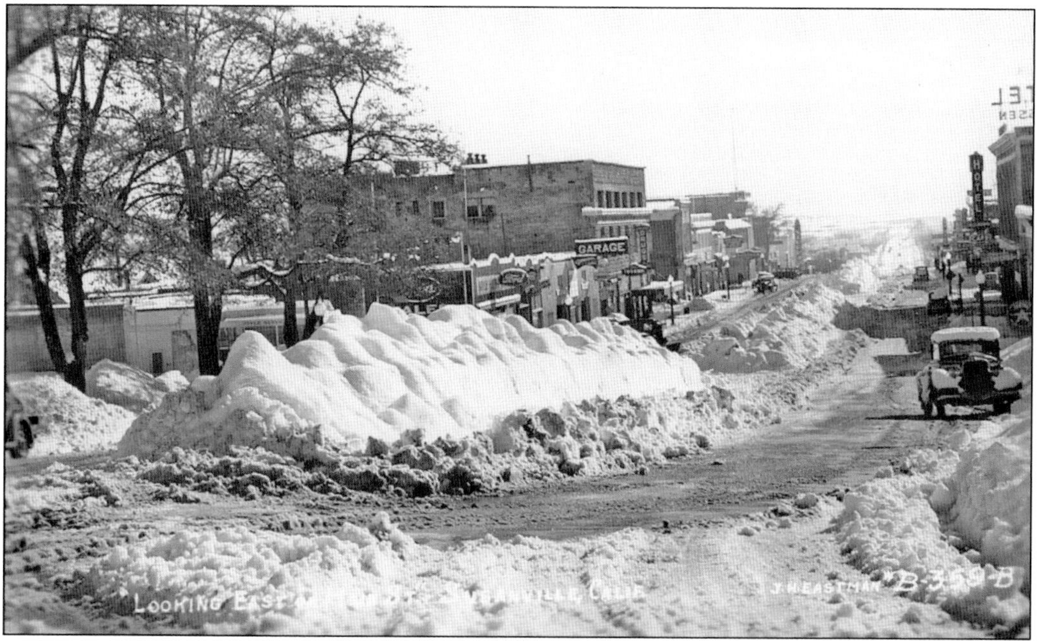

Susanville, California, offers visitors a number of intriguing winter activities. The Bizz Johnson Trail is an abandoned railroad line that opens up to the Susan River before it empties into Honey Lake, and Coppervale is a skiing/snowboarding destination located between Susanville and Westwood. Temperatures often drop to 20 degrees in November, December, January, and February.

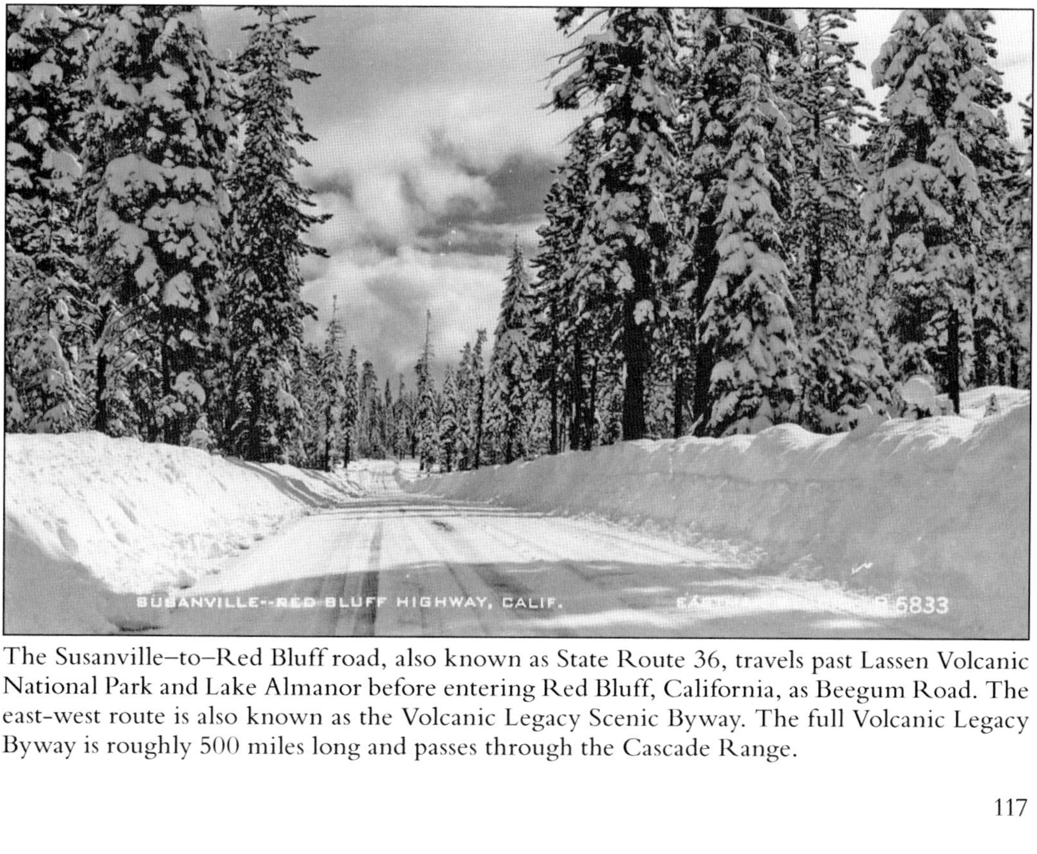

The Susanville–to–Red Bluff road, also known as State Route 36, travels past Lassen Volcanic National Park and Lake Almanor before entering Red Bluff, California, as Beegum Road. The east-west route is also known as the Volcanic Legacy Scenic Byway. The full Volcanic Legacy Byway is roughly 500 miles long and passes through the Cascade Range.

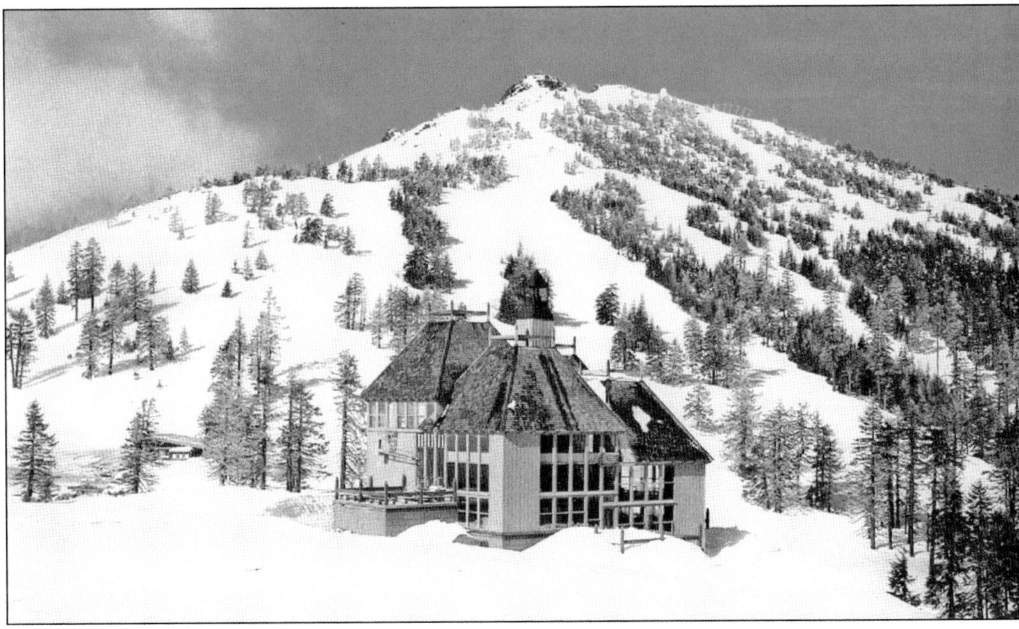

The Mount Ashland Ski and Snowboard Resort is located in the Siskiyou Mountains just over the border from California. The mountain stands at 7,500 feet, and the resort offers 23 ski trails in addition to cross-country skiing. The average snow depth is 110 inches, and the resort is open from Thanksgiving to April. Callahan's Lodge is located at the base of the mountain, just off Interstate 5.

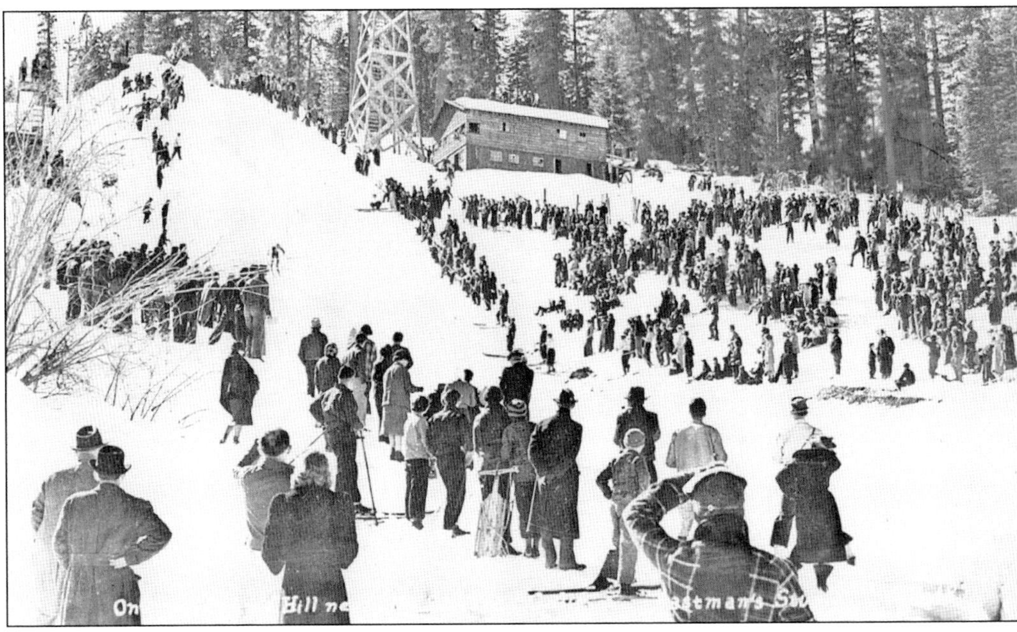

Snowman's Hill is located at the McCloud Summit between the cities of Mount Shasta and McCloud. It was developed in the 1930s after a group of winter enthusiasts carved out a toboggan run. Located nearby on the outskirts of McCloud, California, and situated in a wooded area along the McCloud River is the majestic, but private, Wyntoon Estate, owned by the Hearst Corporation. The medieval-inspired estate was Phoebe Hearst's summer home.

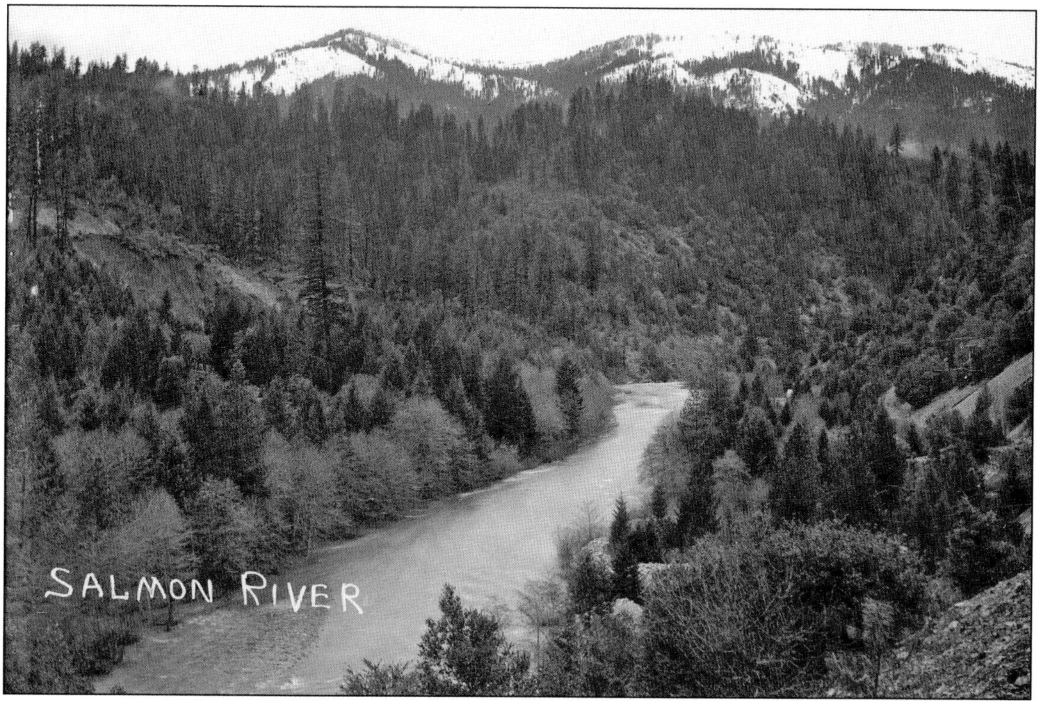

The Salmon River country, located in western Siskiyou County, California, was discovered by miners in the 1850s–1860s. The main fork of the Salmon River, the South Fork, actually begins in Trinity County; it flows north, then turns and travels west toward the Pacific Ocean. Cecilville lies at the confluence of the South Fork and East Fork, while the North Fork joins the South Fork at Forks of Salmon.

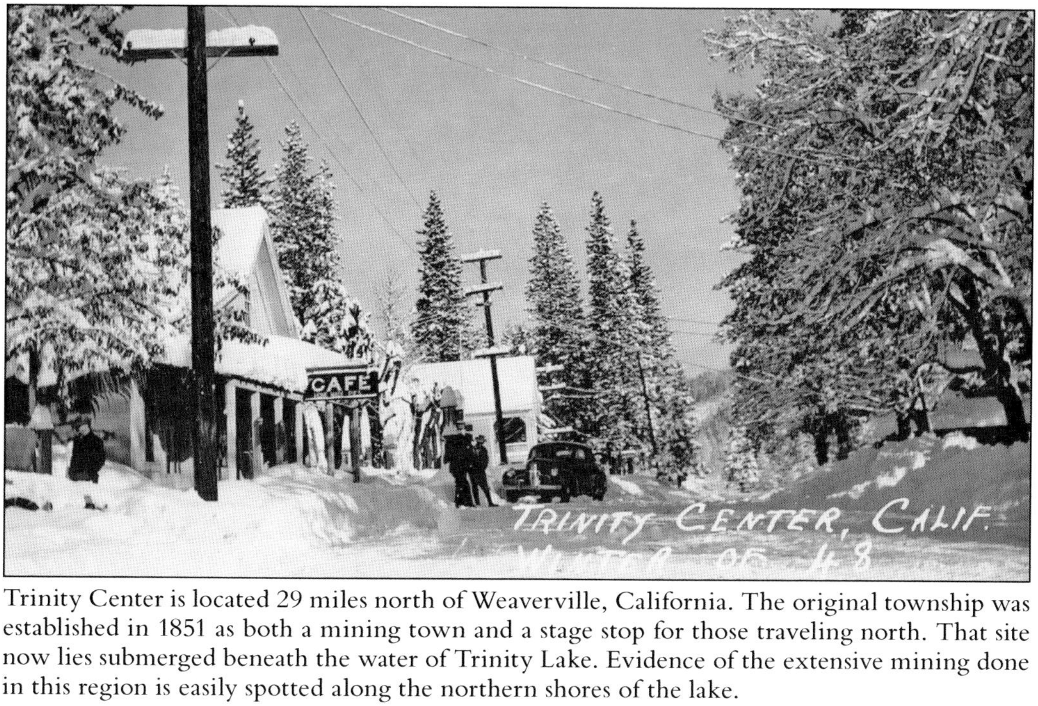

Trinity Center is located 29 miles north of Weaverville, California. The original township was established in 1851 as both a mining town and a stage stop for those traveling north. That site now lies submerged beneath the water of Trinity Lake. Evidence of the extensive mining done in this region is easily spotted along the northern shores of the lake.

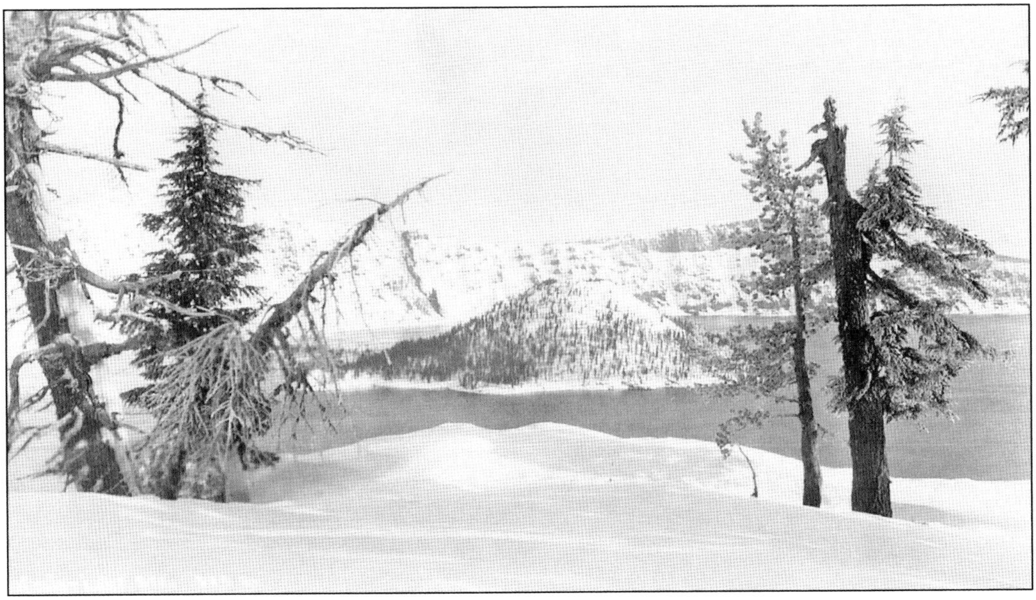

Snowfall at Crater Lake averages 533 inches a year. The lake, at 1,943 feet deep, is the deepest in the United States and seventh deepest in the world. Wizard Island, at the west end of the lake, is a volcanic cinder cone that rises up 755 feet above the surface of the water. William G. Steel, inspired by the crater at the top of the island, named it Wizard Island in 1885. In 1909, Steel convinced Alfred Parkhurst to build a lodge. Unfortunately, neither Parkhurst nor the architect understood how destructive the winter snows could be. Construction fell behind schedule, the exterior was covered in tarpaper, many rooms remained unfinished, and the lodge had no private bathrooms. Not until the National Park Service took control and the public demanded the great lodge be restored was it renovated. It cost $15 million.

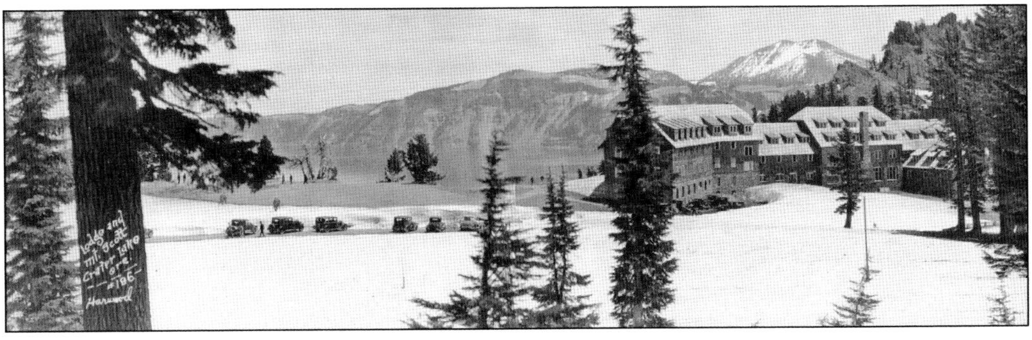

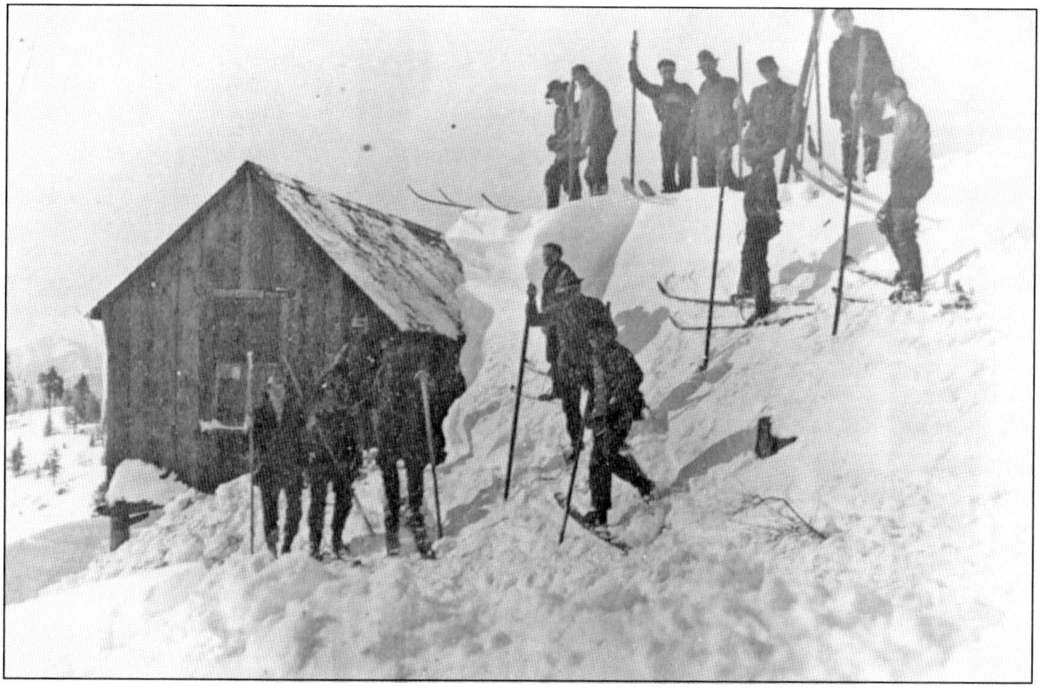

The first placer gold on Salmon River, in western Siskiyou County, was found in 1850. In 1860, gold-bearing quartz was discovered on the lower end of White's Gulch. The Highland Mine was discovered in this region about 1900. It was located in the Liberty mining district, in the Klamath Reserve on the Salmon River. At the Highland, workings consisted of tunnels, but because conditions were harsh, development was slow. Other mines in this region included the Jumbo Mine, Hickey's Mine, the Victory Mine (worked by John Nephroney), the Advance Mine, the Big Cliff Mine, and the Cub Bear Mine. Supplies had to be hauled in over a three-mile trail by pack mules. Note the "snowshoes" worn by the mule in the photograph below: these were specially designed shoes, first developed by William "Bill" Smith of Etna, California, that allowed mules to walk through snow drifts without falling through as easily as they might otherwise.

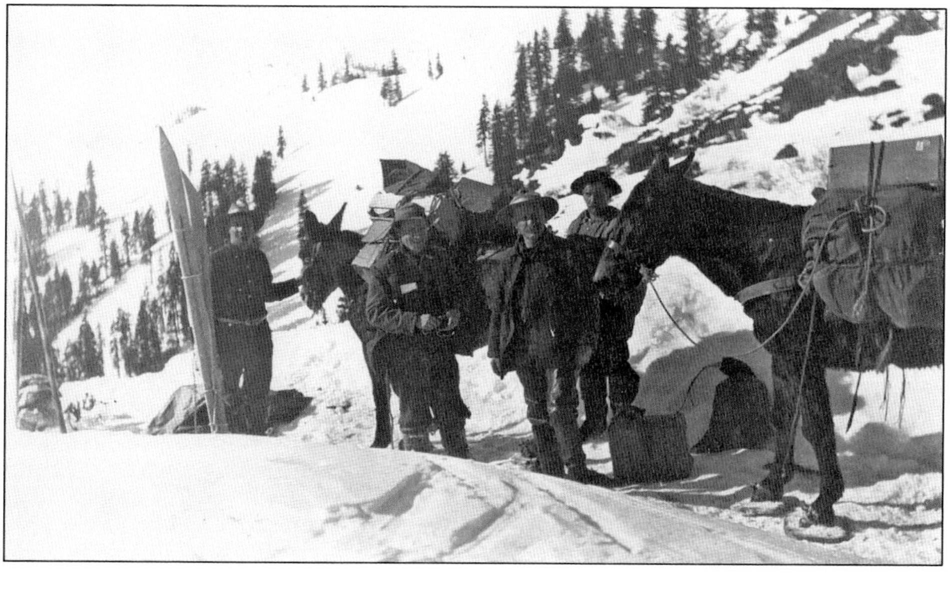

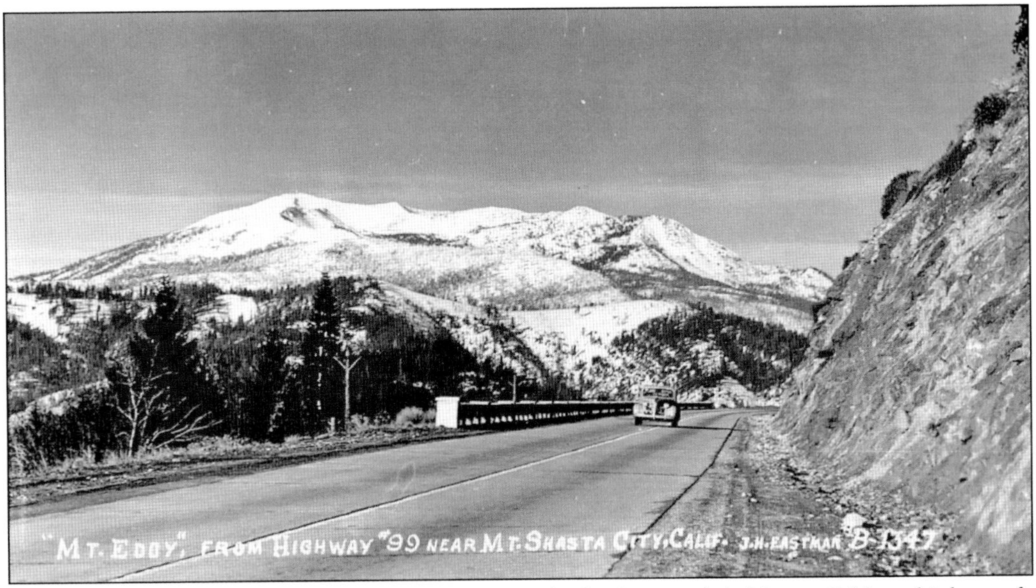

The Eddys are located west of Weed, California. The highest peak is Mount Eddy, which stands at 9,025 feet, right across the valley from Mount Shasta, which towers another 5,000 feet higher. Mount Eddy was named for Olive Louisa Paddock Eddy, wife of pioneer Nelson Harvey Eddy. They settled at the base of the mountain and became prosperous ranchers and farmers. Olive Eddy was the first woman to climb Mount Shasta.

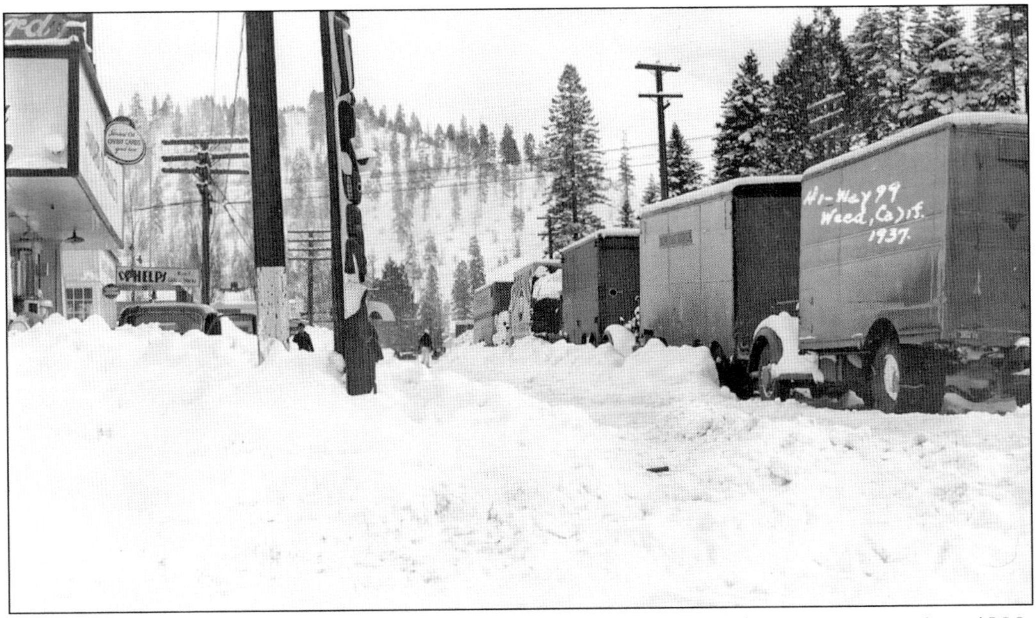

Weed, California, has been a major lumber and wood-product manufacturing center since 1900. Weed is also one of the larger communities in Siskiyou County. Other population centers include Dunsmuir, Mount Shasta, and Yreka. College of the Siskiyous' main branch is located at Weed, at the base of majestic Mount Shasta. The 250-acre main campus is accessible from Interstate 5 and Highway 97. (Courtesy of Sandra Elam.)

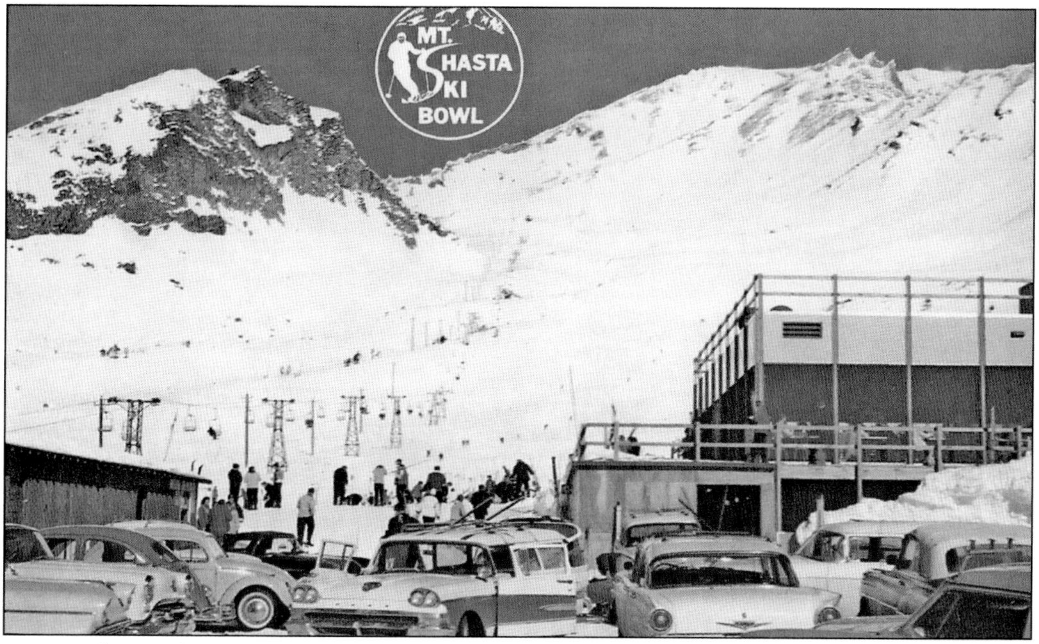

Mount Shasta Ski Park is located between the city of Mount Shasta and the small lumbering town of McCloud, California. Mount Shasta's elevation, recently revised, is 14,179 feet, making it the second tallest peak in the Cascade Range (Mount Rainer is the tallest). The first Mount Shasta Ski Bowl was built in 1958; a massive avalanche destroyed much of the park in 1978. The new ski park was opened in 1985.

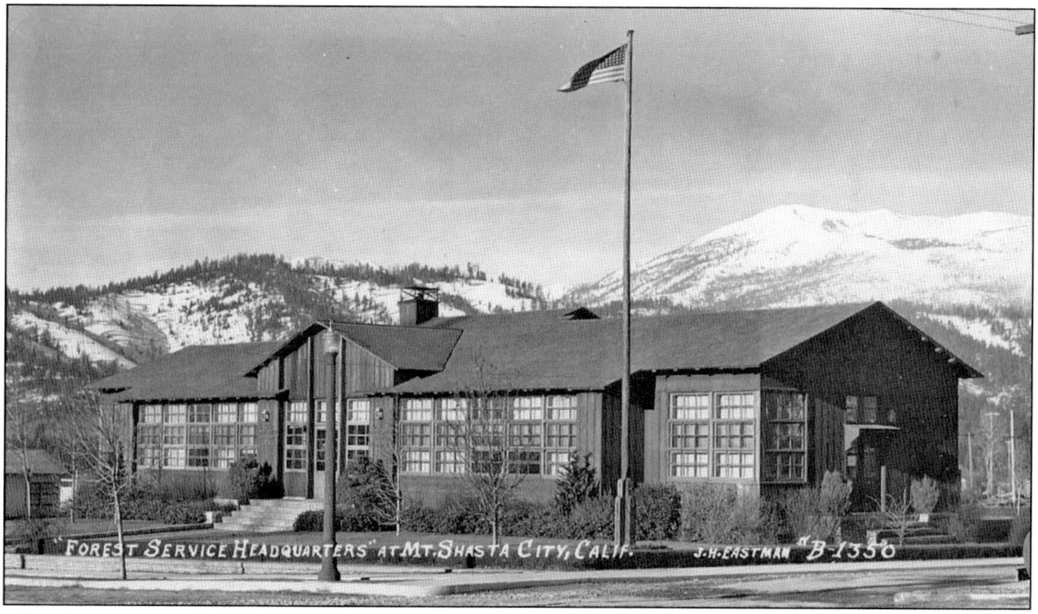

The Shasta National Forest headquarters are seen here around 1937 in Mount Shasta, California. In 1954, the Shasta and Trinity National Forest designations were merged into the Shasta-Trinity National Forest. It is the largest national forest in California and encompasses 2,210,485 acres in six counties, including parts of Trinity, Shasta, Siskiyou, Tehama, Humboldt, and Modoc. There are five wilderness areas and over 6,000 miles of streams and rivers.

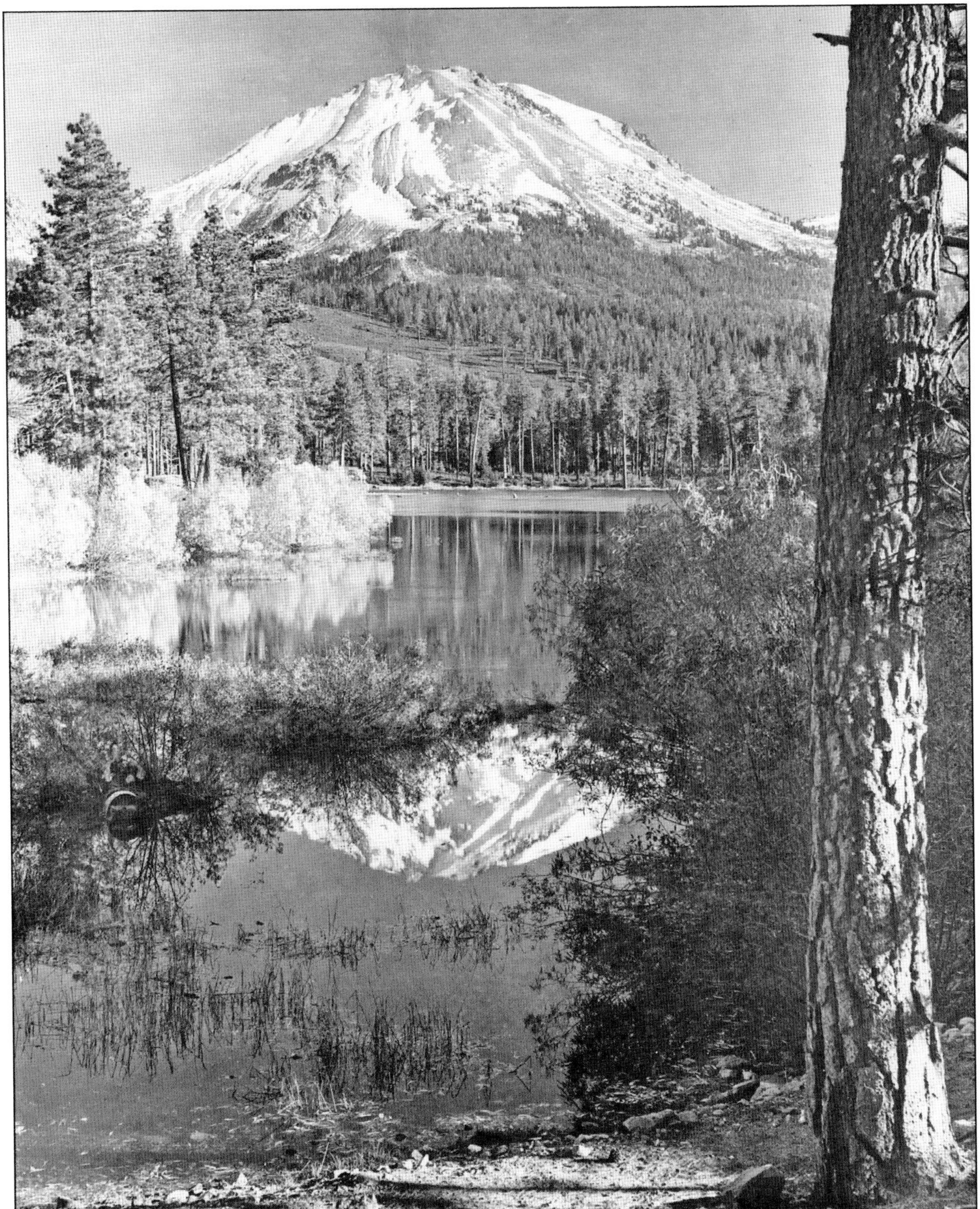

Mount Lassen peers down into Reflection Lake in Lassen Volcanic National Park. Often referred to as "California's Yellowstone," Lassen has amazing geothermal and geologic features, including Bumpass Hell, with its steaming fumaroles and boiling water. Easy trails follow the edge of Manzanita Lake and Helen Lake.

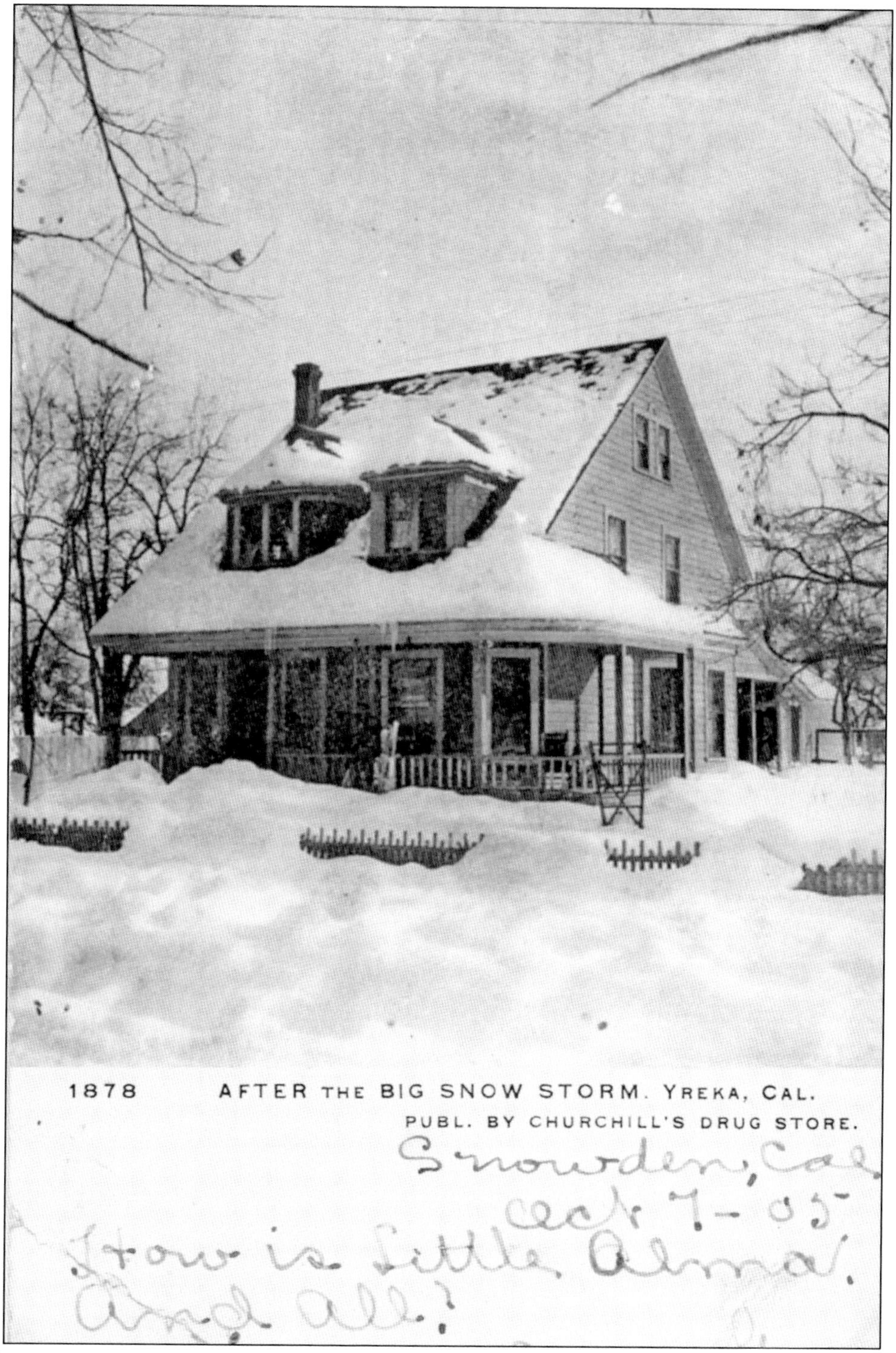

Yreka, California, was hit by a major storm in 1878. It came on the heels of an outbreak of diphtheria in 1877 that first hit Red Bluff, California. In Yreka, fear was doubled when a handful of children were hit with scarlet fever. Even a Christmas tree festival was cancelled in town in order to prevent any spread of disease.

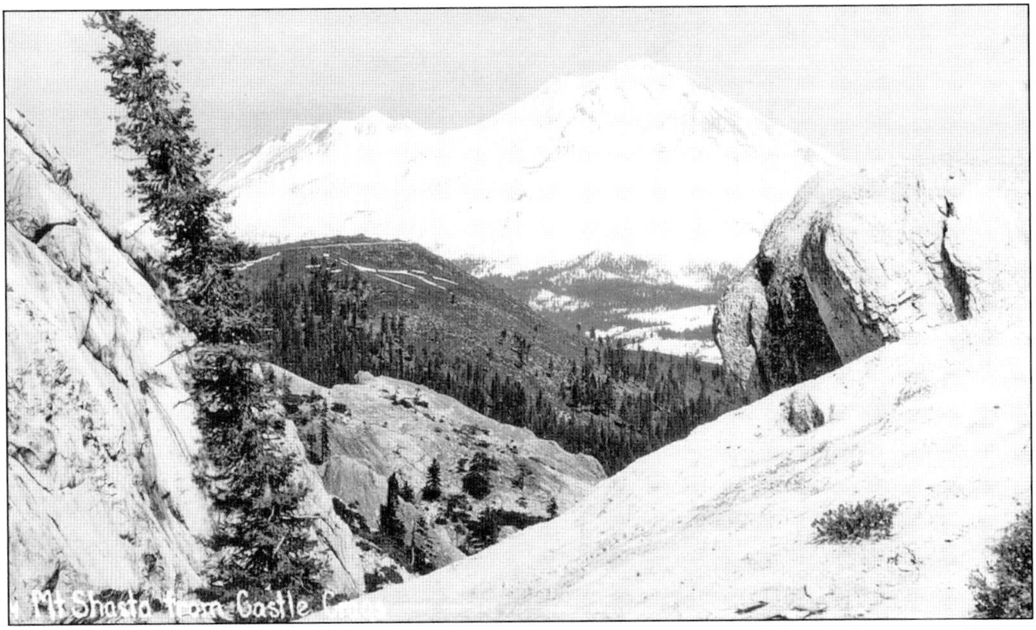

In 1844, when John C. Frémont spotted the mountains of northern California, he wrote, "They have never yet known the tread of human foot; sternly drawn against the sky, they look so high, so steep, so snowy and rocky, that it appears almost impossible to climb them." It has been written that Frémont tried three times to return to Mount Shasta in the hopes of climbing the mountain. Perhaps Frémont studied the peak from this vantage on Castle Crags.

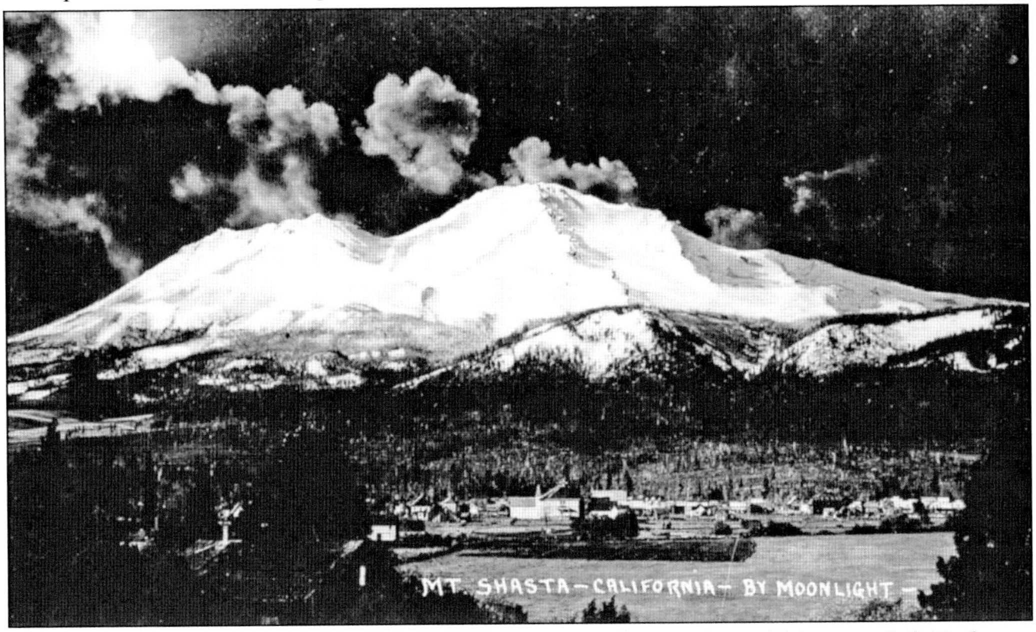

Elias Pierce is credited with the first ascent of Mount Shasta. He and his party left Yreka on August 12, 1854. They camped on Shasta's northwest slope, crossed the steep Whitney Glacier snowfields, then reached the summit. He wrote, "In many places we had to crawl over and around rough, craggy rocks, in single file." In order to convince a disbelieving public, he and another party climbed the peak again in September.

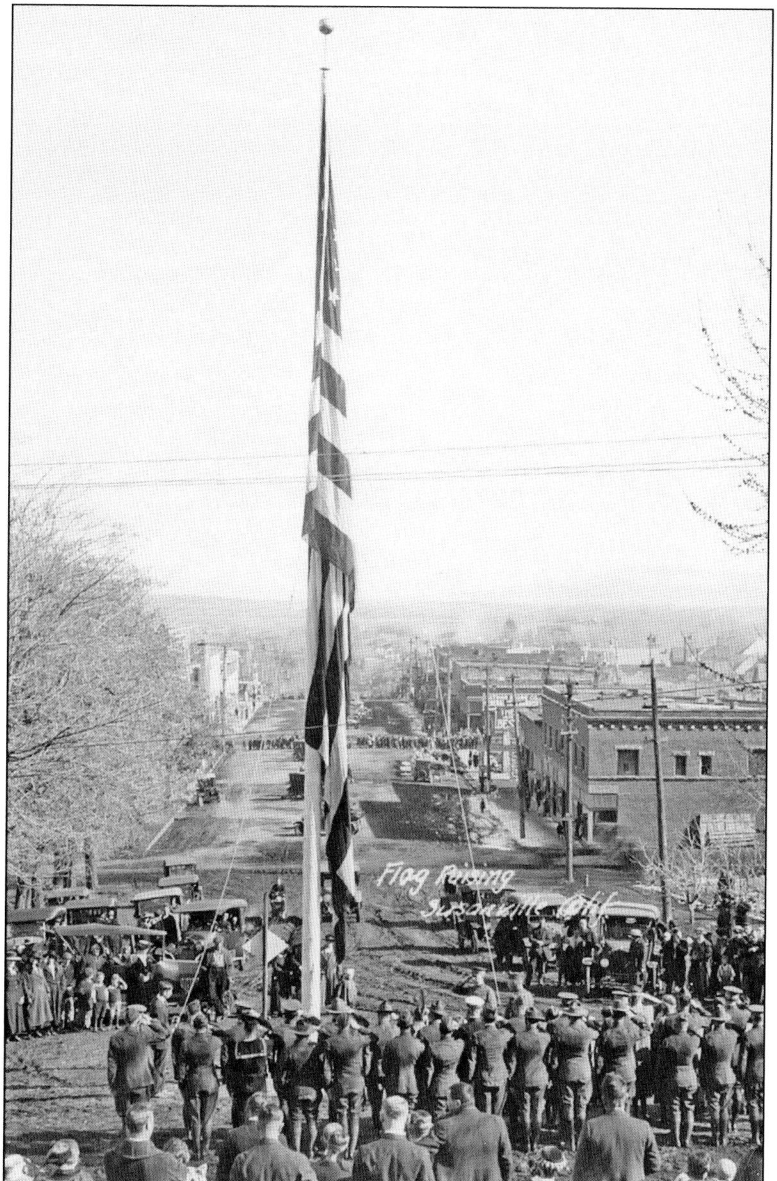

Susanville, California, has had a rich history, beginning with the summer of 1854, when Isaac Roop built his trading fort along the Nobles Emigrant Trail. Formerly called Rooptown, the name was changed to Susanville in honor of Roop's daughter. In 1860, the post office was established, and in 1900, the city was incorporated. The railroad arrived in 1913, and with it, Susanville quickly became a major lumber town. The Lassen Lumber and Box Company, Fruit Growers' Supply Company, and later the Paul Bunyan Lumber Company and the Susanville Logging Company all established mills here. When the lumber industry fell into decline, Susanville became the site of the High Desert State Prison as well as the California Correctional Center. The Army post at nearby Herlong also impacted the growth and development of Susanville. It sits at the crossroads where going north leads to Klamath Falls, Oregon, going west leads to Red Bluff, California, and going southeast leads to Reno, Nevada. Honoring the town's strong ties to service, this c. 1920 photograph depicts a winter's day flag-raising ceremony at the Susanville courthouse.